Confessions of a
Recovering Type

A

By Wendy Bowen

Confessions of a Recovering Type A

Copyright: 2009 © by Wendy Bowen

First Printing February, 2010

Editor: Catherine Frenzel, Cover Design: Jennifer Casey
Photo: Allison Mignery

ISBN: 978-0-615-34642-7

Published by: New Street, Inc.

For information on additional Recovering Type A offerings, to invite the author to speak to your group, or to make a tax-deductible contribution supporting the Recovering Type A message, please contact:

New Street, Inc.
Box 30
7633 Pineville-Matthews Road
Charlotte, NC 28226

704-999-4908

info@recoveringtypea.com

www.recoveringtypea.com

Follow Recovering Type A on Facebook and LinkedIn.

Table of Contents

Prologue

Enough

A man in my mind was chasing me
And I didn't care what he said
As long as I couldn't hear Him
I was safe clear up ahead.

I had to continue moving
Gain momentum for a faster pace
The man in my mind couldn't catch me
And I would keep winning each race.

I once wondered what He was saying
His faint yell from far away
I wondered what I was missing
Ignoring Him each day.

But slowing down would be too hard
What if I heard something bad?
Or worse, what if, I lost a race
One that I should have had.

One day I just stopped to listen
That day I just stood fast
And then I heard the unexpected
I love you, I love you, at last.

~ Laura Danforth

Acknowledgements

The quotations used in this book were gathered unscientifically from several sources over several years. Sources include original versions, books of quotations, notes I have taken from speeches, radio, television, and numerous scriptural translations, mostly New International Version and New King James Version unless otherwise noted. Because of this wide variety of sources, some quotes may be imperfectly worded or attributed. To authors, contributors, and original sources, you have my thanks, and where appropriate, my apologies. ~ Wendy

Special Thanks

There are so many people who have supported me on this journey. Big hugs and great thanks to all of you, especially:

JeLo, Cherpie, Tim, Silke & Brian
Dana, Emily & Victoria, Forest Hill
and of course, Mom & Dad

Introduction

At some point in each of our lives, we figure out that society does not know what is best for us. I've been a perfectionist, workaholic, and over-achiever since approximately birth. I've read all the right books and applied all the right messages like, *"You can do anything you set your mind to,"* *"Don't let anybody stop you,"* and *"Don't care what anybody else thinks about you."* I've been on the fast track to everything our culture endorses as the ultimate life, and yet somewhere along the line, I found myself unfulfilled, lonely, sad, empty and disappointed. While society looks at my fast-track life and says, *"Wow!"* I look back at my fast-track life and ask, *"How?"* How did I get here? How did this happen? How have I missed years, even entire phases of life?

This is not an autobiography, so throughout the book I have deliberately blurred the lines of my history in order to stay clear and focused on the issue at hand, which is Type A and its glories and downfalls. To give you proper insight, here is a quick run-down of my professional background, leaving out names to protect the innocent. I spent five years as an Investment Banker with a private equity firm in New York; I was the youngest one ever to make the executive team. I spent the next four years on the West Coast of Florida, in Wealth Management with a major Wall Street firm and then as Vice President of Private Banking for a top-ten bank. Opportunity knocked, and I went to Denmark for six months, meeting royalty, ambassadors and international businessmen. Upon my return to the States, I moved to Charlotte, North Carolina, where my Type A make-over has taken place.

Through major soul searching, and by the grace of God, I have gone through a complete metamorphosis. Because of this transformation, I have a new sense of fulfillment, love, joy, peace and wisdom that I have never had before. The purpose of this book is to encourage you on your own journey – even if I have to use myself as a transparent example – so that you, too, can experience this kind of satisfaction. There are many times I have said to myself that I am soooooooooo not qualified to write this book. I have no idea if it will mean anything to you, but it has meant a lot to me. I humbly present it to you with a great deal of gratitude.

Depending on where you are in life right now, you may prefer certain sections of this book over others. For some of you, section one (written from a Type A perspective) will feel like you are talking to yourself, while for others of you, it will be intense and exasperating. Similarly but in a different way, for some of you, section three may be the answer to your prayers and what you have been seeking for some time, while for others of you, it may feel awkward and uncomfortable. All I ask is that you stick it out through sections that push your buttons and boundaries. Getting out of your comfort zone is part of growing.

My mission is to inspire positive change through spreading the good news and through the loving application of compassionate conservative values. I invite you to take this journey with me, and I ask you to help me spread the good news. Share your journey with me at wendy@recoveringtypea.com, and see *Spread the Message* at the back of this book for ways you can help.

Are you doing everything right, and yet you are still not satisfied? Then I just have one question for you: Are *you* ready for change?

Let the words of my mouth and the meditation
of my heart be pleasing in Your sight, O Lord,
my Rock and my Redeemer.

Psalm 19:14

Disclaimer/Warning

Hi. My name is Wendy, and I am a Recovering Type A.

You respond: "Hi Wendy!"

Yes, yes. Very funny. Like all those other 12-step programs with their meetings and stuff. Well, I've got a news flash for you. This is not a 12-step program, because if you are truly Type A, you don't have time for 12 steps and you would probably skip the most important steps because they are the steps that take too long. This is not a "ten things you can do to change your life" or a self-help kind of book. Why? Because there is no magical set of steps or combination of things to do in this world to make your life better. Sorry to be the one to break it to you.

I am not a psychologist and could probably never be one because as a Type A, I'd just tell all my clients to "get over it" and that would be bad for business. This is the same reason I could never be a waitress, but that's a different story. Frankly, I am not an expert at anything, and I'm sure there will be plenty of real experts out there who disagree with everything I'm about to say. So what? They probably weren't ever Type A themselves, so what do they know about it other than what they might have read in some text book that was written from an academic, psychological or generational perspective? Unlike them, I am uniquely qualified to discuss this issue with you because I have personal experience living the life of a full-blown Type A *to the max*.

If you seek to enter into Type A recovery based on any information or insight you gain from this book, let me warn you: I cannot guarantee or predict your results and I will not be held accountable for your results or lack thereof. Additionally, if there are things I say that bring up issues for you, offend you, resemble you, or cause you to resent me, that is really not my problem; it's yours. If I touch upon your insecurities, unrealized expectations, baggage, unbecoming motives, frustrations, hurts and/or disappointments, those are yours, not mine. Believe me, especially because of my Type A background, I don't really enjoy discussing the mistakes I've made along the way. My only hope is that instead of throwing the book away or burning it in the fire when you get upset with me, you allow what you read to open your thoughts to a new perspective of someone who's been in your shoes and changed.

If you can relate to what I'm saying because you are Type A yourself or have someone in your life who is Type A, that's great! I hope that you will let me know of your Type A experiences by writing to me at wendy@recoveringtypea.com.

If you can't relate to anything I'm saying, maybe you are a hermit who lives under a rock, or have been completely secluded from society for an extended period of time. Or maybe you have always been Type B, and just don't get what all the excitement is about. Even if that's the case, I'm sure you know someone in your life who is Type A who could benefit from this book, even just a little bit. If nobody comes to mind, think of that person you wish you could tell to just chill out, take the scenic route; that their priorities in life are all wrong, that they are shallow and stressed out, and stop being such a stuck-up, snobbish, workaholic, egomaniac, narcissistic, bling-bling, possession-centered jerk. Think of anyone yet?

Section One

A to the Nth Degree

Written from an Entirely Type A Perspective

Chapter 1: *I'm AAA*

Let's start at the beginning. What is Type A? If you are Type A, join the club. Being Type A is the only way to be, and people who aren't Type A really tick me off because they tend to be slow, sloppy, unmotivated, emotional disasters that get in my way. If you want a full assessment to see you if you are Type A, there is a quiz in this book to help you find out. If you already know you're Type A, you don't have any time to waste, so let's jump right in.

By definition: Type A is a noun,

> of or pertaining to a pattern of behavior characterized by competitiveness, tenseness, a sense of urgency, impatience, aggressiveness, perfectionism, and assertiveness...

Beyond the definition: Type A individuals can be described as excessively time-conscious, insecure about their status, highly competitive, over-ambitious, business-like, hostile, aggressive, incapable of relaxation in taking the smallest issues too seriously and are somewhat disliked for the way that they're always rushing and demanding other people to serve to their standards of satisfaction. They are often high- and over-achieving workaholics who multi-task, drive themselves with deadlines, and are unhappy about the smallest of delays. Because of these characteristics, Type A individuals are often described as "stress junkies."

If you read this and you think, "What's wrong with that?" you are Type A. Like me! I totally agree with you! I mean seriously, don't you people understand that time is money? And there are only so many hours in the day, and days in the year, and years of my life to accomplish everything I want to do! I have goals, ambitions, things to do, and plenty of people that I need to make insanely jealous of me, even though I'll be really cool and they'll like me for who I really am. I have a five-year plan and I've got to do everything precisely right to make it happen!

I've heard the whole *"Money isn't everything"* line, but that's mostly said by people who don't have any and aren't motivated enough to work hard enough to earn it for themselves. Money is power and status and possessions and all the other things that make me better than everybody else. And that, my friends, is the whole point of this game called life: beating the other guy because I am smarter, better, faster and have more stuff. I mean, unless you are Mother Teresa (who at least is the best at what she does, so I give her credit), you are in this game, and you have to *play to win*. Second best is not enough. I move through life at the pace of a NASCAR speed racer, making quick decisions based on hard facts and where I want to go. I keep my calendar jam-packed with appointments because people who are not busy are just wasting time and will never accomplish anything. *Eat my dust, you losers!*

I've been called a workaholic, but that's why I'm successful. You're probably thinking I have no personal life, right? Well, maybe not right now, because I don't have the time, but believe me, I can multi-task. So while I'm climbing the corporate ladder, it is on my To-Do list to find a husband, live in a mansion, pop out a few kids and hire a nanny, a housekeeper and possibly a driver. It's just that I can't do that until I've reached a certain point in my career where I can make time for it. Right now, I think the best relationship for me is probably a long-distance one. One night a week and every other weekend sounds like an ideal arrangement. Then I don't have to feel so alone, but my relationship won't get in my way and I don't have to get weighed down with someone else's neediness. All that emotional stuff is really annoying.

The second part of the definition of Type A is:

...often resulting in stress-related symptoms such as insomnia, indigestion and possibly associated with an increased and even double risk of coronary heart disease.

Whatever!! I am not going to have those problems because I eat right and work out. I've got everything in my life under control and that means my health, too. Did you really expect any different? This size-two figure of mine doesn't maintain itself, you know. And I don't have any sleeping problems because I never stop being busy. I have only two speeds: warp speed and stop. Stop means I'm sleeping. Duh. Yeah, sometimes I work until 2 a.m. because I can't stop my brain and I don't want to lose any of my fabulous ideas. But that's just hard work – totally different than sleeping problems.

What are the other symptoms? According to Meyer Friedman's *Type A Behavior: Its Diagnosis and Treatment*, symptoms include:

An intrinsic insecurity or insufficient level of self-esteem, which is considered to be the root cause of the syndrome, though this is believed to be covert and, therefore, less observable. Time urgency and impatience, which causes irritation and exasperation. Free-floating hostility, which can be triggered by even minor accidents.

Intrinsic insecurity? I'm not insecure!?! Give me a break! You are what you think you are, and I am a Superstar!! Anybody who lets insecurities get in their way is just a sissy who shouldn't be in the game in the first place. Nobody would ever say that I am insecure. I am confident, assertive, intelligent, and professional – I've got it all together! Never let them see you sweat! And I don't! Ha!!

So what, if I sometimes wonder if it's all going to collapse around me, or if someone is going to figure out that I'm really not that special or smart or beautiful after all? Who cares that in my private thoughts I wish I were further along by now? Even though I'm ahead of my peers and getting recognized, I'm not even halfway to where I want to be. Being satisfied with the status quo is not the formula for success, so I'll keep busting my butt every day because *I want more*. Yeah, sometimes I feel like I'm doing "Fake it 'til I make it," because I keep getting these promotions to positions that I'm not sure I deserve or even know what I'm doing. But one of these days, I'm going to catch a break and I won't have to work so hard at keeping up with myself, and then I can finally relax. But I will *never* let *anyone* know that I feel this way because that would show weakness, and the weak get beat.

I am proud to be a Type A. I'm sure my boss likes it, and I know my clients appreciate it. I was an investment banker in New York, and Private Banker to the rich and famous on the glamorous West Coast of Florida. I am on the fast track in my career because I am Type A. I know exactly how many calls I need to make per day, how many appointments I need to have per week, how many accounts I need to open per month, how much revenue I need to produce per quarter, and I know my annual goals (according to the company, though the goals I set for myself are actually much higher). I always achieve my goals because I will do whatever it takes to win, to be #1, to slay my competitors and get all the recognition as The Best.

Once I achieve all of that, I know exactly how I will be spending my bonus money. So depending on what level of over-accomplishment registers this quarter, I will have more and better stuff, gadgets, clothes, and things to show off to everyone around me.

At the end of the day, or at least by the time I'm 35, I see myself in a 10,000-square-foot house in the best neighborhood, preferably on the water somewhere, so I can dock my yacht out front. I'll have a five-car garage filled with a BMW X5, a Mercedes E500, a Maserati, a Bentley coupe convertible in black or powder blue, and of course a tricked-out Range Rover. My luxurious and extravagant life is all on my Dream Board, and I visualize it all the time, so therefore I know it will come true. This is what successful people do, and I know this because that is what I was born to be: a Superstar!

I will also have the perfect husband, the perfect children, the perfect dogs, the best clothes, go on the best vacations and live an all-around fabulous life. We will be the power couple building an empire, both of us at the top of our game professionally, with people watching us in awe wondering, *"How do they do it all?"* and wanting to be us. He'll probably cheat on me, but that's to be expected in this day and age, isn't it? Besides, a long-term relationship is really just a business deal anyway, so I'll just look the other way or sleep with the pool boy as revenge or something, but we'll continue our otherwise fabulous life together.

I am in control of my life, and I am in control of my emotions. Well, actually, I think emotions are pretty useless and will only trip you up. Having a heart is completely over-rated. It's much more important to achieve your goals in life than it is to get all sloppy and sentimental. Besides, having a heart takes too much time.

As for how I achieve my goals, if you haven't noticed, I don't waste any time and I am super-organized. It really bothers me when things take too long because I know I could be doing ten other things in the same amount of time. I stop moving only to sleep, and I try to do that quickly. My To-Do lists constantly keep me on track so that nothing ever slips through the cracks. That simply cannot happen because I am me, and nothing slips through the cracks with me. Even at home, I have everything outlined on my computer, on an excel spreadsheet, in order of importance, color coded, with formulas and page-links. And I re-organize my closet at least four times a year so my wardrobe is rotated, color categorized, and nothing is worn too frequently. You could eat Thanksgiving dinner off my kitchen floor because bleach is the best invention ever, and I don't miss a single spot. Eventually, I'll have a maid or housekeeper who can do all of these petty chores for me, but right now, I do them perfectly myself. I have everything under control at all times, which is a really important part of achieving your goals and making your dreams come true.

I also surround myself with all the right people and I don't bother with people who can't benefit me in some way. I can quickly size someone up by what they do, what they have, how much they make, where they live, or what they drive. If they can be useful to me, I stick close to them. Most people, however, just get in my way, slow me down and don't understand me. That's probably because I am more motivated, driven, and successful than they are. I can't help it if they are jealous and insecure because they don't have what I have. I've worked so hard to accomplish everything in my life, I deserve it and I'm not going to change. I don't really want to be around them anyway; I want to be around people who are higher up than me, so I can keep advancing. No matter what, though, I always remind myself that everyone is going to disappoint me at some point, so it's best to rely only on myself.

People do disappoint me a lot. I just don't understand people who say they are going to do something and don't do it! Ugh! It is these same people who also don't know how to set goals. What, are they just aimlessly walking around the planet with no purpose? How do they even get up in the morning without knowing exactly what they want and how to get it? If you are one of these people, let me explain. The basics of goal setting can be read in countless books about how to decide where you want to be in five years and then breaking it down into SMART goals. I didn't come up with this term, and I don't care who did, but SMART stands for Specific, Measurable, Attainable, Realistic and Timely. Then you set different levels like base-goal (expected), mid-goal (higher) or over-achiever stretch-goal (the one I aim for and am most likely to meet). I am so advanced at goal setting that I set only stretch goals because if you shoot for the moon, at least you land on a star. And, no, I don't know who came up with that expression, either.

The other thing to keep in mind when goal setting is who your competitors are. But it's not politically correct to acknowledge that, so if anyone asks you, just say that you compete with yourself and view others as your teammates. Between you and me though, it is important to know who you have to beat and by how much you have to beat them in order to get the recognition you deserve for being better than everybody else. I mean, your first or second year in a new job, you should totally be outperforming the people who have been in the business for 10-20 years... otherwise, you're probably slacking off.

Everyone tells me I should pace myself or I will burn out. I think that's crap. Burning out will happen only if you let it. I don't know about you, but burning out is not on my To-Do list, so I don't have time for it. Plus, these people are probably telling me that because they're lazy and jealous and don't want me to succeed the way I know I can and will. If you're a Type A, and people tell you that, don't listen to them. They don't know what they're talking about. But in case they are someone important who could help you later down the line, smile and tell them they are right, and then keep doing what you are doing anyway. At least, that's my approach.

I have too much to do to pace myself. My calendar is so packed that I have to rush to get where I'm going. The other day, for example, I needed to take a left turn at a traffic light, but the left turn signal was red, so instead I went straight through the green light, looped around at the first U-turn, came back around to the intersection and took a right to get where I wanted to go. I know it added a little distance, but at least I kept moving and got there faster. When I used to live in New York City, I was always thinking the sidewalks should have lanes on them like highways. The lanes would be *slow*, *fast*, and *outta-my-way*! Even in high heels, I would always be in the *outta-my-way* lane. I've got places to be and things to do, people!

I've also been told that I should get a hobby or something. Seriously? Hobbies are stupid unless you are the best at it. I own a set of golf clubs so I can do that for networking and getting business. It's fun, I guess, but it would be better if it were just nine holes so it didn't take so much time away from everything else I have to do. And I have a good excuse for why I'm not very good because I'm just a beginner and I don't play very often. I tried fencing at one point, but all the people were weird and nobody had anything that could benefit me, so I stopped. I really like the polo-playing high-society crowd, but I can't afford horses right now, so that's out. I also can't afford a yacht yet, and having a boat under 40 feet is not even worth it. Besides, I usually work on Saturdays when nobody else is in the office, and Sundays I might log in to my work computer using my remote access from home, so I'm really just too busy for hobbies.

If I'm too busy for hobbies, I'm definitely too busy for a boyfriend, so like I said, I don't have one right now. I have plenty of people hitting on me all the time, don't get me wrong... there's just nobody special. When I feel the need for companionship, I usually pick someone who is not a long-term possibility in order to get some temporary companionship and physical benefit. Before we sleep together, we have a clear and concise discussion about how we are not going to fall in love and how this will come to its rightful end in due time. Clear-cut relationships are the ones that work for me. I really don't have the time to be worried about how somebody else is feeling today, or add their problems to my life. Frankly, I don't care. I'm not going to ask you to solve my problems, so keep yours to yourself, if you don't mind.

I usually also pick someone who can benefit my business in some way, based on their friends or social status. But I have never slept with a client, because that would be prostitution, and I am not a prostitute, just a savvy player of the game. One of these days, I'm going to find my Prince Charming who will sweep me off my feet, and we will build our perfect life together. I'll know him when I see him because he will be everything I've outlined on my excel spreadsheet *Husband Checklist*.

What I do in my spare time, which is why I don't have any spare time, is philanthropy. I'm on the Board of Directors of a few non-profit organizations, and I've even been elected to leadership positions on the Boards. It's really good for my reputation, and it gets me in with all the wealthy socialites. I go to the best charity events, black-tie affairs and cocktail parties with the most important people in town. I get my picture in the paper all the time with the heavy hitters, and that's good for my business and status. Plus, it's a good dress rehearsal for when I'm even more important and high-ranking, and they are doing articles on me in all the national papers. I'm not even close to where I'm going to be yet, so this is really just a warm-up.

When I go out, it has to be first class all the way. Only the hot spots and finer places for dinner, lunch, and drinks, where I can see and be seen. I also live in one of the most elegant, high-rise, condo buildings in town. It impresses people when I tell them where I live. When I am home watching television, I watch only the news, TLC, Discovery, History or anything educational in order to know things that most people don't know. When it comes to clothes, I would rather wait and save up for a really impressive item than buy something cheap. I need to project the image of success at all times, so I shop at Nordstrom or Saks and buy mostly brand names.

What else...? I feel like I'm forgetting something... Oh yeah... God. I won't talk too much about Him because it's not polite to talk about religion or politics, but I can tell you that God is totally on my side. I wasn't raised in a very religious household, but a few years ago I made a deal with God, and so now we understand each other. My favorite prayer is the Prayer of Jabez, an example in the Bible where you pray for yourself first. You pray for expanded territory and wealth, power and influence, and then you promise God that if He blesses you with these things, you will bless other people. I pray it all the time, so I know it will come true, and God is going to make me a Superstar so I can help other people through my own power and influence. Isn't that awesome?

So pretty much, that's me. I've got everything under control, and everything in life is going to go according to my plan. I hold myself to these high standards because I don't want to be like everybody else. I can't think of anything worse than being "normal" or "average." What would the point be? I want to be exceptional. If you were a paint color, would you want to be taupe? Please! I've always been a standout from the pack, and I can't imagine being anything else. I mean, if I'm not going to be the best at something, why bother? That way, I never look like a loser.

I've been told to dream big and, therefore, I do. I'm doing everything right. I'm reading all the right success books so I'm making all the right moves in order to make my dreams come true. Yeah, I work too much, but it will all pay off in the end. Yeah, I'm competitive, but that's part of what drives my success. Yeah, I've been called a stone-hearted bitch, but I play to win. Yeah, I don't have much of a personal life, but it will all come together at some point in the future when I have more time. I'm just driven to achieve more in this life than the average person. Therefore, I will accomplish more in this life than the average person. What's so bad about that?

What's so wrong about being Type A? Why on earth would I ever want to recover from it?

Chapter 2: Are you Type A?

Do you want to find out if you are Type A? Here's a quick test to see if you are or not. I bet you can't beat my score! Type A tests are based on the Jenkins Activity Survey that was created in 1979. That's the year I was born, so obviously I was meant to be a Type A!

Disclaimer: This personality test and its results do not constitute a clinical or medical evaluation. It cannot psychologically diagnose you as a Type A. For further investigation, please consult your doctor. There are also lots more unofficial quizzes available online.

TYPE A QUIZ

Section One: 20 Questions			
Do you agree or disagree with the following statements? Check the box according to your answer. *A = Agree, S = Sometimes Agree/Sometimes Disagree, D = Disagree*			
	A	**S**	**D**
I am more competitive than most people.			
The more money I make, the happier I'll be.			
I can't tolerate people who slow me down.			
I usually pursue relationships with people who can be useful for my advancement.			
Talking about emotions is a sign of weakness.			
I set goals that are ambitious.			
I would take a less interesting job for more money or position.			
Having nice things is important to me.			
I consider someone's motive when they do something nice for me.			

11

	A	S	D
I think hobbies are mostly a waste of time.			
They should make driver's licenses harder to obtain to reduce the idiots on the roads.			
I find it difficult to maintain personal/romantic relationships because I don't have enough time and work too much.			
I will do whatever it takes to get that promotion, first place/# 1, better title, bigger office…			
I am the most efficient person I know because I can fit more into one day (one hour, one minute) than most people do in a year.			
In a few years, after I achieve more success, I will have more time for a girlfriend/boyfriend, social life and some hobbies.			
Sometimes, even a tasteful peck between a loving couple in public makes me think, "Get a room."			
I get frustrated and even angry when things do not go according to my plan.			
I find it difficult to admit when I make a mistake.			
If the doctor told me to stay home from work for two weeks, I would work anyway.			
I rarely confide in others.			

Section Two: 8 Questions			
True or False? Circle F for False, T for True			
In general, I'm a trusting person.	F		T
I find it easy to unwind.	F		T
I can accept when someone performs better than me.	F		T
I live up to my own expectations.	F		T
I have never missed a family event because I needed to work.	F		T
It does not bother me if I don't finish what I planned to do for the day.	F		T
Even if I have important work to do, it is more important to spend time with family and friends.	F		T

I am satisfied with where my life is right now.	F		T

Section Three: 11 Questions

Do you relate to the following statement often, sometimes or never? Check the box according to your answer.
O = Often, S = Sometimes, N = Never

	O	S	N
I feel like I am rushing.			
I tend to think of others in terms of what they can do for me.			
I feel uneasy when I am not doing something productive.			
I compare myself to others.			
I find it difficult to relax.			
I eat on the run.			
I have everything planned out, and my actions are calculated steps towards my future goals.			
I view my teammates/colleagues as competitors.			
When my boss gives me a goal of 5-X, I make it my goal to accomplish 15-X.			
I wonder why I'm not doing better.			
I get lonely, or feel like people don't understand me.			

Section Four: 11 Questions

True or False? Circle Y for Yes, N for No

The following things really annoy me:

• When the person in front of me in the 10-items-or-less line has 15 things	Y		N
• When the cashier at the 10-items-or-less line wants to have a conversation with everyone when s/he should just shut up and do their job	Y		N
• Traffic in general, or even just a red light	Y		N
• When your taxi driver wants to take the scenic route or any route that is not the absolute most efficient, even if the cost is only pennies different	Y		N

13

▪ When I have to wait for someone who is late for any reason	Y		N
People consistently tell me that:			
▪ I am impatient.	Y		N
▪ My life is too stressful.	Y		N
▪ I am a perfectionist.	Y		N
▪ I am a workaholic.	Y		N
▪ I am too hard on myself.	Y		N
▪ I should take more time to smell the roses.	Y		N

Calculating Your Results (see Table below):

1. Count the number of checkmarks and circles in each column (remember to count all four sections).

2. Write each column's total in the space provided in Row 1 Column Total.

3. Multiply Row 1 results in each column by the number provided in Row 2 for that column.

4. Write the result of step 3 in Row 3: Points in This Column.

5. Add all the Points from Row 3 together to calculate your Total Score.

Calculating Your Results			
Row 1: Column Total (Add Each Column From All Four Sections)			
Row 2: Multiply Row 1 by:	x3	x2	x1
Row 3: Total Points in this column:			
Add All Three Columns Together: Total Column 1			
+ Total Column 2			
+ Total Column 3			
Total Score:	=		

Results:

Less than 50 Points = Probably B

Type B's are usually relaxed, laid back people who are friendly, accepting, patient, at ease and generally content. They are usually in a good mood... *Blah, blah, blah...* Type B's are usually the people that Type A's think are lazy, passive, aimless, and will never accomplish anything. But you should keep reading because you'll probably like where this book is heading.

50-100 Points = Almost A

Almost A's (also referred to as Type A/B) want to succeed and believe in healthy competition. They occasionally struggle with work-life balance, but make it a priority to take time to re-charge. From time to time they are impatient or skeptical, but they are well-grounded and surrounded by people they trust... *Yeah, yeah...* Almost A's are people that Type A's are suspicious of and **do not trust.** Type A's view you as competition, even though they assume they can beat you. Even though you are not fully Type A, you should keep reading.

100-150 Points = Absolute A

You are a Type A! Awesome! This whole book is for you! You are probably pretty proud of yourself for passing the test, huh? And you are probably thinking you are even more Type A than I am, or any other reader who's reading this, because you strive to be #1 at everything you do. Congratulations; you are totally Type A.

Chapter 3: It's Not Easy Being A!

It is so awesome being Type A, isn't it? Ha! We totally have the world under control, and someday we're going to rule it all! You can own the mansion next to mine, and we can smoke a cigar together on the back deck and blast Frank Sinatra's "My Way" through the neighborhood. That's going to be so much fun, I can hardly wait!

I know that sounds egotistical, but if you're really Type A, you are probably told all the time that you are too hard on yourself, so I'm going to take this next section and go through all the many positive aspects of being Type A. You're going to like this part a lot.

List 1: Compliments for Type A's

Driven	Bold	Strong-willed
Organized	High-powered	Strategic
Successful	High-energy	Tactical
Motivated	Positive	Calculated
Focused	Doing Well	Deliberate
Intense	Talented	Productive
Accomplished	Thriving	Efficient
Super-achiever	Proficient	Resourceful
Multi-tasker	Expert	Professional
Determined	Highly Capable	A Winner
Ambitious	Passionate	Acclaimed
A Go-getter	Concentrated	#1

Feels pretty good, doesn't it? Let's face it: In today's world, it pays to be Type A. We are facing the challenges of some of the most difficult and demanding careers paths, and our jobs require productivity, efficiency, intelligence and determination. We should

16

thank our lucky stars every day for being Type A, don't you agree? But I'm just warming up; let's keep going.

We Type A's tend to be successful because it is our mission to achieve and advance ourselves. We do well in our careers, especially the dog-eat-dog corporate world. We are very precise, and nothing falls through the cracks when we are on the job. We are often getting recognized as the top producer, employee of the month, or the "up-and-comer." We are usually the apple of our boss' eye. We make it our mission to succeed and, therefore, we do.

We Type A's are competitive and we thrive on winning. We aren't the best team-players, but our teammates can rest assured that we will do our part to make the team #1, even if we alone deserve all the credit. We're not against teamwork, but it's a little annoying when other people can't keep up with us, and we really don't have the time or interest in bringing them up to our level. We would rather do things by ourselves because nobody else can do it up to our standards. I mean, it's sad for them, but we usually walk away from meetings with our co-workers and colleagues, thinking, "I'm the only one who really understood what the boss was talking about" or "I better start my strategy for outperforming everyone... again."

Furthermore, we prefer to remain skeptical of our colleagues, and constantly remind ourselves that they are the competition. We sometimes give them nicknames (that we never tell them about) that highlight their weakest trait, to remind us that we are better than they are. Don't hate the player, hate the game. We know it's a game, and this is how we win and why we win. If someone is doing better than us, it's safe to assume that they had a lucky break or a rich uncle. We've been known to take advantage of a situation or two, but if we didn't, somebody else would – right?

We are excellent corporate navigators and quite good at convincing others to our way of thinking. In this process, we are also masterful at packaging the truth to guide people to our conclusions. We are adaptable, even chameleon-like, which is such an asset to producing the results we want. I don't know about you, but people have told me a thousand times that I should run for office. No interest there, but at least I know I'd have their vote, which means my methods are working. Anyway, the reason we have perfected the skill of influencing people is to maintain control over our agenda for advancement. Other people are really just tools we need to use to accomplish our objectives.

Our motto is, "Feed your lions, ride your horses, beat your dogs" when it comes to clients, prospects, co-workers, people reporting to us and, sometimes, friends/acquaintances. (*Note: For those non-Type A's reading this, that basically means you pay the most attention to the people who can do the most for you, and you treat people who can't do much for you like crap.*) We have been called a bulldozer, bulldog, firecracker, the terminator, or told that we are ruthless, pushy or demanding… and we take these as compliments.

There are people in this world from whom we need approval, and we need to get them to like us in order to be selected for advancement. That means that we generally find a way of getting along with people who are useful to us, no matter what it takes. We know our assets and we use them, including good looks, charming accent, foreign language skills, or even a love of football to draw the right people in. We'll use the full arsenal of every life experience we've ever had (including things we haven't personally experienced, but read in a book or saw in a movie, or had a friend that did it) in order to be considered "one of them" with the people we need to like us. Even if we're not particularly good looking, that can be used as an asset, too. Get people to underestimate you and then the surprise attack wins the battle, the war, and demolishes the competition that never saw it coming!

Yeah, we have strong opinions, but we also make it our business to be right. If you are not Type A, you could learn a lot from us because we view being the smartest as an important part of being the best.

We'll thoroughly immerse ourselves in a topic to be an expert at it, and we usually try not to talk about things or topics where we can't showcase our superior knowledge. Which brings me to another point: If you think you have ever won an argument with a Type A... you didn't. They simply decided you were too stupid to waste any more of their precious time with, and walking away was a better option than trying to prove to you how right they are. Sorry. All you Type A's out there know exactly what I'm talking about. Ha!

People sometimes (ok, often) tell us Type A's we're impatient. And we are, but that's only because we want to be achieving more. We wish that sleeping didn't take so long because we could really use the extra hours every day to get more accomplished. I mean, since we're already working 80-100 hours per week, while also taking additional or continuing education courses in our spare time, we truly don't have time for people or activities that slow us down. We are fully invested in our professional advancement, and we'd like that advancement to move along quickly, thank you very much. Our level of dedication is unsurpassed, but we are willing to sacrifice everything because we know it will pay off in the long run when the rest of you are reporting to us.

Another great advantage of being Type A is that all the bosses and employers out there are looking for us! I'm used to getting at least two to three recruiting calls per week from competitive firms – aren't you? We are ideal candidates for jobs because we don't screw up, we over-achieve and we're efficient. I mean, we A's could all win gold medals at the Multi-Tasking Olympics! And best of all, we don't bring our emotional baggage into the office. That's because we think emotions are for sissies, so we don't have any emotions or baggage! Even if there was a death in the family, we'd probably miss only a few hours of work to attend the funeral, and nobody would really be able to tell the difference by our work product. And health issues, we don't have any of those, either. Well, we might, but we don't really take time to go to the doctor, so ignorance is bliss. The point is: You won't catch us taking time off for stupid stuff like that.

The best part of being Type A is all the recognition we get. It is sweet to be #1, the winner, the top dog. We get to enjoy those brief and fleeting moments after the award has been handed to us and we get our photo taken shaking the CEO's hand. We get the compliment of a knock on the door with a smile and thumbs up from our boss, saying what a great job we did. We get that passing bliss of vindication over anyone and everyone who ever told us it wasn't possible, or we weren't good enough, or hurt our feelings about anything, ever. We get the joy of composing a "nice guy" routine as a consolation to anyone who tried to compete against us, and lost. And we get to figure out where in our office the plaque is going to go to showcase it for all the world to see that we are the champion. And then we get into our awesome car, and go back to our perfect home that's full of great stuff, and figure out how we're going to do it all over again.

Let's face it: We're always two steps ahead of everyone and every obstacle. And yet, we are still motivated to achieve more, be better, improve ourselves and out-do our competitors.

It's Not Easy Being A

Whew! It's not easy being A. I mean it. It really isn't easy being A.

I mean, if you're with me so far on all these positive aspects, then you'll be the only person I can talk to about some of my frustrations. I can't believe I'm telling you this... but... well... I get the sense that you could relate.

You've probably read some of the same success books that I have. They tell us all the techniques and methods used by the most successful people, so if we follow them correctly, we should be successful, too. Aside from the goal-setting and tactical stuff, some of which we covered earlier, I also have books about things we do consciously and things I might be doing unconsciously to sabotage myself. If it is not a success-making thing to do, I don't want to be doing it, right?

Here are a few of the lessons I've picked up from these books (these are not my original ideas; they are truly a collection from some very respected success books):

- ✓ Don't pretend it's not a game, or play the game safely within bounds. It's a game. Play to win. Never underestimate your opponent. Fire your mother if necessary.
- ✓ Always take the job that offers the most money. If you want power, you must take power; nobody is going to just give it to you. There is no such thing as *too aggressive*. Move like a shark, eating as you go. Acquire your neighbor. Think BIG.
- ✓ Kick ass and take names. Don't help other people too much; you're not a teacher. Keep a profile on everyone in your office. If other people aren't doing their own work, let them hang themselves. Be quick and decisive on your own authority. Record your own mistakes.
- ✓ Make one more call.
- ✓ You don't need other people's opinions. Don't believe that others know more than you do. Don't put the needs of others before your own. Don't let other people's mistakes inconvenience you.
- ✓ Use office politics to your advantage. Make allies of your peers' subordinates. Cultivate a few enemies. Exploit yourself only slightly less than you exploit others. Use quid-pro-quo in *all* relationships.
- ✓ Make one more call.
- ✓ Avoid superiors while travelling. Skip all office parties. Don't go for drinks.
- ✓ Sometimes doing a *good* thing is not doing the *right* thing for yourself and your advancement. You don't always have

to tell the whole truth and nothing but the truth.

✓ Have fun. Laugh. Be in love with your destiny. Be upbeat. Do what you feel like doing. Say what you feel like saying. Cherish your boss. Say things to make people feel good about themselves. Win as many awards as you can.

✓ Make one more call.

✓ It's not about how good you are; it's about how good you want to be. Do not seek praise, seek criticism. Don't take no for an answer. It's wrong to be right, it's right to be wrong. Getting fired can be a positive career move. Do not try to win awards.

✓ When sitting at a conference room table, try to take up as much space as possible in order to appear more intimidating. Always dress one level above your co-workers; dress like your boss. Walk confidently with your shoulders back, your chest out and your chin up. Don't tilt your head when listening to people. Style your hair in a professional manner; the office is not a glamour show. Wear a watch that demonstrates your success. Wear or carry something with a company logo on it whenever you can.

✓ Meetings are not about the content of the meeting, they are about seeing and being seen, meet and greet, show and tell, and marketing yourself for promotion. Don't give a speech; put on a show.

✓ Make one more call.

✓ Don't share too much personal information or bring too many family photos to the office; you don't want people to think of you as a person. Don't be buddies with your boss.

✓ Don't be naïve. Don't be too nice. Don't be too humble. Don't be modest. Don't use your nickname. Don't wait to be noticed. Don't smile too much. Don't read paperbacks. Don't be too patient. Don't explain yourself. Don't deny your own power. Don't protect jerks. Don't care if people like you or not. Never cry. Never apologize.

✓ Make one more call.

It's hard to keep up with all these rules sometimes, isn't it? Do you ever feel just totally exhausted? Are there times when you sleep through Saturday afternoon because your week has totally beaten you up? I mean, provided I'm not working on Saturday, I can't count the number of times I've cancelled plans by saying I had something else come up, but really I needed to sleep to be ready for the upcoming week. Have you ever done that?

Do you ever feel like you are trying to put a square peg in a round hole? Or that you've adapted yourself so much that you are becoming a round peg, even though you're not one? I know we've got to play to win, but sometimes what I really want and what I'm actually doing are two different things. For example: Deep down, I really want to be that sweet and endearing kind of girl. But I curse like a sailor and I have a repertoire of dirty jokes that could make a whore blush. It's just that I had to prove I was tough enough to be taken seriously. I mean, after eight years in New York City, I guarantee you'd be swearing, too! I'm told to use my superior vocabulary, but when I do, I feel like nobody understands what I'm saying. In general, I feel like I'm banging my head against the wall. I'm doing everything right, but I'm still not where I want to be. To add to that, I think I'm failing at work-life balance. I don't like failing. Do you ever feel that way?

Do you ever feel like if you don't let it out, you might burst? For example: I'm always saying I just want some peace and quiet, but I always have noise going in the background. When I'm driving, I blast my music at top volume, and I sing along and dance in my seat to get the oomph out of my system. At home, I always have the television on or music playing, because when it's too quiet, I get anxious. Or, from the outside, I am known for having a really positive and optimistic outlook, but sometimes I get so angry, my blood boils. I try not to let it show or take it out on anyone, but I have been known to grunt a visceral animalistic growl, just to let off some steam. I also curse a lot *(I know I said that already, but I do mean a lot)*, especially when I get fired-up about something. I can use the f-word as a verb, noun, pronoun, adverb and adjective all in the same sentence. It's a skill. Do you ever do that?

Do you ever feel the need to hide things or "omit" telling someone something about yourself because you think they wouldn't like it? I mean, for example, sometimes I get tired of all the gourmet first-class food and I crave Chick-fil-A. I'll go through the drive through and chow down on an original chicken sandwich, waffle-fries and coleslaw – YUM! But I hide it because I doubt the major philanthropists in town would find Chick-fil-A as charming as I do. And sometimes I watch trashy reality shows because they really make me laugh. I just don't admit to watching them because I'm afraid it would make me look immature. Or my condo: I couldn't afford to buy, so I'm renting. But it's better if people think I own it, so I don't feel the need to tell them the whole truth and nothing but the truth. It's none of their business. Same goes for clothes. Sometimes I go to a Target that's way out of the way so I don't run into anyone, and I can sneak a few things into my wardrobe that nobody would ever know aren't designer, but they look fabulous anyway. I feel so stupid admitting this. Maybe these are lame examples. But have you ever done anything like that?

Do you ever wonder if anyone is ever going to love you? I know I do. I've been betrayed by everyone I ever loved, except for my parents, I guess. And then most of the people who seem to want to love me are needy and annoying. Who can I trust to open up to with the truth about everything? I mean the real truth, not just the image I project. What if when they get beyond the show I'm putting on, they don't like who I really am? Sometimes I look at couples that seem so happy together. Their lives seem so simple. I have a much better lifestyle than they do, but for some reason, I'm a little jealous of them. My life is not simple. Maybe there's not room for someone else. I just don't know how I'm ever going to find someone who loves me and I love them back. All that emotional stuff scares me. I've made bad decisions in the past; maybe I'm just a fool when it comes to these things. Do you ever feel that way?

And what about changes at work? Aren't you a little stressed about it? I know I get nervous sometimes about management changes. I mean, what would happen if I get a new boss and my new boss doesn't like me? If I'm not the favorite, that's going to affect my entire career, and then the future I'm trying to create could get all thrown off. A bad boss can add years to your plans, and take years from your life! I can't let that happen! If I don't create the future I want, then people won't like me anymore! People like me because I'm successful. People like to be around a winner. If I'm not a winner, they won't want to be around me. And if I don't get my mansion and cars and fabulous life, then people won't know that I'm a winner that they want to be around. And then I wonder why I'm not further along by now. It's so frustrating, isn't it? We work harder than everyone else, and yet, we're not there yet. I wish I could just skip a few stages in life and be older and more successful already. A little gray hair wouldn't be so bad. It would probably be good for business. Why do I have to go through every step? This whole thing takes too long. Do you ever feel that way?

And watching the movies, don't you ever feel like you are that guy who has it all going for him, but loses everything important in his life (i.e., family, friends) because he works too much? I watch those movies and I *know* I am that guy! Ok, I know I'm technically a girl, but you know what I mean. *Family Man* with Nicholas Cage – totally me. *Click* with Adam Sandler – totally me. *It's a Wonderful Life*, Ebenezer Scrooge, maybe even the Grinch! But even though I know this, there is nothing I can do about it right now. I'll have to take care of it later. I just don't know exactly when later is going to come. Do you know what I'm talking about?

I'm such a disappointment. All these sacrifices I've made and nothing to show for it. I think I need to read a self-help book or a

25

book about empowering myself. I think I'll plan to watch the movie *Wall Street* tonight to remind myself not to be such a wimp. I think I should play my theme song, Frank Sinatra's "My Way," right now to keep my eye on the prize of what I'll be listening to when I finally get where I'm going.

Listen to it with me:

*...la la la......***I did it my way.**

Regrets, I've had a few; but then again, too few to mention.
I did what I had to do; and saw it through without exemption.
I planned each charted course; each careful step along the byway,
And more, much more than this, **I did it my way.**

Yes, there were times, I'm sure you knew,
When I bit off more than I could chew,
But through it all, when there was doubt,
I ate it up and spit it out.
I faced it all and I stood tall, **and did it my way.**

*...la la la......***I did it my way...**

To think I did all that; and may I say, not in a shy way –
Oh, no. Oh, no, not me; **I did it my way.**

For what is a man? What has he got?
If not himself – Then he has naught.
To say the things he truly feels
And not the words of one who kneels.
The record shows I took the blows
And did it my way!

Ok. Type A batteries recharged!

Uh-oh. Um, all those things I just confided in you... please don't tell anyone. I really don't like admitting that I have any problems whatsoever. I don't want anyone's pity and I certainly don't want their suggestions for solutions because their solutions probably wouldn't work. Besides, it's none of their business, and they probably wouldn't understand. I don't want them to think I'm weak, because if they think I'm weak, then they'll probably try to take advantage of the situation, and that could set me back on my plans, and I don't want that to happen. There's nothing I can't handle. I'm going to keep recharging, and by tomorrow, I'll be back in the swing of things again.

I'll do it my way. I'll have it my way. I'll get it my way. I create my destiny. I am in control. I am the CEO of my life.

Chapter 4: The Outcome of A

Hi. My name is Wendy, and I am a Recovering Type A.

You respond: "Hi, Wendy!!!"

No, I'm not repeating myself. But I do have to tell you that from here on out, you are dealing with the new and improved Wendy who has already gone through the transformation process and is living life as a Recovering Type A.

I have written section one for you in the perspective of a Type A, so you would know beyond a shadow of a doubt that I have walked in your shoes. This is the way I was for many years of my life, especially during the investment banking years. I must admit, it's difficult for me to re-live some of that stuff. It must be how a recovering addict feels when they watch themselves on A&E's *Intervention*. I know I was that way, but I'm not that way anymore.

I have made significant changes to my life, my perspective, my priorities and my actions. I don't know if I'll ever *not* be Type A, but I'm doing the best I can, and I take one day at a time. If you are really Type A, you probably hear that and think, "Oh crap, not another mushy, emotional, weak wannabe who just wasn't tough enough to make it in the real world, which is why she dropped out like a quitter *(loser)*, and now she's going to try to tell me what to do and how to live my life?" Yeah, I would have thought that, too. But, I am not mushy, emotional or weak; I am not a wannabe, and as a matter of fact, I am tough as dirt. I used to receive accolades and praise for my chutzpah all the time. People would remark in awe of my straight-shooter style and toughness. I would simply smile, thank them, and remind them that *"My balls are so big, I have to wear a skirt."* No, I am not making that up; I actually said that.

The point is this: There are reasons to recover from being Type A. No matter how much you think you can't change, or the world has sucked you in; or you want to change, but you can't do it right now. It's going to catch up with you sooner or later. It caught up with me, and I was doing a fantastic job of maintaining my Type A priorities. The catching-up-with-you process is painful, and the whole reason I'm writing this book is to spare you from even a morsel of that suffering. The best of you Type A's out there are still thinking, "This really doesn't apply to me." Yes, it does.

If you don't want to listen or believe me, suit yourself. Just know that there will come a day when you will be wishing you had listened. There will come a time when you are striving to perform and achieve by every standard of measurement you can think of in this world, following all the formulas for success with perfect precision, doing everything right, and yet you will come up unfulfilled, lonely, disappointed, anxious and feeling foolish. The opposite of your ambition. Believe me, I'm not wishing this on you; I'm just saying there's an insanely high probability of it happening, whether you like it or not.

Even if you escape a short-term downfall, you'll still face long-term consequences. After you retire, you'll discover a few things. First, you'll quickly become useless to the corporate world, and your best contacts and acquaintances will be the first to drop out of your life. Then, you'll discover you have no real friends except for people who say they are your friend, but all they really want is your money or what's left of your influence. Of course, you'll have no companion, spouse or partner since you called it quits on marriage after three to four devastating divorces, or never being able to replace *the one that got away.* So you will sit there and ponder life, alone in your mansion, bitter and old, and choking on your Botox, with only your maid or butler to listen to you; but they listen only because you pay them. Won't that be nice for you?

~A~

Case Study: The Economist

I have had the good fortune to meet a few of the leading economists of our time. I won't name names, but there is one in particular I'm thinking of, whom I met at a private dinner party. During his career, he was highly revered in the top circles of society, received honor after honor, lectured at Harvard, Yale and the rest of the best, and served on numerous Boards of Directors of publicly-traded companies, philanthropic organizations, and the like. However, once he hit 70, he was circulated off the Boards, which nudged him into retirement.

To meet him now: He is one of the crankiest, most cantankerous, bad-tempered, irritable, disagreeable, and just plain crabby egomaniacs you will ever encounter. You know why? Because his entire identity was wrapped up in his status, his positions, his possessions, his high-society friends, and his accomplishments. When whittled down to just being himself, he doesn't have a clue who he is without the external accolades. He doesn't really have any friends because he discovered that a lot of people were just using him. It's hard for him to make new friends, because he is so arrogant. And he spends all of his time telling you about his past accomplishments to prove how important he once was. He's obviously very smart, but he lacks true wisdom. He also lacks true self-worth.

Case Study Query: Are you on the path to being that guy? Will your journey to accomplishing everything society dictates take you so far away from yourself that you no longer know how to be yourself? Have you ever known how to be yourself?

~A~

Let's face it, the only reason you picked up this book in the first place is because you thought you could relate to it in some way, or you already know you are a Type A. Maybe you thought it could give you a different perspective, or you thought it could help you figure something out, or even make your life just a little bit better. The truth is, all of us want to live a better life. The best possible life. As a Type A, you are no stranger to envisioning your future, and I hope in some small way this book will help you create the future you really want. As Henry James said, "It's time to start living the life you imagined."

Intermission: How I Got Here

The purpose of this book is not autobiographical. Though I do share relevant stories from my experience and use the "case studies" collected from many people I have known along the way, I do that strictly for the purpose of transparency with you. My mission is to help you, and sometimes that means I have to use myself as an example, even if it is, unfortunately, an example of what *not* to do.

If this were an autobiography, I would go into much more detail about the events leading up to this next chronicle. However, since it is not an autobiography, I'm not going to go on tangents like that, and will instead stick to what is relevant to Type A's. Though I'm *recovering*, I'm still a Type A, so I like to get straight to the point.

I returned from an extended time in Europe with no job, no man, and no place to live. My decision to go there was based on both personal and professional opportunities. I thought I would return to the States engaged to be married and engaged in the highest levels of international diplomacy. The guy I thought I was getting engaged to had been requested by the Queen as the next US Ambassador to Denmark. I know it sounds crazy, but what can I tell you? That's why going into the details would only take us off track.

So, like I said, I returned from an extended time in Europe with no job, no man, and no place to live. I had made decisions along the way that seemed like fantastic opportunities, but they blew up in my face. I had left my job before departing for Copenhagen, and by the time I got my computer up and running overseas, there were half a dozen e-mails waiting for me from former competitors wanting to hire me upon my return. That had been a great feeling. However, by the time I was back in the States, the economy had completely tanked, and nobody was hiring. I evaluated my options. Neale Donald Walsch says, *When Things Change, Change Everything.* So I did. I moved to a city where I thought there would be more opportunity for me to make a fresh start.

But something strange happened. As I went through a long period of unemployment, I realized that everything I had previously centered my identity around had been stripped away from me. Instead of being Wendy with the job, title, and income that were years ahead of my peers, I was Wendy the unemployed girl. Instead of living in one of the newest and nicest, high-rise condo buildings in town, and even the most prestigious and luxurious neighborhood, I was living in someone else's guest room. Instead of being able to talk about my plans and projections for my fabulous future, or the fabulous private cocktail party I went to last week, I was all hat and no cattle. All the things I was accustomed to taking pride in and branding myself with were pushed further and further into the past, and talking about them became a useless performance that had nothing to do with my current situation.

My professional experience was all in the financial industry, and since most every financial institution was making major layoffs, not hiring, I knew I had to reinvent myself in order to be the perfect candidate for some other kind of job. But what was that going to be? I panned over my resume and experience, considering the options and possibilities. I wrote ten resumes, encapsulating my experience in ten different ways, highlighting the many aspects of my know-how and expertise. Truth be told, there were some great jobs out there that I was qualified and even overqualified for. Unfortunately, the thought of doing most of these jobs day in and day out was absolute torture. Then I started negotiating with myself like, "I'm going to take a job like that only if it pays me X. I've made XX in the past and I'm not going to go backwards at this point in my career. At least if I'm making X, then I can have the life I want, even if I'm not happy *(miserable)* at work." Negotiating with myself didn't work. Even the money couldn't get me excited. The account I needed to draw from was overdrawn, and I don't mean my bank account. My spirit account was bankrupt. My enthusiasm was gone. My passion was flat. My chutzpah had left the building.

Who was this unmotivated person I'd become? I had always been the first one to step up to the plate for new challenges and more responsibility. I had been a prime representative and networking maven for my employers. I was the deal-maker, the one on the fast track, the go-to girl with a knack for even the most difficult clients. People liked me, trusted me, enjoyed doing business with me, believed in me, and wanted to be a part of my future. I served on Boards of Directors of non-profit organizations and was always elected to leadership. I'd even been featured in magazines and newspapers with articles, highlights, and pictures in the social section. I had built a reputation and a name for myself. As I sat pondering the amount of energy I had put into creating that reputation, the thought of keeping up the pace I had set was exhausting. To add to it, I had moved, and the thought of re-building such a reputation in a new city was completely overwhelming. I knew I didn't have it in me. Instead of the spotlight, I craved anonymity. Instead of representing and networking, I yearned for peace and solitude. Instead of the society pages, I wanted to be nobody. Instead of responsibility and being the go-to girl, I needed to be relieved of duty.

As I was reviewing and reflecting on all this experience of mine, it occurred to me that I'd never had a job that fully satisfied me or ever could have fulfilled me. It's not that I wasn't good at my job or didn't have enough potential or talent. It's not that I didn't have enough encouragement or support. It's not that I didn't try hard enough or have enough passion or determination or vision. I even made good money, especially compared to my peers, but it was never enough. Every time I acquired or achieved something, there was more to make, more to get, more to achieve, and it was further off in the distance all over again.

The things that could fulfill me were things I didn't have time to do since I was completely committed to my 80-hour/week job and career path of a champion. There are certain things you can't do at home when you're travelling for business every week, and it's hard to have a personal life when you're always at the office. But that was part of making the right sacrifices associated with long-term success, wasn't it? I had all the quotes of so many masters running through my head, telling me that being dissatisfied with the status quo was a good thing; that I should focus on where I want to go; that the sacrifices of today are the payoffs for tomorrow; and that I should never, ever, give up. This was the prescription, and I'd followed the instructions perfectly.

I looked at my Dream Board, and some of these images staring back at me had been there for years and I still didn't have them. They were laughing at me. Betraying me. Mocking me. I'd been following the formula perfectly, so how was it possible that these things had not manifested their way into my life yet? I had read all the success books, seen *The Secret* twenty times, envisioned it already being mine; even prayed about it. I'd done everything right, so where was my stuff?

How had this happened? I'd lost my drive, and to add insult to injury, the life I envisioned hadn't arrived. The prescription for success did not come with a side-effects warning, but I was kind of thinking it should have. If it had, it would have read like this:

> Potential side effects include: exhaustion, frustration, misery, loneliness, loss of authentic identity, disappointment, exasperation, anger, resentment, jealousy and distrust of others, and bouts of being an arrogant and narcissistic egomaniac.

As I continually asked myself what I wanted to do with my life, I realized that all my priorities were out of whack and had been for some time. I was a Dream-Board junkie, shooting for the moon and hot-wiring my rocket ship to try to get there faster. I'd been pumped full of so much information about how much potential I had, how much I could control my destiny, how nothing was impossible for me, and how I could do anything and everything I set my mind to do. I had taken the reins in my life and set out on a path to the other side of the rainbow and the pot of gold. But how many perpetual Dream Boards was it going to take for me to be satisfied? When would this cycle ever end?

I was living in the future. I was making decisions today based on projected circumstance. I was sacrificing the moment for a prospective upcoming chapter of my life. To paraphrase Tim Connor, I was mortgaging my present for a future I couldn't guarantee I would have. Or as Eric Hoffer said, "We are warned not to waste time, but we are brought up to waste our lives." Or Thoreau: "As if you could kill time without killing eternity!" Ouch! You mean to tell me that all the effort and sacrifice I've put into using every minute of every day is not the path to success, but the path to wasting my life? Why didn't anybody tell me that?

I thought I could control everything. I was doing everything right, and somehow everything turned out wrong. The decisions I'd been making with my Type A priorities were throwing me way off track of the life I really desired. How did my identity become so wrapped up in my career and the stuff I had? Did I really need any of that stuff to be happy? Who am I really, under the layers of bling bling, title, status, and society? Had I become a living, breathing version of my public profile? Had I repackaged the truth of my life so much that it was no longer accurate? Had I become too advanced at justifying my decisions through society-driven, culturally-endorsed excuses, whether they were right or not? Did I even know how to be myself anymore? And what about those people I'd stomped on in the process? People whom I'd fired, out-performed, or at least out-maneuvered?

What do you do when you discover that the priorities you thought were of utmost importance turn out to be ones that aren't important at all? Everything I knew of myself was shot down. I had completely lost my identity.

A friend of mine compared it to what she experienced when she had her first child and stayed at home. Her transition from professional woman to stay-at-home mom changed her world so drastically that she went through a "Who am I?" crisis, because everything she had known herself to be was gone or different. Instead of designer suits, she was wearing t-shirts and blue jeans with spit-up on them. Instead of a stylish new briefcase, she carried a diaper bag. Instead of conferences, trade-shows or trainings, she was watching Barney and Elmo. Instead of being the top producer, or on the fast track to making partner, she had the responsibility for the life of a child and raising a person into this world. Instead of being the chief bitch that could combat any conference-room drama, she now had to protect her little one from the evils of the world. Instead of advancing and manipulating the system to her advantage, she became a teacher of right and wrong, hoping beyond hope that her daughter would make good choices and stay on track. Instead of competing to be the best at everything, she wanted the absolute best for her child in all circumstances, no matter what.

I didn't have a baby. In my case, I discovered that I was the baby. Well, more like simultaneously the mother and the baby because I had to re-teach myself and re-learn life's lessons through a new lens. And in order to raise myself up in a new life, protect myself from the evils of the world, stick to the basics of right and wrong, make good choices and hope the best for myself, I needed to make some serious changes.

~*A*~

Case Study: The Millionaire

Bravo's show *The Millionaire Matchmaker*, and specifically Patty, the Matchmaker, is absolutely hilarious. She speaks the truth, which is often a sharp contrast to what her millionaire clients are used to hearing from people who spend all day pandering to them. She sets up matches, and we get to watch what happens.

In one episode, there was a millionaire who was extremely concerned that women were after his money and were attracted to him only because of it. As the show progressed, he found the woman he wanted to bring on a date. When he took her out, he picked her up in a shoddy old truck, and brought her to an apartment in a shady neighborhood, telling her this was where he lived. Then he took her out to dinner at a second-rate restaurant; no, that's giving it too much credit, it was more like a pub. *(Not that there's anything wrong with eating at a pub, but remember the girl is expecting a millionaire date.)* Over dinner he tells his date that he had lied to Patty the Matchmaker and isn't really a millionaire. His date handled it like a champ and told him she was having fun with him and didn't care. They finished their dinner. Through their conversation, he gained comfort and a sense of security that this girl liked him for who he really was and was not after him for his money. So, they got back in the truck, and he brought her to the other side of town, to his multi-million-dollar mansion, with Range Rovers and Ferrari's in the garage. Showing her everything, he proceeded to tell her that this was actually the real him, and what he really had to offer her. She had passed the test of liking him without the riches and now this was all her prize.

I'm sure some of you successful guys out there are thinking you should try this method, if you haven't already. Don't. It's not about the money. If you are basing your entire identity on your money and status and what you have, how can you expect anyone to like you for anything else? What you're getting back when a girl likes you primarily for those things is exactly what you asked for and exactly what you deserve. Only after you base your identity and worth on *who you are on the inside* will people start to appreciate and value you for your best qualities.

Just as an FYI, the girl was ticked that he had lied to her and staged this whole production. He got himself kicked out of the Millionaire's Club, and he didn't get a second date.

Case Study Query: What are you basing your identity on?

~*A*~

At this point in my journey, I was already a believer in God, but I realized I had turned my back and wandered away from Him. Now I knew I needed to turn back around, apologize for straying, and snuggle up on His lap for protection, guidance, and love. I needed to really, truly, once and for all, *give it to God.* You've heard that expression a thousand times, I know. So, why are we so in the practice of giving it to God and then taking it back and doing it ourselves? I knew it would be challenging for a control-freak like me to trust in God and His ways. But now, regardless of that, I knew I needed to be accountable to God – and God alone; to give Him control, keep Him first in my life and allow Him to restore my soul.

This was a major turning point. The beginnings of that inner change I'd heard people talk about, but hadn't really experienced myself. I wanted God to direct my every move. I knew that the more I had taken things under my own control, the more I had screwed things up. For once in my life, I didn't want to be responsible for the results. I was willing to give God credit for whatever happened to me, and trust in His process for my life, no matter what.

But I'm getting ahead of myself. Let's first talk about why you might want to consider recovering from being Type A.

Section Two

To A or Not to A?

Part I

Chapter 5: Why Do I Need to Recover?

I'm glad you're still with me. I know some of you aren't convinced yet. You are probably thinking something like this: "Why do I need to recover from being Type A? What's wrong with being successful or wanting to be successful? What's wrong with enjoying luxury or wanting wealth? What's wrong with wanting more power and influence? If I'm not controlling things, then someone else will be, and I'd rather be in control." You'd probably like to say something to me like, "Welcome to earth, idiot; don't you know how it works here?"

I'm not here to tell you that working hard to achieve your dreams is bad. But I will tell you that your dreams may be focused on things you *want* instead of things you *need*. What happens when you get things you want instead of things you need? You wind up empty. You always wind up wanting more... and more... and more... because your needs aren't met. You will never meet your needs through the lousy imitation of filling your wants and desires. Plus, you will lose yourself in the process. If you're telling yourself that money solves everything, you are lying to yourself.

So here's the question: What do we need? You, me, all of us... what do we need to create satisfaction and happiness? It is not a simple question. Just asking it makes my mind race across the world to all the people who already have less than I have. The whole, "There are starving people in the world, so finish your dinner" theory. But let's not get extreme and lose the point through worst-case examples. There will always be those more fortunate, and there will always be those less fortunate than us. I'm not talking about them right now,

43

I'm talking about you, so please resist the Type A tendency to be flippant about this process or things that come up and make you uncomfortable.

I'm going to take a shot here, and say that our deepest needs are: fulfillment, love, joy, peace and wisdom. I may be missing a few, but if you had fulfillment, love, joy, peace and wisdom, do you think you would be satisfied and dare I say, happy? I must admit I think I'd be pretty satisfied if I had those things.

Those probably aren't the words you were expecting me to say. They're probably not the things you've been focusing on in your life. If you are Type A, you were probably thinking I was going to say success, wealth, fame, power, and control, because those are the things you have been focusing on. So, let's do the math. If our deepest needs are fulfillment, love, joy, peace and wisdom, and you add that together with the Type A priorities of success, wealth, fame, power, and control, what do you get? Here's my experience: Deepest Needs + Type A Priorities = Dissatisfaction, Loneliness, Disappointment, Anxiety and Feeling Foolish. For some reason, Dr. Phil is in my brain asking me, "How's that working out for you?"

I fully understand that you are probably getting defensive and trying to convince yourself that you are not dissatisfied, lonely, disappointed, anxious or foolish. You may not be totally dissatisfied, or you may think that dissatisfaction is a good thing and a fuel for positive change. You may have someone in your life right now, so you don't feel that lonely – for now. You might have just accomplished something great, so you don't feel disappointed at the moment. You're probably anxious, but you brush that off because it comes with your high-stress job. What about feeling foolish? Anyone looking at what you've accomplished in your life would know that you are not a fool, right? Welcome to denial, my friends. What I'm getting at is this: If you are about to try to slip by and tell me that this does not apply to you, cut the crap. Stop. Turn around, go back, and check your score to the quiz in section one. If you are Type A, this does apply to you.

Why do you need to recover from being a Type A?

The problem with living life with a Type A set of priorities has four primary interwoven symptoms. In no particular order, they are: trying to control everything, living in the future, focusing on wealth and possessions, and compromising or neglecting character. I'm sure there are more, but that's enough to tackle right now.

Our future is so close we can taste it, but it isn't here yet. So we're all sitting here with Dream Boards and affirmations thinking we can control and manifest everything we want in our futures while completely forgetting to take advantage of the present moment. We wind up existing instead of living, and the existing we're doing is totally stressed out. When something happens that is out of our control, we have no method for coping, other than to try to control it more. This is the path to fear and disillusionment.

And then, because we've been trying to control the future, we have made so many sacrifices of the *now*, that our desire to pay ourselves back (the justification of "It'll be worth it when...") can be summarized as a bling-bling, extravagant lifestyle. We center and attach our identity and security to wealth and money, thinking that once we're rich, we'll be safe, secure, and satisfied. But we won't be. Instead, we'll be running on the Type A treadmill of expectation, never having enough to satiate ourselves. This is the path to remorse and exhaustion.

And we're so busy controlling things and making sure we are still on the path to this fabulously wealthy future of our design and creation, that we make character compromises to guarantee results. We build up an accumulation of personal and spiritual concessions, hardening our heart for the battlefield and competition, selling our soul with minor and major infractions, bargaining with our conscience, bordering ever so close to the line of emotional depravity. This is the path to bitterness and spiritual bankruptcy.

So, if you take a look at that, Type A priorities lead to fear, disillusionment, remorse, exhaustion, bitterness, and spiritual bankruptcy. Is that reason enough to recover before it's too late?

To examine the four symptoms of living with Type A priorities, we're going to take a look at them in the next few chapters through different lenses. The symptoms are so interwoven, that picking them apart and putting them back together again would be a complicated Humpty-Dumpty exercise. Instead, we'll look at Deconstructing the Dream Board, Modern-Day Bankruptcy, and Type A and the Seven Deadly Sins, followed by a Type A Challenge. Hopefully, looking at Type A in these ways will demonstrate how our Type A tendencies can indeed result in dissatisfaction, loneliness, disappointment, anxiety and feeling foolish, instead of fulfillment, love, joy, peace and wisdom.

In these chapters, there will be occasions for you to pause and review your own Type A life and priorities. Every once in a while, I'm going to throw out a series of questions for you to ask yourself. These are the same questions I have asked of myself, and the result is this book. Being a Type A, I know you are in a hurry, and probably don't have time to pause, but I hope you will make an attempt anyway. Here are some to get you started.

Questions:

- ✓ Are you in love with your life right now, or are you in love with where you are going?
- ✓ Do you believe that money, possessions, and power can satisfy your hungry spirit?
- ✓ Are you selling your soul for the purpose of personal advancement?
- ✓ Do you fully comprehend that you cannot control everything?

Chapter 6: Deconstructing the Dream Board

What is on your Dream Board? Oh come on, you know you have one! Isn't it common knowledge that in order to achieve or acquire whatever we want in our lives, we need to put it down on paper, make it a goal, visualize it being ours and maintain a positive attitude, and soon enough it will magically be delivered to us?!

For those of you who don't have one, a Dream Board is basically a collage of images you have cut out of magazines showing the things you want in your life – e.g., a new home or car, a vacation destination, clothes, and the like. Then through the process of visualization, and believing that you already have this stuff in your life, it manifests into existence one way or another. With this technique, you can "treat the universe like your personal catalogue" and get anything you want in this world.

If goal-setting is more your style, you take a gigantic, seemingly insurmountable goal and break it down into short-term, mid-term, and long-term goals. Then you formulate a plan around how you are going to meet these goals, take control of your destiny and step-by-step, you are empowered to make your dreams come true.

Here is a list of things people generally have on their Dream Boards. If you have one, some of these are probably on there. If you don't have one, this will prompt some thoughts for what might be on yours.

- ✓ Having more money than you can imagine
- ✓ Having all the latest gadgets
- ✓ Being promoted to Partner

✓ Having a designer wardrobe, complete with accessories
✓ Owning a Rolex, or other status symbol
✓ Owning a sports car, BMW, Mercedes, or Range Rover
✓ Owning your own business/being your own boss
✓ Being a worldwide expert in your field
✓ Being on the cover of *Fortune Magazine*
✓ Winning an award
✓ Living in a mansion, or just a bigger house in a better neighborhood
✓ Being one-half of the city's "Power Couple"
✓ A bigger office
✓ A better title
✓ A better parking spot, proving that you are the big cheese
✓ Owning properties in four different countries
✓ Owning a private jet or yacht
✓ Being famous, a celebrity
✓ More power
✓ Memberships to all the best country clubs, front-row sports tickets
✓ Going to the spa every day
✓ Living with more extravagance and luxury
✓ Bigger, better, faster, more…

Sounds pretty good, huh? I'd have to agree, but here's where it gets tricky. Hear me out. There is nothing wrong with wanting any one of the things on this list, or even wanting a variety-pack assortment of these things. I am not anti-Dream Board. There is nothing wrong with wanting anything for yourself and working hard to get it. However, when your decision-making process becomes centered on these things as top priority, or when you start to compromise your character with a rogue "anything it takes" justification for getting them, that is where we Type A's fall off the wagon. The mark of an addict is confusing the difference between what you want and what you need. Type A's are no different.

So, then, let's take a look at what's on your Dream Board. Having more money than you can imagine, all the latest gadgets, a designer wardrobe, living in a mansion, and the like. Are these things capable of delivering fulfillment, love, joy, peace and wisdom? Hmm... Now, if you are really Type A, and an expert at justifying your perspective, you're probably thinking, "Well, if I had more money than I can imagine, that would give me peace and joy. And then, I could use that money to do something that I would find fulfilling, even if I don't know right now what that might be. And because I wouldn't have to work, I'd be able to spend more time with the people I love, and then they'd love me more, so that takes care of that. And lastly, because I'd have the time, I could read more, and that would give me wisdom."

WRONG.

Dream-Board Living

You might be wondering why I am picking on Dream Boards. I am not anti-Dream Board. I'm not Henry David Thoreau telling you to go live in the woods, and I'm not even telling you that wanting anything luxurious is bad. However, since we Type A's have a tendency to confuse what we want with what we need, I can share with you from experience that Dream-Board living will not produce fulfillment, love, joy, peace and wisdom. Quite the contrary. Dream-Board living can lead you astray because it encapsulates three of the four major symptoms of being Type A: living in the future, focusing on wealth and possessions, and trying to control everything.

W.T. Grenfell said, "Real joy comes not from ease or riches or from the praise of men, but from doing something worthwhile." The whole idea of "When I get ___, then I'll be happy" is pretty much an act of scamming yourself because even when you get what you want, it could never possibly produce the long-term happiness you assured yourself it would. James Oppenheim said, "The foolish man seeks happiness in the distance; the wise man grows it under his feet."

Being satisfied with what you have is a current, continuous, real-time thing. If you are not content with what you have now, you will never be satiated by what you want. Basing your contentment on money, status, or circumstances forces you to measure and compare with the external world rather than seeking contentment internally. As James Dobson says, "Comparison is the root of all feelings of inferiority." Basing your identity on money, status, or circumstances you hope to achieve in the years to come is doomed to be disappointing. And, trying to control everything to bring that future to fruition is certain to be disastrous.

Society's band-aid is to tell us to keep our eye on the prize, persevere and maintain a positive attitude. You can make your dreams come true if you just believe in yourself and work hard. But guess what? No matter how positive a spin you put on it, or how great your attitude is, the whole thing is driven by negativity and lack of appreciation for your current abundance. It is destination-style thinking instead of enjoying the moment before you right now. In the words of Ken Keyes, Jr., "When will you realize that *today* **IS** the *tomorrow* you hoped for yesterday?" Why is it that even when in the depth of your soul you know that what you really want is fulfillment, love, joy, peace and wisdom, you still keep creating a Dream Board that continually drives you back into the rat race? As Lily Tomlin said, "The problem with the rat race is, even when you win, you're still a rat."

How did this all start? Why has society lied to us? There are variations on this generalized example (including my own), but let me break it down for you:

Once you get out of college, you are thrust into the real world and all its realities. First off, you've been pumped full of confidence by your professors to believe that you possess the most valuable thing in the world to offer employers, and that is your education, from their school, which is the best. Your expectations have been lifted to shooting for the moon and you'll land on a star. *(Dream Board – conquer the world.)* Then you get a job filing papers, and it dawns on you that no matter how far you tried to shoot, the star you landed on sucks.

Then you feel bad about yourself and your situation because this job is obviously not to your academic or intellectual level. Then you have an identity crisis when the reality of who you must be for a few years to prove yourself to the real world is different from what you thought you would be. As you do the office walk of shame to your cubicle, it is a stark contrast to your fantasy of walking into your own personal office every morning in a designer suit with your Starbucks in hand. *(Dream Board – image of success)* Then, because your short-term plans are so out of whack with your current reality, you start wondering if your long-term plans have any merit whatsoever and how "long-term" they actually are compared to your original projections.

Then, when you get home, you look around your crappy apartment while trying to block out the noise coming from your roommate(s), and realize this is not the luxurious loft you thought you'd be living in by yourself at this stage in your life. *(Dream Board – better home)* Then, because you hate your lifestyle, you start freaking out that you are not earning enough, so you put even more pressure on yourself at work to be an achiever and fierce competitor, so you can get a raise or promotion. *(Dream Board – promotion, more money)*

Then, when you run into someone else in your peer group, or just anyone, really, you start assuming that they must be doing better than you (whether they are or not) and you'll do everything in your power to make it seem like you are doing just as well, if not better, than they are. Nobody wants to feel like a loser – or worse, admit that they feel like one, or might even be one.

51

So basically, you're working your tail off in a menial and repetitive job in the hopes that you'll be promoted someday so you won't have to live a Third-World lifestyle anymore, while keeping your misery a secret, which only compounds the problem, but you've heard about the power of positive thinking, and how you have the power to make your dreams come true, and you don't want people to think you're a failure, especially after all the money you invested in your education, so you decide that "Fake it until you make it" is your slogan for living, you put on a happy face, and hope your big break is coming soon.

All of this together is essentially the reason people are having what they call a quarter-life crisis because the reality of life is hitting them so hard, they give up before they even start. When did building wealth shift from being a lifetime endeavor to being a moment in time that changes everything? That one account we open that puts us in the Chairman's Club... That scientific discovery we make that becomes the next best-selling pharmaceutical... The audit we perform that saves the company and gets us promoted to partner... The legal case we win that makes headlines and secures our client base for years to come. Why are we so obsessed with *America's Got Talent* and all those other reality shows? Because everyone wants to believe that their moment is coming. Their 15 minutes of fame, their opportunity to make millions, that personal miracle that changes everything for the better and then you never have to worry again.

I'm telling you right now, that moment never happens for 99% of the population of this world. Oh, we all have great moments in our life, no doubt, but very few of us will ever have a never-have-to-worry-again moment. Why? Because even if you have that moment, it may not be all it's cracked up to be. Do you realize that the majority of people who win the lottery wind up going bankrupt? Or if you think you're too smart for that, I had a wealth management client who won the lottery for $90 million. Even though he was smart with the money, the aftermath of winning almost tore his family apart.

But still we're waiting for our big break because we aren't satisfied with where we are now. We're living our life on our Dream Boards and in the future, instead of in reality and the present moment. We're working our tails off, but are still unhappy with where we are and disappointed that we can't seem to get all the way through to where we want to be. We feel unfulfilled and alone and wonder if we have made the right decisions. We feel aimless, wondering if we're on the right path at all. And even if we take a step forward, at the precise moment that we take that step, the target changes, the stakes go up again, and we're back feeling dissatisfied with where we are, here and now.

~A~

Case Study: The Goal-Setter

Let me give you an oversimplified example. A Type A friend of mine was starting a business. She read all sorts of books about making her dreams become a reality, and how she had the power to succeed. She felt empowered, as if she could accomplish anything. She had crossed all her *t's* and dotted all her *i's*. I was really proud of her.

Then she told me her goal. I didn't want to rain on her parade, so I didn't say anything to her at the time, but her goal was so big, so *shoot for the moon*, that I feared it was terribly unrealistic. Regardless of her specific business, as I calculated in my head how many "widgets" she would have to sell in order to hit her target, I knew that only with divine intervention could she achieve those results. Even though she is really good at what she does, when she didn't reach her goal, she was completely disappointed and felt like a failure. Nobody else thought she was a failure, but she did. Her disappointment didn't stem from anyone else's expectation of her, or any pressure put on her by anyone but herself.

And so the cycle goes like this: unrealistic goal → failure to reach goal → frustration → feeling like a failure → reading more about positive thinking → setting a new unrealistic goal → failure to reach goal → frustration → feeling like a failure → wondering if you are a failure → reading about never giving up → setting new unrealistic goal... you get the drift... → waiting for big break → eventual disheartening, demoralizing and giving up.

Case Study Query: Are you setting goals that are unrealistic? Is the pressure you are putting on yourself resulting in you feeling like a failure?

~A~

Our expectations have been distorted by what we see on television, read about it magazines and see in movies. Everything in our society is measured externally, constantly forcing comparison of ourselves to others to measure our status and worth. We idolize money and possessions. We idolize accomplishment and power. We become egocentric worshippers of ourselves. Everything in our culture encourages us to maximize pleasure and minimize pain. Then we turn our passions into businesses until it isn't fun anymore. In the process, we are draining ourselves of spirit and enthusiasm until we become cynical and hard. We shoot for and expect the moon and, instead, wind up dissatisfied, lonely, disappointed, anxious and feeling foolish.

That's not to say that expectations come only from within. There are plenty of external expectations placed on us. For example, when I worked at a major Wall Street firm, and was one of the few women in my particular office. Being Type A as I was, I received a lot of positive re-enforcement and encouragement from the people around me for my drive, determination, and work ethic. At the top of the top of the executive team in New York was one of the most powerful women on Wall Street. People told me I was going to be her – all the way to the top. What a huge compliment. But what a load of pressure. I mean, what if I don't even hit next month's breakpoint? Does that mean I have not only disappointed myself, but everyone who told me I was on my way to the top? My goal was just to be good; or at best, to be the top producer in the office or the region. Had their expectation of me now become my objective, only because they said I could? Maybe you've experienced something similar. And the higher you climb, the pressures only intensify.

We are told to mimic the career paths of those holding the positions we seek. How did they get to that position? What steps did they take and how can we take them? What do we need to do to get on that track? How do we need to be more like them? This is garbage. Trying to recreate someone's personal experience, happenstances, timing, connections, relationships, and just pure blessings on the way to attaining a position of power is impossible and ridiculous. You wind up trying so hard to be something you're not, and then when somebody else gets the position because they are naturally the right fit, you become bitter and angry. You feel robbed, and you were. You feel robbed of the position, but what you were actually robbed of was yourself.

And yet, society still tells us that we are in control of our destiny. Put it on your Dream Board, set goals, visualize it happening; the power of positive thinking, positive attitude, is the key to every success. It's really easy to find all sorts of readily available sources to support and justify your choices. And the "Go conquer the world" self-help and motivational books will only feed you and fire you up even more. Create your dreams, persevere, never quit, there are no limitations except the ones you put on yourself... and all that other stuff. If you are doing all these things perfectly, then why do you feel so empty? You are a perfectionist, a Type A. You are good at everything you set your mind to. So why are you so disenchanted? Why do you keep convincing yourself that you should keep applying the same formula again and again and again until it delivers your perfect life?

While planning, goal setting, visualization, positive thinking and attitude are all time-tested and proven techniques, over-planning, unrealistic goal setting, ungrounded visualization, and naïve positivity will send you on a painful path straight to mega-frustration. It's true that positive thinking works. Visualization works. Accomplishing things makes you feel temporarily triumphant. But jumping from one thing or accomplishment to the next only serves to create perpetual bouts of short-term satisfaction, to the degree that you might even think it is long-term, when it is really just a sequence of temporary substitutions. You'll start believing that you really are in control. You'll start to think you're better than everybody else. You'll feel like anything you had to do to produce results was totally justified. You'll enjoy the envy and approval of others. You will have more freedom of choice. But you will NOT find satisfaction or happiness.

Living in the Future

If you are looking at your Dream Board and making sacrificial decisions for today on the basis that it will be worth it later, you are living in the future. You are also fooling yourself. We Type A's are so focused on our goals, and *getting where we're going*, that we completely neglect the now. Saying, "I want to be *there*" is the same thing as saying, "I don't want to be *here.*" You think you're taking on the world with your positive attitude, but you are actually sowing seeds of negativity and dissatisfaction. Those seeds can only grow into bigger displeasure and greater discontent.

Living in the future is reflected every time someone tells you to stop and smell the roses. If you are Type A, you are probably sick of hearing people tell you that. I remember one week where seven different people said that to me, and all I could think was, "I don't have time for roses!" The "roses" expression is the one you always hear from people who are older. Why? Because they wish they had smelled more roses along the way. Take their advice. Take your time. Savor the moment. Slow down. Now go get yourself a treat, no matter how many calories are in it, and enjoy it!

You can also tell if you are not living in the now when someone asks you, "If you were told you had one week to live, what would you do?" If your answer demonstrates great disparity with what you are currently doing with your time, you've got work to do on your priorities. Someone asked me that once, and I responded that all I wanted to do was party. It became so obvious that I'd been working so hard for so long that I had completely forgotten to have any fun. Many people's response to this question is, travel. These are usually the same people who have not prioritized taking vacations. The biggest response to this question is, to spend more time with friends and family or those we love. Could that possibly be because we are neglecting our friends and family in our constant striving for those items on our Dream Boards?

~A~

Case Study: Hanging Out

For example, while I was building a business, I was cramming five to six appointments and an uncountable number of phone calls into every day. In the process, I met some really great people. I genuinely enjoyed them. But, no matter how cool they were, all I really wanted was their business, so I could advance my own agenda. I would laugh and joke with them, but all I wanted to do was open their account and get them into one of my previously ranked customer-retention programs. Their value to me was based entirely according to the revenue produced by their accounts.

Then one day, a couple I had been advising as clients invited me to hang out with them sometime. Of course I said yes, but I had no intention of going. Why? Well, first of all, they were not Platinum and not even Gold clients, so I had no guarantee that there would be other potential clients there for me to network with, and even if there were, they probably wouldn't be Platinum or Gold either, which really didn't do me much good. And secondly, I had completely forgotten *how* to hang out. What is hanging out, anyway? Just sitting around doing nothing but enjoying each other's company? What a complete waste of time. Do you know how much work I could be getting done during these precious hours, even if it is the weekend? And what about the people and potential clients I could be meeting if I weren't here with you? And if I'm not working or meeting potential clients, I want to be home taking a nap on the couch because I'm exhausted.

Case Study Query: How are you spending your time? Have you forgotten how to relax and hang out?

~A~

How can you determine if something is a priority? Look at your calendar and your checkbook. Case closed. If your calendar and your checkbook are full of things contributing to your Dream Board's realization, there is a very good chance you are living in the future.

57

As George Bernard Shaw put it, "The statistics on death are impressive. One out of one dies." As a Type A, I would hear this and still think that meant I needed to cram ten appointments in per day instead of six. I was so overpowered by idolizing accomplishment that I believed gaining status through accomplishing as much as I could in every minute of every day was my measurement of success and rank in life. Are you doing that? Check your Dream Board.

Focusing on Wealth and Possessions

If you are looking at your Dream Board and thinking that material things, accomplishments, and even money will fulfill you, you are focusing on wealth and possessions. You are also fooling yourself. We Type A's are so consumed with the external competition of who has what, keeping up with the Joneses, and where we rank by comparison. We're in a culture where *"What do you do?"* is more important than *"How do you do?"* and we build our identities around what we have, where we live, who we know, what we drive, and every other outward aspect of ourselves. We actually start believing that possessions are our joy, wealth is our security, and our professional or social status determines our value as a human being. But the Joneses will always have more than you, money cannot buy happiness, and having more stuff or a higher position doesn't make you better than anybody else.

Material things and accomplishments cannot satisfy you in the long-term. Why? Because they are temporary. You are seeking enduring happiness, but using impermanent objects to try to achieve it. Most of the things you want are completely unnecessary. Many of the things we seek need regular maintenance, or quickly become last-year's model. Everything from homes to clothes to cars goes in and out of style so quickly, it's impossible to keep up. Activities that once gave us joy become boring and repetitive. Once you get a promotion, you are at the bottom again. You have momentary merriment, but it's never enough. The result is, no matter what attain or achieve, we always feel at the bottom. Triumphs and possessions are just notches on the bedpost, and completely incapable of giving you lasting fulfillment.

When you introduce yourself to someone new, what are the most important things you want to mention about yourself? To make a good first impression, you probably want to tell a new person the things you are most proud of about yourself. What are those things? As a Type A, you probably include your profession and title at work, what college you went to and the highest degree you have, and a few other things about you or what you have that demonstrate your special style and flair. What if someone took your responses individually and asked, *"Who cares?"* about each one?

So, you have a great job and big fancy title. Who cares? You went to a great school. Who cares? You live in the best neighborhood, drive a BMW, and go to the best parties. Who cares? If you get as defensive as I did in this process, you are probably thinking, "It means I make good money and outrank you; it means I'm probably smarter than you are; it means I have a better life than you do." So what? Your value as a person is not tied to any of those things. Some of the wealthiest, most successful, most powerful people in the world are also some of the most broken, lost, and lonely people on the planet.

~A~

Case Study: The Empty House

I met a guy who seemed to have it all together. He was good looking, had a good job, was well-spoken and was a gentleman who held doors for ladies and didn't cuss in front of them. It didn't hurt that he drove a Porsche and owned his own place in a really good neighborhood. This guy seemed like a bona-fide great catch. We went on a few dates, and then one night after dinner, we went back to his place for an after-dinner drink. We took a slick ride in the Porsche to the great neighborhood, and pulled into the driveway of a beautiful house. He opened the door, and we walked in.

With my hand on the Holy Bible, I tell you the truth: He had no furniture, except in his bedroom. I guess his priorities were pretty clear. He had spent everything he had on the outward extravagance to keep up a façade that was completely fabricated, and lure people into his fantasy-land existence. He tried to make up some stupid story to explain why his house was totally empty, but I wasn't falling for it. Needless to say, he didn't get another date. I later found out that he was mortgaged to the hilt, was leasing the Porsche, and had kleptomaniac tendencies.

Case Study Query: Are you leveraging yourself to the hilt to present an image to the world? Have you jeopardized your security for the attainment of the latest product? Is the image you are projecting the truth or a façade?

~A~

How can you determine if something is a priority? Look at your calendar and your checkbook. Case closed. If your calendar and your checkbook are full of things contributing to your Dream Board's fruition, there is a very good chance you are focusing on wealth and possessions.

Ken Boa puts it perfectly when he says, "People are spending money they don't have on things they don't need in order to impress people they don't even like." Looking back, this conjures an image of that evening gown I purchased on my credit card, in order to never wear the same dress twice during black-tie season. Not to mention living in the right building in the right neighborhood, so people would say things like, "You must be doing well if you live there" and, of course, driving the right car to go along with it. Idolizing money and possessions through maintaining my lifestyle and displaying what I owned, led me to believe that the amount of bling bling I had to exhibit was a demonstration of the sparkle I had to offer as a person. Are you doing that? Check your Dream Board.

Trying to Control Everything

If you are looking at your Dream Board and thinking that because you can see it in front of you, you have the power to make it become a reality, you are trying to control everything. You are also fooling yourself.

60

There's no easy way to say this: You are not in control.

You don't control the world. You don't even know what's going to happen tomorrow. You cannot control what other people do. You cannot control what other people think. You cannot control the outcome of a situation. And you can control your emotions only for a while until you feel like you need to burst. *(This is where the self-help books would say, "But you can control your attitude.")*

Society tells you, "You are in control of your destiny," "Yes, you can," "Have it your way." That quickly converts to and becomes the excuse for our *me, me, me* mentality and supreme selfishness. That then leads to ruthless, heartless, bottom-line thinking, as other values are pushed aside to make room for our *ends-justify-the-means* approach. Trying to control as much as we can about every aspect of our lives, we get anxious about screwing something up. Anxiety turns to fear, and we're terrified that if we make one wrong move, if we get one strike against us on our permanent record, then we'll be working at the drive-thru the rest of our lives. We can't let that happen! What's the only answer? Try to control it more! Do you see how this could be problematic? I'm exhausted just thinking about it. As Type A's, we have major issues with this. How many times has someone told you that you are a *control-freak* or *perfectionist*?

~A~

Case Study: Me and the Diplomat

Trying to control everything led me down a very wrong path in my personal life. Well, first I must set the scene by starting with the fact that a man who was not established did not stand a chance with me, and that meant men my own age need not apply. I had worked hard to establish my reputation, and I didn't need some less-cultured or immature "significant other" embarrassing me or acting inappropriately in a way that would ruin it. Have you noticed how difficult it is to control other people? Instead, I opted to go to the other extreme, and started dating a man many years my senior, who was well established, internationally recognized, spoke nine languages fluently, and could hold his own in any classy crowd. Even though I knew he was not right for me, he was doggedly persistent, and eventually I caved.

61

At least with him, I knew what to expect and I felt in control of the situation.

Besides, what did I cave to? An upgrade in lifestyle? What could be better for a Type A? I thought it was a good, solid, methodical, never-have-to-worry-about-money-again decision. And he would tell me all the time that I never had to worry again, so I chose to believe him. Eventually, he gave me the news that he had been requested by the Queen of Denmark to be the next US Ambassador to that country. Though it is an appointment of the President of the United States of America, and the Queen doesn't always get her way, he told me the odds were greatly in his favor and he wouldn't go without me. He stroked my ego about skills and abilities with people, and painted a picture of how I, too, would have an opportunity to make my own impact on the international scene. He described the life we would have together in Copenhagen, living in the Ambassador's mansion, entertaining the highest levels of international businessmen, intellectuals, peacemakers and socialites. He even promised a marriage proposal to make it official. It all sounded like a good deal to me. I caved again. I left my job and got on a plane to Copenhagen.

The marriage proposal never came. The Ambassadorship never came. The fruitful, independent, strong-woman life I had built was left thousands of miles away with six-hours-time difference. Over the months that I lived there, I met socialites and royalty, executives and diplomats, but my spirit was forlorn and wasting away. The upgrade in lifestyle was interwoven with a downgrade in reciprocal love, happiness, hope, and possibility. To add insult to injury, by the time it was all over, I was three times worse off financially than I had been when we began. Quite the opposite of never-have-to-worry-about-money-again. (And in case you're wondering, I know it was three times worse because I maintain a Type A personal balance sheet. Did you expect any different?)

Turns out that even though I thought I had everything under control and had made good choices to protect my future, I didn't have anything under control and it wound up being a gigantic mess.

Case Study Query: What are you trying to control that could be blinding you to other truths?

~*A*~

How can you determine if something is a priority? If you are trying to control it! If you, as a Type A, are not trying to control something, it probably doesn't matter that much to you. If you are trying to steer, maneuver, strategize, and make plans to bring your Dream Board to realization, there is a very good chance you are trying to control things too much.

Lawrence LeShan guides us, "Don't worry about what the world wants from you; worry about what makes you come more alive. Because what the world really needs are people who are more alive." As a Type A, I would have heard this and, ignoring intuition, convinced myself that my perfectionist, workaholic, over-achiever, and control-freak ways were exactly what made me more alive. "I can." "I will." "I am the CEO of my life." My ego took over and was so caught up in creating my destiny, that releasing control was just not an option. Are you doing that? Check your Dream Board.

Deconstructing Your Dream Board

Deconstructing the Dream Board is just what it sounds like. Taking it apart piece by piece, the same way you put it together. What do you have on your Dream Board that is going to give you fulfillment, love, joy, peace and wisdom? If you read the last chapter, you can probably tell what was on my Dream Board. And I was well on my way to achieving most of it. Did I know what I was doing? Yes and no. I knew I was striving for the things that were on my Dream Board. I knew I was making decisions that would be on the path to achieving what was on my goals list. But I did not fully realize that I was living in the future instead of living in the present. I did not fully realize that in the process of achieving and acquiring the things on my Dream Board, I might be abandoning the best aspects of myself, or straying from the path that could actually produce satisfaction and happiness in my life. My life became a never-ending journey to the pot of gold at the end of the rainbow. My Dream Board projected where I was supposed to be and what I was supposed to have, and every day that ticked by just added more pressure to the fact that I didn't have it yet. And since time always marches on regardless of the Dream Board's realization or not, my Dream Board items had to swell bigger, better, faster and more to compensate for the passage of time. I'll use myself as an example.

Dream Board Item:	Gigantic mansion (includes having enough money to also have a maid to clean it for me)
Why it's on there:	Symbolizes status, success, power, superiority; Impresses people
What it will produce for me:	Sense of accomplishment, ego gratification, show-off appeal
Will it or can it directly produce fulfillment, love, joy, peace or wisdom?	Um... Not sure... Probably Not Oh, come on! **NO!!!**
Therefore, do I need it?	No.... sniff, sniff, tear running down cheek...

Ok. Your turn. Believe me, this can be difficult. This exercise requires absolute honesty with yourself, and that can be uncomfortable. You may not like what you hear yourself saying about what you want and why you want it. I know I didn't. Here are some additional questions to guide your thinking:

Questions:

- ✓ What is on your Dream Board?
- ✓ Why are those things so important to you?
- ✓ What lengths will you go to in order to get it?
- ✓ Are the things on your Dream Board capable of producing fulfillment, love, joy, peace and wisdom?
- ✓ Do you think you will be satisfied once you have it, or will you get there and need to make another Dream Board full of more stuff, and you won't quite be satisfied until you get that stuff?
- ✓ How many perpetual Dream Boards is it going to take until you feel satisfied? Loved? Wise?
- ✓ Does having a Dream Board full of great stuff cause you to become a greater person?
- ✓ Did it ever occur to you that what is on your Dream Board might be wrong?

- ✓ Is it possible that what you think you want may not be what you need?
- ✓ Have the accomplishments of your life become tied to your material possessions or your competitive ranking?
- ✓ Is the stuff on there really for you, or to show off to other people? Do you actually need it, or do you just really, really want it?
- ✓ Are fulfillment, love, joy, peace and wisdom a part of your Dream Board or just your presumed side effects of what's on there?
- ✓ What are you idolizing?

Repeated Case Study Questions:

- ✓ Are you setting goals that are unrealistic?
- ✓ Is the pressure you are putting on yourself resulting in you feeling like a failure?
- ✓ How are you spending your time? Have you forgotten how to relax and hang out?
- ✓ Are you leveraging yourself to the hilt to present an image to the world?
- ✓ Have you jeopardized your security for the attainment of the latest product?
- ✓ Is the image you are projecting the truth or a façade?
- ✓ What are you trying to control that could be blinding you to other truths?

~A~

This is the part where you deconstruct your Dream Board. Remember, the purpose of this book is to inspire positive change in your life. Don't just read about this exercise – go and do it!! Then come back and keep reading.

Thank you.

~A~

The exercise of deconstructing your Dream Board is all in pursuit of what is driving your decisions right now. I'll say it again: There is nothing wrong with working hard and wanting more. However, if you are not satisfied with what you have now, you are never going to be satisfied with what you want when you get it. Plus, if your Dream Board has you on the wrong path, you certainly don't need encouragement to go faster. Persevering will only take you further into the wrong and this results in disillusionment. Even if your Dream Board does not have you on the wrong path, it may cause you to approach things with the wrong motives. Achieving things for all the wrong reasons results in hollow victories. Plus, unfortunately, you can't take back the things you've sacrificed or the ways you've justified your actions or hurt other people in the process. Eventually, you arrive at a place in life where you realize you've been trying so hard to perform and achieve by every standard of our society's measurement, and yet somehow you've still come up unfulfilled, lonely, disappointed, anxious and feeling foolish. I can tell you from experience – it sucks.

Maybe the pursuit of these things has become so central to your existence that you don't even know how to deconstruct your Dream Board. Maybe you are sitting there, reading this, thinking I'm a quack or that this is useless garbage. If that is the case, you are in *Justification-land*, and I've been there. I completely and totally understand. But that doesn't make it right. Unfortunately, justification is exactly what leads to the fourth symptom of Type A priorities, which is compromising or neglecting character. Have you been selling your soul in pursuit of your Dream Board? Have you thought about your character lately? You probably don't get asked that question very often because you are probably surrounded by a lot of people who have their own Dream Boards to achieve and really don't care about your soul. But that doesn't mean you shouldn't.

Chapter 7: Modern-Day Bankruptcy

Do you guard your character, or are you making personal and spiritual concessions as you harden yourself for the brutalities of life? Are you negotiating with yourself – "I'll just do it for a little while" or "Everybody else is doing it"? Are you selling your soul for the purpose of your own advancement?

The problem with even the most minor infractions of soul selling and character compromise is that they accumulate. You deny your conscience, you make a deal with your integrity, and you go into debt with your soul. As the offenses mount up against you, your core character and spirit are worn down, and the secrecy and shame of it add interest to the arrears. We all know what Einstein said about the wonders of the compounding of interest. The problem with going into debt with your soul is that it quickly crosses over the point of repayment, and the only possible result is complete and total spiritual bankruptcy.

Modern-day bankruptcy is of the spirit. It is an eventual consequence of living by Type A priorities, with special emphasis on the symptom of compromising character. It includes the other three Type A symptoms, so there is overlap with Dream-Board living, but there are subtle differences in the nuance of underlying motives. On the path to spiritual bankruptcy, we compromise our character *because* we're living in the future. We compromise our character *because* we're so focused on wealth and status. We compromise our character *because* we're trying to control everything around us to create our destiny.

I'm not saying you are a bad person. Not at all. I don't think you are.

The smallest soul-selling happens with such frequency, it becomes almost indiscernible. It has become such a part of modern-day living that it's easy to get distracted from what is right, even while in pursuit of legitimate things. It's amazing, all the many ways we can justify a *means-to-ends, whatever-it-takes* mentality. Everybody else is doing it, and if I don't do it, I'll look like a slacker. That's the nature of the beast. Don't hate the player, hate the game. It will all be worth it in the end. Nobody else is looking out for me, so I have to look out for myself. Besides, we are a culture that endorses a *whatever-it-takes* mentality, where being a maverick or a rebel is admirable as long as you are rich, no matter who you stomped over in the process. And the pressures are so great, it's difficult to exist in the world without making some difficult choices, some of which result in us choosing the soul-selling option.

The strange thing is when it comes to soul selling, you know you're doing it, and you probably don't like that you're doing it. However, if it works, you may brag about whatever you did in order to show other people what a fierce competitor you are. I'll give you the benefit of the doubt and say that you **are** a good person. You justify your actions by saying that someday you'll be rich and powerful enough to not have to do it anymore. The problem is that by that time, your habits will be so ingrained in your behaviors and reactions that you'll most likely either continue doing it or revert back to doing it to keep getting to the next level. And at that point, you'll justify doing it by saying that it always worked for you before. Do you see where this cycle is going?

In *The Cheating Culture,* David Callahan suggests we have developed two moral compasses: one for life and the other for our advancement and success. Having our morality divided makes it easier to "be a good person" even though we're doing bad things in the name of accomplishment. George Washington said, "Few men have virtue enough to withstand the highest bidder." But what is the price for your soul? Callahan contends that the cycle of justification has become an inherent part of our culture and is starting to take hold earlier than ever before as new generations step up to the plate. In high school, the pressures to get into a good college are so immense, kids who would be earning excellent grades without cheating, cheat anyway in order to guarantee their success. This only continues through university where sustaining good grades is critical to maintaining your scholarship, getting into an advanced degree program, or being recruited by a top firm. It takes long hours of studying, and you have fewer hours because you probably have a job or two to pay for your education or earn some spending money. The demands increase, the stress intensifies, the weight of the burden seems to force you to adjust your priorities just to keep up. We already discussed what happens after you get out of college from the Dream Board perspective, and so the cycle continues.

I feel terrible for the generation coming up with the mentality of *everybody gets a trophy*. They have some huge surprises coming their way when they get into the real world. First of all, in professional life, not everybody gets a trophy. Frankly, very few people get trophies or even recognized. Depending on your work situation, you may go weeks without seeing or hearing from your boss, and when you do, it's not guaranteed to be pleasant. You don't automatically move up to the next level, unless you deserve to be there. There are office politics to contend with, and there are people who are manipulative liars with hidden agendas while they are smiling in your face. Nothing ever feels secure, so job hopping seems like a good way to move up, and the recruiters sure do seem to appreciate you. But then once you are in a new job, you are the "new guy," so you've got to prove yourself all over again. The only way to do that is to achieve and aim for that trophy that's oh, so hard to obtain.

For the validation of achievement, we wind up doing and pursuing things that are against our nature in order to build our resume and state our case to the world that we are worthy. We think we've got the whole thing under control and that we can dominate our inner man as long as it takes. *I'll do this only for a little while*, we tell ourselves. *A few years isn't that bad*, we negotiate with ourselves. *This is the path to success, and it will all be worth it in the end*, we convince ourselves. Believe me, I know there are unbelievable temptations nowadays. That, combined with a dog-eat-dog environment and *yes-you-can* reinforcement, is a deadly combination. It all fuels the fire of our Type A competitive nature because achievement and acquisition of external rewards becomes the basis of validation and substantiating ourselves and our existence. What happens when this competition goes awry and you start cutting corners, skipping steps, misrepresenting the truth, cheating, or using people as objects in order to accomplish your self-driven purposes? At what point have you completely abandoned your convictions, your integrity, and your principles in order to achieve results? The competition skews our thinking that our status in the workplace is our status in life. We look to our financial wealth for security, significance, and comfort. We look to our status to feel important and safe. Every time we move up in our careers, we feel like we are better than we were, and better than everyone below us. Wealth makes us proud and over-confident, and we start to think we got it all because of ourselves and our own powers. And if anyone tries to take it away from us, we must fight to the death to maintain whatever level we have achieved thus far.

Again, I'm not saying that you are a bad person, please let me be clear about that. Greed and dishonesty have become almost completely acceptable, if not expected, in US society, especially in business. Fraud by employees totals over $600 billion per year. The divide between the rich and the poor is expanding day by day, and we all know which side of that is more fun. It's survival of the fittest, and the winner takes it all. We idolize money and possessions. We idolize accomplishment and power. We become egocentric worshippers of ourselves. Selfishness in the *me, me, me* approach to life is overshadowing and overpowering our most important values.

The stakes are high, and the rewards are bigger than ever before. Living by traditional values and beliefs may hold you back and keep you from winning. Charles Dickens said 150 years ago that "Americans are always ready to forgive rogues – as long as they're rich."

The pressures we are exposed to nowadays, especially in the stressful jobs that Type A's flock to, have a tendency to make the lines of ethics blurry. Just the simple fact that everyone is referring to corporate existence and struggle as a game only serves to enable us to take our character infractions and the implications of soul selling just a little less seriously. We negotiate with ourselves and set our morals into battle with our worldly self-interests. *"I'll just do it this one time"* is how it all started for most of history's greatest criminals. Competition is fierce. Greed is pervasive. Everybody else is doing it. If you don't do it, you'll look like a loser. Compromising your character is more tempting today than it ever has been. The rewards are bigger. The bling bling is easier to show off. Everyone is on the hunt for status, and they envy those at the top. The winner takes it all.

We're obsessed with winning. Do you watch *Glee*? The character Sue Sylvester, played by Jane Lynch, is the epitome of character compromise under the guise of self-love and self-empowerment. She will use anyone, tell any lie, create any excuse – from the sublime to the ridiculous – to propel her agenda at any cost, in order to win. For example: tripping an old lady down the stairs, pitting people against each other, saying one thing to one person and the opposite to another, rigging coin tosses with a double-headed coin, pointing out others' failures or downfalls at every opportunity, fabricating stories to conceal ulterior motives, instituting an environment of fear through irrational and random terror, threatening law suits, blackmailing people with personal information, raiding people's space to gather that personal information, staging walk-outs on meetings to dismantle the competition, enlisting traitors or moles from the opposing team, cutting deals behind the scenes to rig results, throwing anyone under the bus to the point of getting them fired for preservation of self, and of course, hugging someone to make everything appear wonderful on the outside while the voiceover from her thoughts is saying, "I'm about to vomit down your back." One of my favorites is when she was recounting a story of selling her house to a nice young couple, but before she moved, she salted the backyard so that nothing could grow there for over 100 years, all because they made her pay the closing costs.

Ok, so Sue Sylvester is an exaggerated example. She clearly has no moral compass whatsoever, and has no compassion or even regard for anyone but herself, unless she can use them to her advantage. But would her character be so hilarious if it didn't reflect so many people we know, even including ourselves from time to time? Isn't she just an exaggerated application of everything you've read in the self-empowerment and business books?

We're in a world of corporate scandals, tax evasion, steroid use by professional athletes, and fraud in its many forms, just to name a few. It all starts with someone compromising their character for their own personal gain. Have these terribly destructive things just become par for the course? Are we numb and blind to the immorality of it all? There is a good possibility that as you are reading this, your heart is so hardened that you think I'm just stating the obvious about what's going on in the world. I know this sounds cliché, but every time you control, manipulate, lie, or cheat, you are really only controlling, manipulating, lying, and cheating yourself. With each offense, you are making a withdrawal from your character account, and eventually that account will dry up. And with each step you walk further away from fulfillment, love, joy, peace and wisdom, and closer to dissatisfaction, loneliness, disappointment, anxiety and feeling foolish.

Additionally, we can't help but allow these lowered moral standards to creep into our personal lives. That is, of course, if we even have time for one. No emotions. Harden your heart for battle. The life partner you select must be a good business decision, someone who will not get in the way of your career. Don't base anything on your feelings; it will only get you into trouble. No wonder we can't hold relationships together – we are all tin men in need of a wizard! And as Type A workaholics, it's more likely that we don't even have a personal life, and that's not nourishing to the soul, either.

Character Case Studies

Before you start thinking that you've never committed any of these offenses, and before you go into Justification-land – or even worse, complete denial – let me prompt your thoughts. Describing character compromise and soul selling is one thing, but illustrating it will be far more effective. Have you ever taken a ream of paper home with you, submitted exaggerated or false expenses, used office postage for personal mail, or anything like that? Those are minor examples, possibly in the gray area even, but it gets far more complicated. So I've assembled a bunch of Case Studies for you, with minimal commentary in between.

~A~

Case Study: The Young Lawyer

Here's an example I'm borrowing from a speech Callahan gave about a smart, ambitious, young guy who went to a top law school, and was recruited by a big firm with a huge starting salary. In return for this salary, he is expected to bill the firm's clients for a certain number of hours every year. After a few months of 100-hour work weeks, he figures out that no matter how hard he works, he cannot *honestly* bill the number of hours expected of him. Then he finds out that the other Associates are padding their bills to meet the firm's expectations. It was commonplace; no big deal. If he didn't pad his bills, he was at the bottom of the billing stats, and looked like a slacker who wasn't working as hard as his peers. If he's not working as hard as his peers (or if the partners think he isn't), then he's not going to be top of mind when it comes time for bonuses or promotions. So, what did he do? He padded his bills. He cheated. He violated State and possibly even Federal laws, not to mention the code of ethics of his profession.

73

And what happened? I'm not really sure because Callahan doesn't give the ending. It's one of two outcomes: The guy either got a promotion, or he got fired. I'm betting he got a promotion.

Case Study Query: Are you compromising your character or ethics to get ahead? If everybody else is doing it, does that mean you have to do it, too?

~*A*~

This young lawyer took control for his future and compromised his character for the aim of wealth and status. How does the story end? What would you do in his situation? How long do you think he got away with it before somebody caught him? Once they caught him, did they let it slide because he was billing so well and bringing in money? Did they use it against him if or when he did something else wrong, or just aggravated one of the partners, so they decided his fate and wanted him gone? Can you see how this gets very sticky very quickly?

~*A*~

Case Study: The System-Worker

Take Tucker the banker for example. Tucker wanted to be a top producer. Marcia was his boss and wanted him to be her shining star. She proposed a plan where she would help him be a top producer so she could get a promotion and he would step into her position. All they had to do was work the system to their advantage.

Tucker used the internal systems to identify attractive clients to transfer to himself, even though that meant stealing them from other people, many of whom he knew and shook hands with on a regular basis. Marcia worked the senior managers to get approvals for loans for Tucker's clients who were outside of guidelines. It worked. Tucker became the top producer, and even got an award at a big fancy dinner where he got to shake the CEO's hand. They both received sizable quarterly bonuses and eagerly awaited the big money to come in their end-of-year bonus.

Unfortunately for them, neither one of them made it to the end of the year. Marcia was the first to be terminated. After she was gone, those loans outside of guidelines that she had pushed through the approval process blew up... big time. Of course they did. The clients were way outside of guidelines for approval based on assets and cash flow. The loans should never have been approved, and wouldn't have been if it weren't for her manipulations to benefit her dually self-centered scheme with Tucker.

The result of the exploded loans was that Tucker's compensation plan was turned upside down. Even despite the revenue from stolen clients, he was so far in the hole that he wouldn't be getting a bonus for the foreseeable future. With a lifestyle and a family to support in a heavily bonus-driven industry, his best option was to re-package the truth. It went something like this: "I'm the top producer in my department, and the bank is screwing me on my bonus." He sang his sob story to a competing institution. He included the revenue from the stolen clients in his transfer estimates, even though he'd never met those clients. The competing institution bought the story and hired him. After six months, he was bounced out of that institution because his over-inflated estimates did not match up with his lack of results.

Case Study Query: Are you working the system too much? Would you want everything you are doing in your work day on the front page of the *Wall Street Journal*?

~A~

Tucker took control for his future and compromised his character for the aim of wealth and status. Can you honestly say that you would resist this type of temptation, especially when your boss is the one plotting the scheme? Is the important element of the story here that it backfired? Would you be applauding them if it hadn't?

~A~

Case Study: Me, the Protégé

Unfortunately, I have my own example of this. I'm not proud of it, and I don't think I'm a bad person. I'm a good person who made a bad mistake. It's uncomfortable for me to tell you this, but I always want you to know that I have walked in your shoes, and having you know that is worth more to me than secrecy about my faults. Here goes:

I had been working on some major accounts just prior to a sales breakpoint. I thought the accounts were going to open on time for me to hit the breakpoint successfully, but the prospective clients were taking longer to move than I anticipated. My mentor, who had been in the business for almost 30 years, didn't want to see me risk my Top 20 status, which guaranteed a certain class of earnings. He felt especially strongly about this because of the great things I had in the pipeline, and he said the intent of the breakpoint was performance, not a specific date. He wanted to transfer funds for me to open an account that would guarantee my hitting the breakpoint regardless of the real accounts opening on time.

I didn't want to, and fought the decision viciously within myself and with my mentor. It's hard to describe, but I had a lot of other things going on in my life at that time that made faltering over this stumbling block seem intolerable and unendurable. Besides, my calendar was jam-packed with appointments; I was getting lots of positive feedback and was building a great reputation; and not hitting this breakpoint on time would really screw up my plans and my momentum. Not to mention, I had a lifestyle to maintain, and a reduction in income would really cramp my style. Losing that status would dramatically affect my income and would, therefore, even more dramatically affect my life, which was more consequence than I could handle at the time.

I felt terrified and desperate, but my mentor told me he had done it a hundred times for other people he believed were going to be superstars in the business, and there was nothing to worry about. I'm not sure I believed him, but I figured it was incognito enough that I could skate through without anyone noticing. I figured even if I got caught, at most I'd get a slap on the wrist, but all would be forgiven once I closed the major accounts. I allowed him to transfer the funds, convincing myself that this was the way to secure my income, status, position, and superstar career path.

Instead I got fired, and so did my mentor. I deserved it. So did he. I had said so many times to myself and to him that I would rather lose honestly than win dishonestly. But fear, self-protection, and manipulating/guaranteeing the outcome won the day. You know what's worse? On the exact day of my termination, in fact a few hours afterwards, I received a call on my cell phone from two of the major prospects saying, "I'm ready to go, get the paperwork ready." Ugh. I cannot make any excuses for myself. However, in chapter 15, I will tell you what happened next.

Case Study Query: If a senior person says it's ok, but you know it's not, what do you do? Are you protecting your income or your integrity?

~A~

I succumbed to taking control for my future and compromising my character for the aim of wealth and status. Have you ever felt pressure like that? What would you do in that situation, especially when your mentor is saying it happens all the time? Is the important element of the story that I got caught? Would you be applauding my maverick skills if I hadn't?

76

~A~

Case Study: The Wormy Apple

Jill was a successful executive with a spunky personality. From the moment you met her, she was in control of the conversation, and knew everything there was to know about her topic. She had 20 years of experience, a Master's Degree and every license and professional certification under the sun. She could strong-arm anyone who stood against her by stating that she was clearly the expert and they weren't, and in a dog-eat-dog world, that's a positive thing. She was also going for her law degree, just because she thought it would be a good professional-development exercise. From the looks of it, she seemed to be the professional of choice. Who wouldn't want such an expert working for them?

But, if you did your homework on her, the picture started looking very different. Turns out her Master's Degree was from some shoddy online program (not that there aren't good ones out there, but this wasn't even accredited), and she was getting her law degree from a similar place. In looking back through publicly-available information, I discovered she hadn't held a job for longer than two years at a time since 1992, and had filed bankruptcy in 1999. On the personal side, she was on her fourth husband, and he had just filed for divorce.

Ok, it's an extreme example, I know, but in this case, the beautiful apple on the outside had a serious worm crawling through it on the inside.

Case Study Query: Are you presenting your background and capabilities in a completely authentic way? Are you skirting or smudging the truth to serve your purposes?

~A~

Jill took control for her future and compromised her character for the aim of wealth and status. Are you speaking the whole truth and nothing but the truth? Do you blur out parts of your past that make you uncomfortable or embarrassed? Are you trying so hard to present the right image that you've lost track of who you really are? Can you see how doing that ultimately leads you to being exactly like this woman?

What about your personal life? While we're so busy climbing the ladder and winning at work, we have completely lost at work-life balance. Do you know anybody who is succeeding at work-life balance? The lack of security in the workplace consumes our thoughts even when we're supposed to be relaxing. Some level of security is required for psychological development. It's not the way it used to be when people had the same job for 30 years, and could do it in their sleep. They had the opportunity to have a personal life. If you want to get ahead nowadays, a personal life is going to be difficult to manage. Margaret Fuller noted, "For the sake of making a living, we forget to live." And Isabel Lennart points out, "It can be lonesome being that busy."

One of my favorite film examples of this is in the movie *The Devil Wears Prada*. Of course, the movie in its entirety points to these sacrifices of ourselves in the name of success, but there is one scene in particular where Andy, played by Anne Hathaway, and Nigel played by Stanley Tucci, are at a photo shoot and Andy confesses to Nigel that her personal life is on the rocks because of the amount of time she's been spending at work. Nigel's response is classic: "Let me know when your whole life is in a tailspin, then you know it's time for a promotion."

James Truslow Adams said very succinctly, "There are obviously two educations. One should teach you how to make a living and the other how to live." But we Type A's don't really know how to live, do we? If we ever did know, we've now forgotten. It's difficult to have a meaningful relationship in your personal life when we are so accustomed to seeing people as objects or tools to be used as we thrust our way up to the head of the pack. It's tricky to turn emotions off during the work day, and then turn them back on again when we get home. It's tough to be tough, and be human. Here are a few Case Studies of a more personal nature, addressing some other elements of compromising your character for personal advancement or gain.

~*A*~

Case Study: The Sales-Friend

Let's take Annie who is in sales, and gets bonuses based on performance quotas. The woman working for a partner company who controls some of the territory's largest accounts is impossible and domineering. Let's call her Wanda the Whacko. Even though Annie can't stand Wanda the Whacko, Wanda the Whacko holds the key to Annie's success, so Annie slaps on her happy face and makes appointments with her. Despite her inner eye-rolling about everything Wanda the Whacko says, Annie smiles and is gushy nice to her, and soon enough starts to be rewarded with business.

Shortly after that, and because Annie's been so nice, Wanda the Whacko asks about her weekend plans, and Annie starts including her. Being in Wanda the Whacko's good graces, Annie's intention is to go around her to secure the accounts for herself, so eventually she won't have to pretend to like Wanda the Whacko anymore. But in the meantime, Annie continues to include her in her personal plans. Eventually, Annie is spending more of her time being phony with Wanda the Whacko than she does with her actual friends.

When Annie hits her limit, the whole thing crumbles. She can't stand another minute of hanging out with Wanda the Whacko, but it's too late to turn back the wheels of time on the decisions she's made. She loses her real friends because she's didn't spend any time with them. She loses her "friendship" with Wanda the Whacko, but that's ok because she never really liked her in the first place. Then she's also concerned about the business she may lose from Wanda the Whacko because she has probably been blacklisted with the clients that Wanda the Whacko controls. Plus, Annie suffered hours of wasted time with people she doesn't even like, just for business sake.

Case Study Query: Are your friendships and relationships authentic? Have your relationships been rendered down to connections and networking?

~*A*~

Annie took control for her future and compromised her character for the aim of wealth and status. Is there anyone in your life that you would never hang out with if it weren't for business? Do you have an overflowing address book or 1,000 friends on Facebook, but nobody you can really talk to? Do you feel as if people know the real you, or do they know your public profile?

~A~

Case Study: The Money or the Mommy?

Then there is Rebecca. Rebecca is a beautiful woman with an international background and lifestyle. She is 40 years old, has a decent career, is unmarried, and when the alarm went off on her biological clock a few years ago, she never found the snooze button. So, you could say that her main objective right now is to get married and have babies.

She has been dating Nick, who also has an international background and lifestyle, and descends from a very wealthy Greek family. I think the family owns a few islands or something, but I know for a fact that Nick owns a soccer team, a yacht, a few cars, and homes in various countries. They've been dating for seven years. Here's the problem: Nick is never going to marry Rebecca, because his mother has forbidden it due to Rebecca not being Greek. This was made clear to Rebecca from the very beginning. Year after year, Rebecca enjoys the highest level of lifestyle, jet-setting from New York City to Miami to Copenhagen, Athens, Prague, Rome, and beyond; they always spend a few weeks in the summer on Nick's yacht around the Greek isles, including the island he owns; and she gets to brag about how she is wearing Gucci or Versace and display her beautiful Van Cleef and Arpels Alhambra necklace that he gave her.

If you're thinking that sounds like a pretty sweet lifestyle, you are right. But don't get sidetracked! A yacht and Gucci are great, but she wants marriage and a baby! What kind of trade-off is she making for lifestyle and showing off? I can't say that she doesn't love Nick, but I can tell you that she is constantly dissatisfied with their relationship. I wonder sometimes if she will try to "accidentally" get pregnant or if she'll ever dump Nick and marry someone else within a year.

Case Study Query: What trade-offs are you making for personal status in society? Is a luxurious life worth more to you than happiness?

~A~

Rebecca took control for her future and compromised her character for the aim of wealth and status. At the end of your life, will you be telling stories about your children and family, or will you be telling stories about your extravagant lifestyle? Is the point of this story that she's a big girl, made her bed, and now has to sleep in it? Do you think it's possible to leave the lifestyle and find true love and fulfillment?

Bankruptcy Exam

Are you starting to see how an accumulation of these types of character compromises could bankrupt your soul? Can you see how making these choices could lead to dissatisfaction and loneliness, anxiety and ultimately feeling foolish? Not to mention the shame that builds in the secrecy of it all. Like a mold growing in damp darkness, the quiet disgrace festers in us, widening the gap between what's inside us and what other people see.

Ok. Your turn again. Believe me, this can be difficult. This exercise requires absolute honesty with yourself, and that can be uncomfortable. You may not like what you hear yourself saying about what you do and why you do it. I know I didn't. Here are some additional questions to guide your thinking:

Questions:

- ✓ Have you compromised your character at work or in your personal life in any way that you wouldn't want your mother to know about?
- ✓ Do we really have two moral compasses or are we just alienating our decisions from our true selves until we lose sight of who we are?
- ✓ At what point are we so calloused that we've become bitter and cynical?
- ✓ Do you ever take a ream of paper home with you, submit exaggerated or false expenses, use office postage for personal mail, or anything like that?
- ✓ Where does quid pro quo end and prostitution begin?
- ✓ How many happy memories or shared human experiences have you sacrificed along the way in pursuit of wealth, power and fame?
- ✓ Are you starting to see that in our overabundant lives, we are actually bankrupting ourselves in far more important ways?

- ✓ Do you think that the advancement you are selling your soul for will produce fulfillment, love, joy, peace and wisdom?

Repeated Case Study Questions:

- ✓ Are you compromising your character or ethics to get ahead? If everybody else is doing it, does that mean you have to do it?
- ✓ Are you working the system too much? Would you want everything you are doing in your work day to appear on the front page of the *Wall Street Journal*?
- ✓ If a senior person says it is ok, but you know it's not, what do you do? Are you protecting your income or your integrity?
- ✓ Are you presenting your background and capabilities in a completely authentic way? Are you skirting or smudging the truth to serve your purposes?
- ✓ Are your friendships and relationships authentic? Have your relationships been rendered down to connections and networking?
- ✓ What trade-offs are you making for personal status in society? Is a luxurious life worth more to you than happiness?

~A~

This is the part where you do some soul searching for yourself. Remember, the purpose of this book is to inspire positive change in your life. Don't just read about this exercise – go and do it!! Then come back and keep reading.

Thank you.

~A~

Most character compromising is done in the name of short-term gain. Unfortunately, short-term gain often results in delayed suffering. Pretty much, we are attempting to feel good *now*, thinking we can deal with the pain and consequences *later*. But, do you see how that could totally spoil your plans of a fabulous life? Are you going to be living in a mansion with everything you've ever dreamed of, making up for all the times you delayed feeling bad? More likely, you will be so far gone at that point, that you'll dismiss what you've done with a flippant, *"I did what I had to do."*

I'm not shoving modern-day or spiritual bankruptcy in your face to make you feel bad about yourself. Rather, I bring it up to help you examine your motives and justifications for things you may be doing to advance yourself. That is the essence of what leads to modern-day, spiritual bankruptcy. When we add compromise after compromise, our debt to our souls becomes immense. Our spirits are languishing, despondent, lethargic, over-drawn. We have been so proud of ourselves by external standards that when we look inward, we find that there is nothing left to be proud of. When our eyes are opened to our own spiritual famine, we have two choices. One is to feed it and nourish it back to health, which takes time, commitment and repentance. The other is to permanently look the other way, and live as hollow, vacant cadavers until our human bodies kick the bucket.

Maybe you have turned your back on the person you once were because of survival of the fittest and playing the game to win. But as I said earlier, if you are not looking out for your soul, nobody else is going to. St Augustine said, "We must care for our bodies as if we are going to live forever, but we must care for our souls as if we were going to die tomorrow."

Chapter 8: Type A and the Seven Deadly Sins

For any of you who are still not convinced that Type A is anything you need to recover from, I've got to break it down for you this way. I'm not trying to make you feel bad about yourself or anything you've done. Examining these things gave me reason to pause, and I thought you might benefit from the same probing. Again, I'm not condemning you, pointing a finger at you, or saying you are a bad person. I'm simply using a commonly known reference *(the Seven Deadly Sins)* to demonstrate my point: *You do need to recover from Type A.*

For you experts out there, I'm approaching this from an entirely Type A standpoint, so please forgive me if I'm not 100% in line with your thoughts on these sins. I am also aware that the Seven Deadly Sins are not Biblical, but it should be noted that these seven sins are called *deadly* because they are considered fatal to spiritual progress. These are the most serious transgressions, and the only ones which could destroy charity in a person's heart. Since we've been talking about spiritual bankruptcy, I thought we'd better take a look. I'll try to make it brief and go through these quickly.

As I go through the Seven Deadly Sins, I will also point out that committing most of these sins is fully endorsed by our culture and society, making it only more challenging to view them as negative or bad. I will also raise my hand in transparency and confess to you my own offenses, before I ask you to contemplate your own verdict.

In no particular order:

84

Deadly Sin #1: Pride

Definition: Pride is having a high sense of your own worth, or an excessive belief in your own abilities. Pride is also known as vanity.

Synonyms: Arrogance, conceit, smugness, self-importance, self-satisfaction, self-gratification, self-respect, self-esteem, honoring self

Isn't this in total contradiction to all those self-empowerment books out there? Doesn't this go against what our entire cultural system promotes? Isn't this the opposite of that Beyoncé *Ego* song? (No offense, Beyoncé. It's not you, it's the song; and usually you are a shining example of grace and humility, including what you did at the 2009 Video Music Awards with Taylor Swift and Kanye West.) The song states our cultural view very well: It's alright to have a big ego as long as you can back it up. In our society, it's the goal to be as self-important as you possibly can be, but it's ok only if you have a lot of money, status, and power. When exactly in our cultural history did pride get converted from a sin to an aim?

Our culture is all about *me, me, me.* Our Type A priorities of success, wealth, fame, power, and control lead us to idolize money and possessions, accomplishment, and power, and we become egocentric worshippers of ourselves. Narcissism is almost necessary for survival. Our pride and vanity are encouraged everywhere we look, from fashion to facial creams to plastic surgery and beyond. It's commonly known that more attractive people go further in life, so we have to look the part, play the part, be the part, affirm ourselves that we deserve nothing but the best, and use our positive attitude to expect nothing but the best. Everything is me-centered. It's all pride.

My Confession: I already told you that my theme song was Sinatra's "My Way" and I meant it. I lived my life by "I will." "I can." "I'll make it." "I'm going to be somebody." "I'm in control." My verdict: Guilty.

What's your verdict?

~*A*~

Deadly Sin #2: Greed

Definition: Greed is the desire to have and acquire more things than you need.

Synonyms: Avarice, greediness, materialism, covetousness, acquisitiveness, avariciousness, cupidity. Also includes acts of betrayal or treason for personal gain, and hoarding of material objects

Aren't we living in a *"Greed is good"* kind of world? Aren't we told that wanting more and never settling until we get it is a good thing? Does that mean that desiring all those things on our Dream Boards such as more money, all the latest gadgets, a designer wardrobe, and living in a mansion are sins? Yup, pretty much.

Our Type A priorities of success, wealth, fame, power, and control are centered on selfish greediness. We idolize money and possessions, accomplishment, and power and we want it all for ourselves. We focus on attaining more things, decorating ourselves, having more than other people, earning more in general, and money, money, money. (Note: This does not mean that people who have things or live in mansions are automatically dirty-rotten, filthy-rich money grabbers. As long as you are generous and have your priorities aligned properly, you can live in a palace, and it won't affect you. We'll talk more about this in section three.)

My Confession: My Dream Board was Bling Bling Central. I've wanted way more than I could ever possibly need. Even when I had more than I needed, I still wanted more. My verdict: Guilty.

What's your verdict?

~*A*~

Deadly Sin #3: Envy

> Definition: Envy is resentment of the fact that somebody else has something you don't, including traits, status, abilities or situation, combined with an intense desire to have what they have.

> Synonyms: Jealousy, desire, resentment, spite; be jealous of, resent, begrudge, hold a grudge

Isn't everyone trying to keeping up with the Joneses (whoever they are)? Aren't we envious of all the celebrities we see on TV as we observe their fabulous lives? Isn't it natural to dislike or even hate that girl because she has the job you want, or loathe that guy because he's dating the woman you want? Aren't most of us a little bitter about the cards we've been dealt while some loser with a trust fund laughs through life?

Again, our Type A priorities and all the success and empowerment reading we've done lead us into a twisted form of envy. We are encouraged to select someone who has what we want and then emulate them, striving to attain and surpass their level of accomplishment. A little envy goes a long way when it comes to motivating ourselves to achieve more.

My Confession: I've had plenty of people to envy over the years, from trust-fund babies to multi-million-dollar executives who've earned every dime themselves. I've been to penthouse apartments in New York City and gigantic mansions, yachts, and private jets. Yes, I was envious. On the other end of the spectrum, I've also envied people for their simple lives. I've envied women who wear sweatpants. I've envied brides at the altar. I've envied retired people who don't have to work anymore. I've envied anyone driving a powder blue Bentley coupe convertible. My verdict: Guilty.

What's your verdict?

~*A*~

Deadly Sin #4: Wrath

Definition: Wrath is forceful and vindictive anger, usually as punishment or retribution.

Synonyms: Anger, fury, rage, antagonism, resentment

But haven't we been told that sometimes the ends justify the means? Aren't we encouraged to do anything it takes to achieve our dreams? Sometimes, isn't it necessary to take down our nemesis or enemies?

Type A priorities get very sticky on the issue of wrath. Even the case studies from the last chapter don't begin to cover some of the extreme cases of wrath that go on every day. For example, the spreading of untrue rumors for personal advancement, blackmail, backstabbing, and more. It gets ugly in a dog-eat-dog environment. I've already given you the example of Sue Sylvester from *Glee*, but if you want to see corporate wrath at its finest, start watching the show *Damages* on FX. Patty Hewes, played by Glenn Close, is cunning and vicious and brilliant. It's almost as if she has x-ray vision for people's weaknesses and isn't afraid to use it, all for her own empowerment, advancement, and agenda.

My Confession: Have you seen that movie *John Tucker Must Die*? I nicknamed a guy in my office John Tucker. He didn't like me stealing his spotlight, and badmouthed me to some of our co-workers. Instead of making a public display about it, I sent out lieutenants to report back to me on his every action, collecting anything he did that was questionable, in the grey area, or just plain dishonest. When the time was right, or if he tried to cross me again, I could use this information to dominate him or take him down. He left the company for other reasons, but it was still wrathful of me to have done what I did. My verdict: Guilty.

What's your verdict?

~*A*~

Deadly Sin #5: Sloth

Definition: Sloth is wasting or lack of use to the point of entropy. Sloth is also apathy or being emotionally inactive.

Synonyms: Laziness, idleness, sluggishness, inactivity, indolence, apathy, indifference

Type A's are not lazy people. *Lazy workaholic* is an oxymoron. But we are lazy in other ways, some of which we've already discussed. We are wasting our souls due to lack of use, to the point of entropy. We are being lazy and inactive, apathetic, and slothful with our character.

As Type A's, we are told to use our heads, not our hearts. Decisions made with a stone-cold heart are the ones that lead to cold hard cash. We've lost our tenderness and sensitivity as we slowly, but surely become numb to our own humanity. Our personal lives are non-existent. Our relationships have degenerated into contacts or networking. We have friends-with-benefits or long-distance relationships, so we can minimally involve our emotions in romance, but still get some physical benefit. Just because we're not couch potatoes, doesn't mean we are not slothful.

My Confession: If I hadn't been slothful with my spirit, I would never have succumbed to compromising my character at work. Not to mention the fact that I was treating personal relationships like a business arrangement. Both behaviors are a demonstration of indifference toward myself. I didn't realize how apathetic I'd become until I heard the song "Goodbye Apathy" by OneRepublic, and realized I was an ice-queen who needed to be melted. *"I kill myself to make everything perfect for you. I don't wanna be you. Goodbye, apathy."* My verdict: Guilty.

What's your verdict?

~A~

Deadly Sin #6: Lust

Definition: Lust is an unrestrained or overwhelming desire or craving, an intense eagerness or enthusiasm for something. To lust is to have an obsessive desire.

Synonyms: Yearn, desire, long for, hunger or ache for, envy, covet, crave; sexual perversion, fornication, adultery

Everyone always thinks lust has to be sexual, but it doesn't. But thinking of it that way can be a great analogy. Do you lust for power? Do you lust for a new Mercedes? Do you lust for that corner office? Do you lust for status? Do you lust for money? Do you lust for love, but wind up with only lust?

As Type A's, we lust for success, wealth, fame, power, and control. Just like we use envy to motivate ourselves to accomplish more, I dare say, with our Type A competitive streak, our envy is lustful. We are literally passionate in our workaholic, perfectionist, over-achiever, control-freak ways because we are lusting after our Dream Board desires.

My Confession: I don't even need to explain myself on this one. If you've been reading this book, you already know I lusted after everything on my Dream Board and then some. My verdict: Guilty.

What's your verdict?

~A~

Deadly Sin #7: Gluttony

Definition: Gluttony is over-indulgence or over-consumption to the point of waste.

Synonyms: Extravagance, unrestrained excess, overload, immodesty, overabundance

How many people could benefit from the food that rots in your refrigerator? How many people could you clothe with what's hanging in your closet that you don't even wear? How many things do you have more than three of, when you need only one?

Our Type A priorities encourage gluttony as proof that we have accomplished and achieved and earned our way to possessing a lot of stuff. Our culture endorses excess. Centuries ago, it was a sign of wealth to be fat because the size of your belly proved that you could afford an abundance of food. This is how we typically think of gluttony. Nowadays, it is a sign of wealth to have five houses, 12 cars, a private jet, a yacht, diamond-studded everything, and a mini-mansion for your dog. Even if you are not at that level of gluttony, you still probably have way more than you could ever possibly need.

My Confession: I don't need 200 pairs of shoes! Wait... um... can I take that back? Please? No? I know, I know... I don't really need them... sniffle... sniffle.... My verdict: Guilty.

What's your verdict?

Intermission: Type A Challenges

No, this is not a competition to see if you are more Type A than anybody else out there. Although you would probably enjoy that and thrive on it, this is quite the opposite. This is a challenge against your own Type A-ness. I dare you to attempt to complete at least five of these challenges and see how you do.

For any of you still not convinced that you need to recover from Type A, this is your call to combat. Test yourself, not through the quiz as before, but by your actions. That means, don't just read it – do it. As a warning to the weak at heart, this is the "Face your fears" section of the book.

Note:

- ✓ If you cannot complete this challenge successfully, you need to recover from Type A.
- ✓ If you struggle, yet complete this challenge successfully, you still need to recover from Type A.
- ✓ If these challenges are easy for you, you probably weren't Type A when you started.

Are you ready? Get set... GO!

The Challenges

Each of these challenges is to be executed for one full week. I do not recommend trying to do all of them in the same week.

Tallying: For One Week: *(Warning: One day of Tallying may be enough to get the point across.)* Keep a tally of how many times per day you do any of the following:

- ✓ Get frustrated or impatient with something or someone that is going too slow
- ✓ Think of yourself as superior to someone else (how many idiots are there in your day?)
- ✓ Snap at someone or treat them rudely (including waiters, clerks, and others in service positions)
- ✓ Feel competitive for any reason
- ✓ Try to control the situation
- ✓ Blur the truth to serve your advantage
- ✓ Justify yourself or your actions
- ✓ Interrupt someone when they are talking
- ✓ Put someone else down (to their face or behind their back) to make yourself superior

Longest Line: For One Week: Every time you go shopping, force yourself to wait in the longest line. Wait patiently, without fidgeting, getting rude or filling your time with other things like texting or talking on your cell phone, or even reading a magazine. Just wait.

Driving with the Governor[1]: For One Week: While driving, engage your cruise control to keep you at the speed limit, and not a single mile-per-hour above it. You may have to exit the left lane in order to do so. Other people may honk at you or give you the finger, as you probably would have been doing to them.

---

[1] Please use safe driving practices at all times, and do not blame me or this book for any traffic accidents that may result from you taking this too literally in any way.

No More Multi-Tasking: For One Week: Do only one thing at a time. Do not open the mail while talking on the phone. Do not eat while driving. Do not work on more than one account or file at once. Do not think of other things while someone is talking to you. Do not talk on your blue-tooth while on the treadmill.

Cursing Cessation: For One Week: No swearing. No cussing. No cursing.

Personal Shopping Suspension: For One Week: Do not buy anything for yourself other than food or medicine. Not major items, not small items. No clothes, no shoes, no accessories, no age-defying creams, no gadgets, no colognes, no books, no magazines. No "It's on sale" excuses.

Caffeine Vacation: For One Week: No caffeine. No coffee, no caffeinated tea, no Red Bull, no pills. No caffeine of any sort... zero... nada.

Hold the Phone: For One Week: Whenever you are with someone, put your phone down. Give the person in front of you your undivided attention. Leave your BlackBerry in the car. Turn your iPhone off. No texting or e-mail or BrickBreaker during meetings, meals, appointments, dates, or any other time you are spending with someone else.

Be Quiet: For One Week: Find and/or make 10-15 minutes each day to sit in silence. No talking. All electronics off. No reading. Do not fall asleep. *(It is best not to combine this with Caffeine Vacation.)*

Identify Your Audience: For One Week: Be consciously aware of who you are trying to impress at any point in your day. Why is their opinion so important?

- ✓ While you are getting ready in the morning
- ✓ While you are walking around the office or walking down the street

✓ When you're talking to your boss or assistant or a client
✓ When you place your order at a restaurant
✓ When you're with your friends
✓ When you get home

~A~

This is the part where you go and try to do some of the challenges yourself. Remember, the purpose of this book is to inspire positive change in your life. Don't just read about this exercise – go and do it!! Then come back and keep reading.

Thank you.

~A~

How'd you do on your Challenges? What did you learn? Did you make it a full week on any of them? I completed these challenges, too, and it is not easy. I have found there is no better way to fess up to my Type A-ness than abstaining from Type A behaviors. The good news is, I also discovered that one week of self-denial makes a big impact and makes it easier to move forward with moderation.

For example, driving with the governor was excruciating for a full week, but now I don't speed (as much) anymore while driving. I focus all my energy on the task in front of me. I told you I used to curse like a sailor, but now I don't curse (as much) anymore. I did shopping suspension for six weeks, and it was hard to resist all the sales that seemed to be going on everywhere, but I made lots of new outfit combinations with what I already have. I failed at caffeine vacation, but I did manage to reduce my intake, and I save Red Bull for special occasions. I am consistently the same me everywhere I go, and basically, I am more compassionate and less concerned with what others think of me.

Share your challenge stories with me. Tell me how you did by writing to me at wendy@recoveringtypea.com.

Section Two

To A or Not to A?

Part II

Chapter 9: The Idols of A

In Part I of this section, we identified four interwoven symptoms of living as a Type A as trying to control everything, living in the future, focusing on wealth and possessions, and compromising character. We also identified that living a life with these symptoms cannot and will not produce fulfillment, love, joy, peace and wisdom, and to top it off, leads us into deadly sins, whether we know it or not.

Since you are Type A, I know you've been paying attention. When you go to the doctor and you give them your symptoms, you want to know what the cause is, so you can cure it. You might be thinking the cause of the symptoms we've been discussing is being Type A, but the cause is much more deeply rooted than that. Type A by definition is *Type A Pattern Behavior* – a collection of things you do that packaged together are recognized as Type A conduct. It is still an outside-in approach to understanding Type A, and has nothing to do with the greater cause.

My theory is that as Type A's, we are worshipping idols. Most of these idols are fully endorsed by our performance-based culture, and worshipping them is only intensified by society's pressures. The Type A idols I can see clearly are these: The Idol of Money (including wealth, possessions, luxury, extravagance, and the like). The Idol of Accomplishment (including status, winning, success, and the like). And the Idol of Self (me, me, me; ego...). Service to these idols is what causes us to be perfectionists, workaholics, control-freaks, and over-achievers. These idols command us to look to them for our worth and value, building Dream Boards as our pledge of dedication. And these idols make us bow down to them by compromising our character as a sacrifice for their glorification. Like the ancient Greco-Roman gods and goddesses, we summon these idols when and as needed, based on situational circumstance because none of them is sufficient on a stand-alone basis.

What defines an idol, really? It's when we take a good thing and turn it into a supreme thing. It's anything we worship and look to for validation. Anything we think has the capacity to solve all our problems and provide us with everything we could possibly need. It's anything we turn to in hopes that it can satisfy our deepest needs of fulfillment, love, joy peace and wisdom, whether it can or not. Culturally, our primary idol is money. Wealth, possessions, luxury, extravagance, bling bling, you name it. It's everywhere; everybody wants it, nobody seems to have it; we are envious, resentful and suspicious of the ones who do have it, and we will justify whatever it takes for us to get more of it.

There are lots of idols in our culture: fame, power, youth, intellect... the list is endless. People who idolize beauty are obsessed with their appearance, and are destined to have multiple plastic surgeries, fighting the good fight against gravity and time. There are people who idolize sex, and they are known as promiscuous players because sex is how they justify themselves and make themselves feel better. People idolize intelligence, and they are known as intellectual snobs because they can always rest on their laurels of knowing that they are smarter than you are. Many people idolize their spouse, and they are known as needy co-dependents because if anything happens to their spouse, they are a nervous wreck and can hardly function through the anxiety. Believe me, I can look back at men in my life who have wanted to be my god. That's really great when they want to be your provider, your comforter, your lover (even in the most innocent sense), but it's not so great when they want to be your master. You get the drift.

But we're not here to get into all the possible idols there are in this world, so we're going to stay focused on the idols of the Type A existence. Those, again, are the Idol of Money, the Idol of Accomplishment, and the Idol of Self. Let's take a closer look.

The Idol of Money

The Idol of Money (including wealth, possessions, luxury, extravagance, and the like) is a cruel ruler that provides friendly captivity. There is no physical affliction to worshipping this idol – as a matter of fact, everything looks great from the outside. Money makes you believe you are better than other people. Money becomes your identity, what drives you, and what defines you. Money becomes how you define greatness in other people and compare yourself to them. Money becomes the center of your life, and you view it as your biggest contribution to other people. You protect the Idol of Money with your life. If anyone speaks against Money, you will put them to shame, aggressively ignore them, dismiss them as ignorant, or discredit them to others.

Your most important consideration when undertaking a new task is whether or not the Idol of Money will be glorified. Meaning, your first thoughts are: How much money can I make? How much money does it cost? Will this lead to more money? Will I get my money back? Is this worth the money?

Your sincere hope when others look at you is that they see Money in you. Meaning, you want people to notice that you are doing well financially, that you have nice or luxurious things, what you do, where you live, what you drive.

When you are going through a hardship, at least you have Money. Sometimes, the only way you are able to withstand things is because of Money. Meaning, you probably check your online bank account a few times a week, if not a few times per day. It is your security, your comforter, your protection, the thing you turn to when you need to feel ok.

The Idol of Money forces you to serve it by putting you constantly in fear of not having enough. You must bow down to it, and be willing to do anything for it, including relinquishing parts of yourself you thought were at your core, and when commanded, even dishonoring your dignity and disgracing yourself. But the Idol of Money can never deliver on its promises. It simply doesn't have the power to provide fulfillment, love, joy, peace and wisdom. It is a slave-master, and there will always be more to be made, and the Joneses will always have more than you do. It is not a provider or teacher, and is incapable of meeting your needs, or lifting you to higher levels of abundance and deeper levels of understanding.

What would it take for you to renounce worshipping the Idol of Money? Any level of suffering such as being robbed, losing it all, going bankrupt, or any other hardship? Any level of success, such as winning the lottery, living in *that* neighborhood, driving *that* car, living *that* life?

People who are in the habit of saying, "It's not about the money" are lying. It's about the money. Why were people, even non-victims, of Bernie Madoff so viscerally and viciously infuriated? Because Money is the god they worship, and Bernie messed with their god.

Money is an addiction. The more you earn, the more you spend. Then it becomes the more you spend, the more you have to earn. The cycle perpetuates, and you have to earn more and more, but more and more produces less and less satisfaction, and you always feel strapped. Money makes you busy, possessions make you proud, but you never feel fulfilled by it. Have you ever received a big bonus, and it's spent before it even hits your bank account? Have you ever acquired something that didn't give you as much enjoyment or satisfaction as you thought it would? Do you feel like you never have what you want or you always want more? That's because unrestrained desires are the enemy of fulfillment. Contentment based on money, wealth, and possessions forces us to compare ourselves to others as a means of substantiating our own existence. We think if we have more money and stuff, we have more value and worth as people. But there will always be people who have more or better stuff than we do, so we never measure up.

Ken Boa observes that "instead of using wealth and serving people, we are increasingly tempted to serve wealth and use people." Isn't that a great explanation of how and why people are taking the path to modern-day bankruptcy? But, the Idol of Money gives us a handbook full of justifications and rationalizations, making it easy to excuse our actions, no matter how ruthless. Add extraordinary levels of temptation to the mix, and you've got good people doing bad things they never thought they would do. All in a day's work for the Idol of Money.

The Idol of Accomplishment

The Idol of Accomplishment (including status, winning, success, and the like) is a cruel ruler that provides friendly captivity. There is no physical affliction to worshipping this idol – as a matter of fact, everything looks great from the outside. Accomplishment makes you believe you are better than other people. Accomplishment becomes your identity, what drives you, and what defines you. Accomplishment becomes how you define greatness in other people and compare yourself to them. Accomplishment becomes the center of your life, and you view it as your biggest contribution to other people. You protect the Idol of Accomplishment with your life. If anyone speaks against Accomplishment, you will put them to shame, aggressively ignore them, dismiss them as ignorant, or discredit them to others.

Your most important consideration when undertaking a new task is whether or not the Idol of Accomplishment will be glorified. Meaning, your first thoughts are: Will this lead to greater accomplishments, status, and success? Will this distract me from larger accomplishments or opportunities to win? How will this help me accomplish more, so my successes and wins are even more superior? Will this add to my accomplishments and status as a winner?

Your sincere hope when others look at you is that they see Accomplishment in you. Meaning, you want people to notice that you have achieved status in your life, and that you are successful, a winner.

When you are going through a hardship, at least you have Accomplishment. Sometimes, the only way you are able to withstand things is because of Accomplishment. Meaning, you probably re-write your resume on a regular basis, making sure everything you have achieved is mentioned. You know that your accomplishments are portable if you ever need to bring your success to a new situation. Therefore, your accomplishments are your security, your comforter, your protection, and the thing you turn to when you need to feel ok.

The Idol of Accomplishment forces you to serve it by putting you constantly in fear of keeping up. You must bow down to it, and be willing to do anything for it, including relinquishing parts of yourself you thought were at your core, and when commanded, even dishonoring your dignity and disgracing yourself. But the Idol of Accomplishment can never deliver on its promises. It simply doesn't have the power to provide fulfillment, love, joy, peace and wisdom. It is a slave-master, and there is always more to be done, and people who have achieved more or have higher status than you do. It is not sovereign nor an endorser, and is incapable of authenticating you, or giving you a sense of contentment and gratification.

What would it take for you to renounce worshipping the Idol of Accomplishment? Any level of suffering such as losing your job or getting demoted, failing or losing, or dropping in status, or any other hardship? Any level of success, such as being the everything-I-touch-turns-to-gold guy, being the top-dog or big-man-on-campus or CEO, a never-ending winning streak?

We all tend to feel more important when we are surrounded by "important" people. Our humility one evening at a private party full of executives turns into our pride and bragging rights the next morning. Our other, more tangible signs of success like plaques, awards, and trophies become our personal displays of majesty. Have you ever seen a grown man cry because his crystal *Top Producer* award fell off his desk and was shattered into a million pieces? I have. That's because Accomplishment is the god he worships, and his god just got broken.

Accomplishment is an addiction. The more you achieve, you are higher than you were, but you are lower than you want to be. The more you accomplish, the more there is to do, and in the meantime you grow weary and insecure. We get caught in the cycle of competing, achieving, and winning just for the sake of competing, achieving, and winning. Achievement makes you busy, status makes you proud, but you never feel secure. Rivalry is the enemy of peace and fulfillment. Competition becomes the platform for us to authenticate our identity and prove that we matter. We start to think that if we do good, we are good. Then we find ourselves cutting corners, skipping steps, repackaging the truth, cheating, and using people to accomplish our goals. This, of course, is the opposite of being good, so our only hope is to continue to over-achieve and base our status as a human on our status compared to others.

If you are not doing work you can be proud of, or doing your work in a manner that you can be proud of, you are cruising at 100 miles per hour down the path to spiritual bankruptcy. But the Idol of Accomplishment gives us a handbook full of justifications and rationalizations, making it easy to excuse our actions, no matter how ruthless. We convince ourselves that living by our convictions and beliefs will mean that we wind up as the loser, so we turn our back on the code of conduct, and kiss our principles goodbye. All in a day's work for the Idol of Accomplishment.

The Idol of Self

Stay with me on this one...

The Idol of Self (me, me, me; ego...) is a cruel ruler that provides friendly captivity. There is no physical affliction to worshipping this idol – as a matter of fact, everything looks great from the outside. Self makes you believe you are better than other people. Self becomes your identity, what drives you, and what defines you. Self becomes how you define greatness in other people and compare yourself to them. Self becomes the center of your life, and you view it as your biggest contribution to other people. You protect the Idol of Self with your life. If anyone speaks against Self, you will put them to shame, aggressively ignore them, dismiss them as ignorant, or discredit them to others.

Your most important consideration when undertaking a new task is whether or not the Idol of Self will be glorified. Meaning, your first thoughts are: What's in it for me? How can I benefit? Is this beneath me? What will other people think of me if I do this? Will this add to who I am and who I want to be?

Your sincere hope when others look at you is that they see Self in you. Meaning, you want everyone to know that whatever you did, you did it all by yourself. You want people to know that you take care of yourself and have self-respect.

When you are going through a hardship, at least you have Self. Sometimes, the only way you are able to withstand things is because of Self. Meaning, you probably value your inner strength and resolve above everything. Nobody else is going to stand up for you, so you've got to stand up for yourself. Therefore, you are your own security, your comforter, your protection, and the thing you turn to when you need to feel ok.

The Idol of Self forces you to serve it by putting you constantly in fear of not being good enough. You must bow down to it, and be willing to do anything for it, including relinquishing parts of yourself you thought were at your core, and when commanded, even dishonoring your dignity and disgracing yourself. But the Idol of Self can never deliver on its promises. You simply don't have the power to provide fulfillment, love, joy, peace and wisdom to yourself. Your ego is a slave-master, and you must push and force your way to what it thinks you deserve, and, despite denying it, you are constantly concerned with what other people think. The Idol of Self is not a creator or guru, and is incapable of composing you, or creating inner peace, serenity, tranquility, calmness, or poise.

What would it take for you to renounce worshipping the Idol of Self? Any level of suffering such as embarrassment, being discredited, public display of disgrace or degradation, or any other hardship? Any level of success, such as promotion, respect, veneration, exoneration?

We make gods of ourselves. We believe it when we are told that we are in control, that we create our destiny and we are the creators of our own lives. We believe it when people say, "You're brilliant." Even if on the outside, we're saying, "No, no, no," on the inside we're thinking, "Yup!" All the psychobabble about self-love, self-esteem, and self-awareness leads us down the path to being self-serving, self-promoting, and self-protective. Ask anyone, there is almost no behavior considered inexcusable when done in self-defense Nevertheless, all of this affirming of self, self, self can be reduced down to ego masturbation. That's because when we worship ourselves, we are the only ones who got the memo that the world revolves around us.

Satiating your ego is an addiction. Even though our ego wants to convince us that we are gods, we know in actuality that we are not. We set out in pursuit of finding ourselves, and wind up sorely disappointed. Then anxiety infuses our existence as we struggle to keep other people from finding out. We feel alone and empty, which leads to being defensive and angry, which leads to taking it out on other people or looking for people to step on while trying to prevent them from stepping on us in the process. Our lives morph into mortal combat between what is on the outside – showing everyone that we are indeed manifestations of our greatest potential – and what's on the inside: constant fear that we are not good enough. Incessantly having to prove ourselves is the enemy of love, wisdom, and peace. Tim Connor said, "If you want a life filled with stress, disappointment, struggle, adversity, and problems, let your ego have the control it wants." We do everything for our own personal interests, putting ourselves first, without regard for other people, and then we wonder why there is no one in our cheering squad. Our only hope is to love ourselves more and continue to convince ourselves that independence and not needing others is the only way to live out our greatest destiny.

Dr. Timothy Keller said, "If you are struggling for glory, power, and fame, you are on a collision course with God." But the Idol of Self gives us a handbook full of justifications and rationalizations, making it easy to excuse our actions, no matter how ruthless. Our own sense of worthlessness, masked by a charade of confidence and even arrogance, spawns an impassioned energy, running on the border between defensiveness and anger. We harden our hearts, and remind ourselves that only the merciless will prevail, and it is kill or be killed, as we slowly and unknowingly self-destruct. All in a day's work for the Idol of Self.

Inverted Idols and Sowing Seeds

Before you move too quickly to the end-of-chapter questions, it's worth noting that each of these idols also has a reverse element, which may not be typically Type A.

Inverse Idol of Money: People who are excessively cheap, meaning they can pinch a penny until it bleeds, are also worshippers of the Idol of Money. Even if they are not being extravagant or luxurious, they are hoarding, protecting, defending, and in love with money and its powers. They give the Idol of Money credit for being able to make anything possible, and they are focused, consumed, and obsessed with finances as their security and life-center.

Inverse Idol of Accomplishment: People who are checking off their *bucket lists* – i.e., non-work related things that you want to do before you die *(kick the bucket)* – are also worshippers of the Idol of Accomplishment. Even though they may not be obsessed with climbing the ranks in their careers, they are still centering their lives on saying, "I did it!" whether that means they travelled to all 50 states, jumped out of an airplane, or completed every task in the book *100 Things to Do Before You Die.* Their sense of success is still tied to and dependent on achievement of a goal, completion, success, and attainment.

Inverse Idol of Self: And lastly, people who have low self-esteem are also worshippers of the Idol of Self. Even if there are no outward signs of arrogance or being an egomaniac, low self-esteem is still constant self-absorption, and how things relate to me, me, me.

These idols are quite sophisticated in the way they creep into our minds and take over our existence. They really don't care how you worship them, as long as you are under their oppression.

Worshipping idols in any form creates major problems. One of the problems is that the problems are so subtle. In fact, the first objective of an idol is to blind you with its promises of goodness until it has you whipped into subservience. Even then, it is easy to surround yourself with other people who are worshipping the same idol, so everything seems kosher... until it isn't.

Another subtle problem with worshipping idols is that you always reap what you sow. If you are constantly working for more money, it is because you currently feel you do not have enough. If you are constantly working for more achievement, it is because you do not feel successful. The seeds you are planting, or as people say, "what you are putting out there," is the opposite of what the idols promised.

But that's the thing: The idols are liars. They convince you that you are sowing seeds of prosperity and achievement, and you are actually sowing seeds of lack and failure. This is exactly how the seeds you think you are sowing – seeds of fulfillment, love, joy, peace and wisdom – somehow reap dissatisfaction, loneliness, disappointment, anxiety and feeling foolish. Every time you go to harvest your fulfillment and instead come up empty, you determine that it must not be time to harvest yet; but you are wrong. Since you have planted the wrong seed, it is not capable of yielding what you actually desire. And the longer you delay reaping the harvest you have actually been planting (i.e. dissatisfaction, loneliness, disappointment, anxiety and feeling foolish), the larger and more painful the consequences become.

Lastly, the worst problem of worshipping idols is that it leaves you wide open for attack and easy prey for predators. Whether you think so or not, everyone around you can tell what idol tribe you belong to, and they can quickly figure out how to use that to their advantage. Your idol becomes your weak spot, and manipulating you with promises can be done with ease. Over time, you develop Stockholm Syndrome, which is where hostages grow affection for their captor because the way you got in appears to be the only way out and the only hope for escape. Eventually, your idol becomes your addiction, the thing that you want so bad, that eventually you'll even settle for a quick-and-dirty street deal just to get another hit, but it will never make you whole. You will be vulnerable to your idol until it destroys and betrays you. Joan of Arc is attributed with saying, "It is not a tragedy to die for something you believe in, but it is a tragedy to find at the end of your life that what you believed in betrayed you." Will the idols you are worshipping betray you?

Questions:

- ✓ Are you worshipping the Idol of Money, Accomplishment, Self, or all three?
- ✓ Are you on their treadmill of expectation and disappointment?
- ✓ Do you feel like you have multiple bottom lines to reconcile and report back to?
- ✓ Is Money, Accomplishment, or Self the center of your life?
- ✓ What seeds are you planting?

Chapter 10: Alternatives and Comparisons

You probably think this is the part of the book where I'm going to tell you to stop everything, turn your life around, and become a weak, emotional, unmotivated slacker who will never amount to anything, but at least you'll be happy. Sorry to disappoint you, but that is not where I am going with this. Do you really think that *I* would be satisfied with a life like that? I am a recovering Type A, not a bereaved shadow of what I once was. I'm still driven to succeed, but my motives have greatly changed and, therefore, so have my results. You don't have to sacrifice yourself or change everything about who you are to find fulfillment, love, joy, peace and wisdom. Not to feed your ego, but you do have really great qualities, and I would never seek to take those away from you. With a few minor adjustments, I think you can be a better you than you've ever been before, and more truly yourself in every situation.

It has been said that "the truth will set you free, but first it will make you miserable." I'm not trying to make you miserable, but part of recovery is identifying what we're doing wrong so we can change it. So far we've pointed out mostly negative reasons why you would want to change. It's time to look at some positive alternatives.

We've examined the core cause of worshipping idols, the sinful behaviors that result, the symptoms of living as a Type A, and how Type A life does not fulfill our deepest needs. On the basis that real change (meaning true, permanent, and fundamental change) develops from the inside-out, we'll look at alternatives starting from the core causes, and work our way outward through behaviors and symptoms to the meeting of our deepest needs, and the overflow of the new you. We will discuss the transformational process in more detail in section three, but this will serve to give you an outline of what the possible outcomes of change entail.

Alternatives to the Consequences of Idols

We examined how Type A life and priorities may be the result of worshipping the Idols of Money, Accomplishment, and Self. They master us as if we were slaves, and the conditions of our servitude to them have consequences. The truth is that only in renouncing the idols can we achieve the best possible results, which we'll talk more about in section three. For now, let's take a look at the idols we've been serving, the conditions and consequences of servitude, and the alternatives possible if we free ourselves from captivity.

Idol of Money, Consequences	Alternative: Fulfillment
Defined by wealth and "stuff."	Defined by character.
Proud. Vain. Selfish. Greedy. Envious. Gluttonous.	Humble. Unassuming. Giving. Selfless. Kind. Self-Controlled.
Dissatisfaction. Disappointment. Anxiety.	Fulfillment. Joy. Peace.
Fear of not having enough. Always feeling strapped. Comparison to others. Keeping up with the Joneses.	Sense of abundance. Satisfaction. Needs met. Simplicity. Steadfast diligence. Love for the Joneses.
Scrooge.	Anonymous philanthropist.

Idol of Achievement, Consequences	Alternative: Humility
Defined by status.	Defined by character.
Proud. Vain. Envious. Wrathful. Lustful. Apathetic.	Humble. Modest. Helpful. Patient. Well-intentioned. Conscientious.
Dissatisfaction. Loneliness. Disappointment. Anxiety.	Fulfillment. Love. Joy. Peace.
Rivalry. Competition. Manipulating others. Trying to control. No trust. No emotions. Fear of keeping up. Never being good enough.	Patience. Endurance. Tolerance. Fortitude. Acceptance. Authentic relationships. Satisfaction. Levelheaded self-worth.

113

Rogue Maverick Executive.	Best friend.

Idol of Self, Consequences	Alternative: Wisdom, Self-Control
Me-centered. Defined by others' opinions.	Others-centered. Defined by convictions.
Proud. Vain. Selfish. Envious. Wrathful. Lustful. Gluttonous. Slothful.	Humble. Modest. Selfless. Helpful. Patient. Well-intentioned. Self-controlled. Diligent.
Dissatisfaction. Loneliness. Disappointment. Anxiety. Feeling foolish.	Fulfillment. Love. Joy. Peace. Wisdom.
Ego. Feeling of worthlessness. Fear of not being good enough. Concerned with what others think. Manipulating others. Bullying. Angst. Fear. Panic.	Sense of satisfaction. Calm in virtuousness. Serenity. Poise. Wisdom. Slow to anger. Observing. Discerning. Levelheaded self-worth.
Selfish Egomaniac.	Mother Theresa.

Seven Heavenly Virtues

We examined how the core cause of serving idols can lead Type A's into Seven Deadly Sinful behavior. If we renounced our service to the idols, it would stand to reason that our behavior would change as a result. It's time to take a look at the other side of that coin. Each sin has a counterpart known as a Heavenly Virtue. Since life with Type A priorities seems to be a living example of the Seven Deadly Sins at work, what would it look like if we became living examples of the Seven Heavenly Virtues? Here they are:

Deadly Sin	Heavenly Virtue	Additional Attributes
Pride	Humility	Unassuming Nature. Modesty. Gentleness.
Greed	Charity	Considerate. Unselfish. Being a "Giver."

Deadly Sin	Heavenly Virtue	Additional Attributes
Envy	Kindness	Being Thoughtful. Helpful to Others. Showing Compassion.
Wrath	Patience	Having Staying Power. Endurance. Serenity. Being Mellow.
Sloth	Diligence	Attentiveness. Conscientiousness. Prudence. Carefulness.
Lust	Chastity	Purity. Innocence. Being Incorrupt. Unblemished. Virtuous.
Gluttony	Self-control	Willpower. Restraint. The Ability to Resist Temptation.

We all want to think of ourselves as people who embody these qualities. Even as a Type A, I knew that these were the qualities I wanted to display. However, these qualities would have to stay hidden until I achieved a certain level of wealth and status for myself, and then they could come out. Here are a few things that stand out to me, a quick Type A look at them, and the possibility that lies in steadfast application of the virtues.

Humility: True humility is tricky because we are so reinforced to be proud of ourselves and all we have accomplished. We can try to fake humility or attempt genuine humility, but nonetheless, as Type A's we're so busy protecting ourselves and building ourselves up, we wind up being cocky, arrogant egomaniacs, whether we want to be or not. And with our pride, we are sowing seeds of antagonism. Instead of wanting to see us succeed, people start desiring for us to fail, get knocked down a few notches, or get a taste of our own medicine. But what if we found true humility within ourselves, and everyone was pulling for us, hoping the best for us, cheering us on through every battle? There are people like that, who will selflessly want the best for you. Can you picture it?

Charity: Being a "giver." Most people consider themselves a "giver," whether they are or not. This concept usually comes up when people talk about their personal relationships, and usually when things are not going well. You hear people say, "Well, I'm a giver, you know," followed by all the ways they have felt taken advantage of. You never hear anyone say, "Well, I'm a taker, you know," because nobody likes to think of themselves as one. But in our society, we are encouraged to be takers. As we shape and try to control and manipulate our destinies, it is natural to reach for and grab whatever we can get our hands on, capturing it and selfishly keeping to ourselves to use for our own advantage. Then we wonder why people want to grab at what we have, and we constantly need to defend ourselves and what we've been able to grab. We are sowing seeds of grabbing, getting, and taking. Even if we give, we're giving on the basis of "what goes around comes around," which isn't selfless giving. It is still giving for the purpose of getting something back, even if that thing is indefinable at this moment. But what if you started selflessly, even sacrificially giving, and other people started selflessly, even sacrificially giving back to you? What if someone walked into your life one day, paid your mortgage, and didn't want anything back? They saw the kind of person you are and want to reward you for it. Stuff like that happens every day. Can you conceive of it?

Kindness: Being thoughtful, kind, and helpful to others also doesn't fit with Type A. Again, nobody wants to think of themselves as a mean person, but yet, I've heard many a Type A brag about "going off to fire someone today" or "beating someone at their own game" or "It's not my fault they can't keep up" or "It's survival of the fittest, and I've got to look out for myself." Then we wonder why we don't have many great, authentic relationships. But it is because we have not sowed seeds of kindness. When you have stomped on so many people, it doesn't really motivate anyone to help you. When you are always comparing and envying anything they may have above or beyond you, it doesn't create a platform for friendship. But what if you started being thoughtful, considerate, compassionate with others, and then – whether things were going your way or not – people did everything they could to be kind to you and compassionate towards you? What if nobody laughed or snickered when you made a mistake, but instead were kind and helpful? There are people like that, who will selflessly stand by you no matter what. Can you expect that?

Patience: Being mellow. Um, I'm trying not to laugh here. A mellow Type A is an oxymoron. A patient Type A is an oxymoron. And yet it is the lack of patience, endurance, and staying power that will defeat Type A's over time because they will burn out, get frustrated, or have their blood pressure become so elevated that their doctor orders them to change their lifestyle unless they want to die of a heart attack. Patience is the counterpart to wrath, and that eventual Type A heart attack is another example of sowing seeds of wrath that somehow get turned inwardly towards ourselves. Not to mention the seeds of wrath being planted outwardly with the people around us. If you have no patience for other people, they have no incentive to be patient with you. But what if we slowed down and somehow morphed into being a more laid-back person? Would people even recognize you? What if you gave yourself the freedom to take one day at a time, and enjoy the moment? It is possible. Can you dream it?

Diligence: The opposite of carelessness is something I know Type A's will love. This one, especially, is reinforcement that I am not telling you to drop all your excellent skills at making things special. I will remind you that you can make things special without making them perfect *(perfectionist),* and things can come together successfully without controlling everything *(control-freak).* Just because you are becoming a recovering Type A, doesn't mean you have to be sloppy. Quite the opposite. The other element here, since we defined sloth as another form of apathy, is that being careful is another way of being caring. Care-full, get it? Sowing seeds of apathy makes the world a bitter, harsher place for us, and we've brought it on ourselves. But what if you started sowing seeds of prudence instead of thoughtlessness, and people started to be more care-full with you? What if you were the recipient of 100 "little acts of kindness" every day? It can happen. Can you feel it?

Chastity: Just like its counterpart lust, we tend to think of chastity as sexual, but it isn't always. For example, we all like to think of ourselves as virtuous, which is chaste in a way. My older brother explained this to me best when we were watching *He-Man* on television as kids. Skeletor was He-Man's nemesis, the evil character. I don't remember how it came up, but my brother explained to me that Skeletor didn't think of himself as evil and, further, Skeletor thought he was doing the right thing. Nobody wants to think they are not doing the right thing, and Type A's are no exception. We've already discussed how sowing even the smallest seeds of impurity can lead us straight down the path to spiritual bankruptcy. What would you give to have your innocence back? What if you started making pure, unpolluted, uninfluenced decisions based on the simplicity of right and wrong? Not in a naïve way, but in a wholesome way, with motives only for the greater good. It can happen. Can you aspire to it?

Self-control: Willpower is not something Type A's tend to lack. However, self-control is not just willpower; it is also being able to choose the right thing instead of the urgent thing. It is having enough control over ourselves that we don't feel the need to control other people or outside circumstances. For example, buying things on your credit card, or any other form of borrowing, to keep up your image is sowing seeds of gluttony and debt. The urgent thing is to have it now. The important thing is to make good long-term financial decisions. When you are at peace on the inside, and you have sowed the seeds of the right decisions, catastrophe can happen around you and you are somehow able to maintain calmness. What if you started stacking your building blocks on the basis of right decisions instead of urgent decisions? You know you've admired the cool-calm-and-collected quality in others. Wouldn't you like to have that yourself? You can do it. Can you commit yourself to it?

Symptoms and Alternatives

We examined how the core cause of serving idols leads to Seven Deadly Sinful behavior, which is also evidenced by the symptoms of trying to control everything, living in the future, focusing on wealth and possessions and compromising or neglecting character. Once we have renounced our service to the idols, causing our behavior to become more virtuous, it would stand to reason that the symptoms or side effects of that behavior would also be changed. Here is a quick Type A look at a few things that stand out to me, and a glimpse at the possibilities that exist through the steadfast application of the virtues.

Symptom	Alternative
Trying to control everything.	Self-control. Acceptance.
Living in the future.	Living in the present. Being in the moment.
Focusing on wealth and possessions.	Focusing on purpose. Being generous.
Compromising. Neglecting character.	Healthy soul. Happy spirit.

Self-control/Acceptance: Even though we covered self-control as a virtue, it is worth discussing again as an alternative to Type A control-freak tendencies. Self-control is a big deal. The more you have self-control, the less you feel the need to control everything else around you. When you have enough solidarity and inner certainty, the world can throw you a tsunami of problems and you will be able to stand your ground. Acceptance is also challenging for Type A's because we are taught by all our business books that acceptance is for wimps who will never accomplish anything. We are told to challenge the status quo, not settle for it. To some degree, that is correct; but on the other hand, a lack of acceptance will result in anxiety, frustration, and dissatisfaction. I'm not talking about *que sera, sera*, or extreme passivity, but trust in the process that everything happens for a reason. I imagine we Type A's are God's worst back-seat drivers and arm-chair quarterbacks. However, when we stop lusting after outcomes and demanding to have our own way in every situation, somehow we are able to relax, observe, and contribute our proper share instead of needing to dominate everything all the time. There is more peace and wisdom in self-control and acceptance than trying to control everything else.

Living in the present: Now has been a popular topic in our culture lately, probably because most of us are living in either the past or the future. As Deepak Chopra said, "The past and the future have one thing in common – they are not here. Yesterday is a memory and tomorrow is imagination. Both are in the mind and do not exist right now." Though we Type A's may base parts of our identity on accomplishments, successes or recognition received in the past, and though we may have issues and baggage that follow us like everyone else, I contend that most of us Type A's spend most of our time living on our Dream Boards in the future. This is problematic. If you are looking through a telescope, you cannot see what is right in front of you. We miss relational and growth opportunities every day because we think we have somewhere more important to be. We are frustrated, disappointed, and anxious because we are not even close to where we want to be, and no matter what we do, we never seem to get closer. We are lonely, and our spirits are languishing because we deliberately abandon our humanity for the purpose of advancement. By contrast, living in the present opens up worlds of opportunity and possibility. As Eckhart Tolle noticed, "To have your attention in the now is not denial of what is needed in your life. It is recognizing what is primary…When the now is the foundation and primary focus of your life, then your life unfolds with ease." There is more wisdom, joy, and real-time fulfillment living in the now than living in the future.

Focusing on purpose/Being generous: Are you in love with your work, or are you working for a paycheck? If you were forced to take a 50% reduction in pay, would you still want to do your job? By contrast, have you ever thought about your purpose in life? Do you have a calling or a recurring theme in your consciousness that is magnetizing you to a path different from the one you are on? Are there images in your mind of you doing or being something that would fulfill you beyond any measure of materialism? I believe each one of us has a unique purpose, calling or task that we were put here on earth to carry out. Material objects could never satisfy us the way that living out our purpose will. Our individual callings utilize and magnify our distinctive gifts to the fullest, and energize us beyond our ability to consume. Once you discover your purpose and start living it out, you become so abundantly fulfilled (not just monetarily, but spiritually and emotionally) that generosity is a way of life. Instead of manipulating things to pull into greedy, self-serving outcomes, you overflow with warmth, kindness, and giving. Instead of walking tightfisted, you move forward openhanded. There is more fulfillment, love and joy in focusing on purpose and being generous than in focusing on wealth and possessions.

Happy soul/Healthy spirit: Have you been on the path to modern-day spiritual bankruptcy? Have you done small things or big things to get ahead? Are you living in the gray area? Are you living a life where the truth and reality have somehow separated and you feel like your existence is perjury on two feet? I contend that nothing is more important than a healthy soul and spirit. Everything could be wrong in your life, but if the spirit is fed, you will find perseverance comes naturally. Everything could be externally right in your life, but if the soul is neglected or sick, just getting up in the morning is difficult.

People talk about selling your soul to the devil, but as Type A's we have sold our souls to the idols we worship. Once we renounce those idols, we get our souls back, but they are worn and pale, battered and in need of resuscitation. Feeding the spirit is like blowing air into an inflatable raft. Without enough inflation, you'll sink; but when it's fully inflated, it can save your life. Once your soul is happy and your spirit is healthy, then functioning with wisdom, joy, and love comes effortlessly, and fulfillment abounds. Quite a contrast, wouldn't you agree?

Deepest Needs: Fulfillment, Love, Joy, Peace and Wisdom

We examined how the core cause of serving idols leads to Seven Deadly Sinful behavior, which is also evidenced by the symptoms of Type A life, which could never meet our deepest needs of fulfillment, love, joy, peace and wisdom. Once we have renounced our service to the idols, causing our behavior to become more virtuous, and the symptoms are cleared, it would stand to reason that our deepest needs would be next to be met. It is not appropriate to make a goal of fulfillment, love, joy, peace and wisdom without going through this entire inside-out process. Furthermore, taking an outside-in approach to arriving here will be totally ineffective in the long term.

That being said, I'm going to highlight what fulfillment, love, joy, peace and wisdom actually mean. I'm not assuming that you Type A's, with your high level degrees, do not know what these words mean by definition, and I'm not trying to over-simplify. However, I do believe that bringing it back to basics is an excellent way of reminding ourselves and painting a picture of what life could be like.

Fulfillment: Definition: (n.) The state of satisfaction, measuring up, full potential. Synonyms: Satisfaction, contentment, happiness, pleasure, gratification

Can you imagine feeling satisfaction? Can you imagine believing at the deepest level that you measure up? Can you imagine knowing that you are achieving your full potential? Can you believe such a feeling even exists? Having that feeling is a Type A fantasy. Not having to keep up with the rat race; having a moment to pause and feel like work is done; the feeling of measuring up in the world for once. As a full-blown Type A, I never – ever – felt fulfilled. But I do now. So can you.

Love: Definition: (n.) A profoundly tender affection for another person; a feeling of warm attachment; affectionate concern for the well-being of others. (v.) To have love or affection for; to take great pleasure in; to need or benefit greatly from. Synonyms: Affection, adoration, friendship, tenderness, have a weakness for

To quote the Beatles, "All you need is love." Have Type A's become so hardened to life that we have lost the ability to love or be loved? Have we become so independent that the desire to depend on someone is outside our emotional vocabulary? I don't think so. We are just like Tootsie Pops, meaning, it takes a lot of patience to get through the hard candy coating, but there is a soft center in there just waiting to be enjoyed. As a Type A, I was an ice-queen with a heart of stone. I never let anyone get too close, and I never cried in front of people. I never knew I had all these emotions. Now, I cry at movies and elsewhere, and even carry tissues in my purse, just in case. I'm surrounded by the most loving, giving, forgiving, and gracious people. You can be, too.

Joy: Definition: (n.) The emotion of great delight or happiness caused by something exceptionally good or satisfying; a state of happiness or felicity. (v.) To feel glad, to rejoice. Synonyms: Delight, enjoyment, pleasure, bliss, elation, thrill

When was the last time you felt joy? And I don't mean the kind of joy that comes when your Type A master plan to sabotage your enemy is perfectly executed. I mean, when was the last time you laughed uncontrollably for more than five minutes, and then laughed about the same thing all week whenever you thought about it? Do you think pure joy is possible? As a Type A, I don't think I believed in joy. But I do now. So can you.

Peace: Definition: (n.) A state of mutual harmony, especially in personal relationships; silence or stillness; freedom from any strife; freedom of the mind from annoyance, distraction, anxiety, or an obsession. Synonyms: Calm, quiet, tranquility, serenity, harmony, end of war

When we think of peace, especially nowadays, we think of the end of war. When are we going to realize as Type A's that our war is with ourselves? When are we going to wave the white flag of surrender? In a culture where being busy is boss, peace can be so elusive. As a Type A, I had no peace in my life whatsoever. But now I have inner peace, outer peace, all-around peace, in-between peace. Shhhhh.... I think your peace is on the way.

Wisdom: Definition: (n.) The knowledge of what is true or right coupled with just judgment as to action; level-headedness. Synonyms: Understanding, insight, perception, discernment, prudence, good judgment

Dr. Timothy Keller said, "If you think you are not a fool, you are a fool. If you know you are a fool, you are on your way to being wise." We mistake knowledge (which Type A's have a lot of, with our drive to be experts) for wisdom. We mistake maturity (which Type A's have a lot of, with all the responsibilities we have) for wisdom. We mistake common sense (which Type A's have a lot of because we reduce and simplify things, so they don't slow us down) for wisdom. But knowledge, maturity and common sense are not actual wisdom itself. Knowledge, maturity, and common sense cannot give us the answers in life that only wisdom can. As I have personally embarked on this journey to Type A recovery, I have discovered that despite my abundance of knowledge, maturity, and common sense, I had a sore scarcity of wisdom. Since the day of that discovery, my wisdom has flourished. Take this journey with me.

Alternative Results

We examined how the core cause of serving idols leads to Seven Deadly Sinful behavior, which is also evidenced by the symptoms of Type A life, which could never meet our deepest needs of fulfillment, love, joy, peace and wisdom. Once we have renounced our service to the idols, causing our behavior to become more virtuous, and the symptoms are cleared, and our deepest needs of fulfillment, love, joy, peace and wisdom are met, what could possibly be next?

In section one of this book, I listed a bunch of positive aspects of being Type A, expressed as compliments Type A's receive with regularity. There are some very noble characteristics on that list, and there are ones that we may need to temper a bit. Since we are examining alternatives in this chapter, here is a new list of characteristics and compliments that could describe you as you become a Recovering Type A. I am not using compliments as a goal, for that would be external. Rather, the things people compliment you on are a result of what's going on inside you. You receive compliments only when other people recognize something in you to such a level that they feel the need to comment or say something about it. Based on the alternatives proposed in this chapter, here are some of the new compliments you may start receiving.

List 2: Compliments for Recovering Type A's

Virtuous	Fair	Kind
Prudent	Honest	Good
Wise	High Integrity	Gentle
Discerning	Truthful	Calm
Clear-thinking	Courageous	Cool
Good-tempered	Resilient	Poised
Patient	Convicted	Unshakable
Moderate	Faithful	Humble
Disciplined	Hopeful	Modest
Just	Big-hearted	Considerate

| Selfless | Compassionate | Honorable |
| Thoughtful | Conscientious | Tolerant |

Pretty awesome, huh? If you are as Type A as I was, you probably think some of these seem mushy and weak. But they are not. These words describe someone who is steadfast in their beliefs and convictions. They describe someone who is well-intentioned, blameless, hopeful, and secure enough with themselves to nourish others around them. They describe the kind of person we all want to be, even though we have somehow lost this part of ourselves along the way.

~A~

Case Study: Home on the Range

(Alternative to Dream Board Life)

Did you ever see that PBS special *Frontier House*? If you haven't, I highly recommend it. It's one of those shows where they take modern-day families and thrust them into history to see how they survive, and get their impressions along the way. In *Frontier House*, they travel back to the homestead years of the 1880's in the American West where you could mark off as much territory as you wanted, and it was yours for free as long as you could maintain it for five years. Each family on the program took over a 160-acre plot, and they were completely immersed in the frontier lifestyle.

One of the most poignant moments for me was a side-bar/video-diary with a guy who was a self-professed workaholic and very successful businessman. In the real world, his family enjoyed the spoils of living in a gigantic 15,000-square-foot villa in California, international vacations, and all the other pleasures and treasures of modern-day living. In this video diary, he had just come in from hand-mowing, meaning cutting grass with a long-handled sickle, and felt such a sense of accomplishment. He said he loved working for his family on the frontier because they could actually see all he had done for them in a day. Whatever chores he accomplished for them in a day, they were grateful, and recognized his contribution to their family. He commented that in the modern world, he worked hard for a paycheck to provide for his family, but somewhere between the work and the material things money can buy, the appreciation got lost in the shuffle.

A man who already has everything on your Dream Board found farm work more gratifying than riches. What do you think of that?

~A~

Case Study: Taylor and Dave

(Alternative to The Millionaire *and* The Money or the Mommy?*)*

Taylor was a struggling artist dating Dave who was a successful investment banker. They loved each other very much, and she knew beyond a shadow of a doubt that he was the one. He provided a wonderful lifestyle for her, and people scoffed and snickered that she was probably with him for the money. I was close enough to Taylor, that one day I asked her what she thought about it. Her response was thoughtful, introspective and loving.

She told me that she, too, had done a lot of soul searching on that issue. Even though Dave was not a glitzy or bling-bling kind of guy, it is easy to get caught up in the spoils of security and abundance. She wanted her marriage to be based on love, mutual respect, and trust. She put herself through litmus tests with Dave to be sure she loved him for who he was and not for his money. Through her soul searching, she realized that the qualities that make a man attractive to her are the same ones that will make him successful. Those qualities being: honesty, integrity, loyalty, confidence, charisma, magnetism, steadiness... and the list continues. Even though success tends to go hand in hand with these characteristics, she loves Dave for these qualities, regardless of his finances.

Dave didn't base his worth on his riches, but on his character and the kind of man he is. Taylor didn't settle for Dave because of his money, she chose him for his character and the kind of man he is. I attended their wedding in October of 2000. They are still happily married, with three beautiful children. Is that the kind of happiness you want?

~A~

If you think it is too late for you to experience these alternative results, it is not. I assure you, it is not too late. It is never too late to change. It is never too late to make a different choice. There is nothing you have done that convicts or condemns you forever into a life of misery. There is no burden you are carrying that you cannot leave behind. There may be consequences for some of your previous actions, and you may still have to harvest the seeds you've been planting. However, positive choices have the power to annul unfortunate or misguided choices. You cannot take back or escape the past, but you can start planting the right seeds. Pretty soon, the seeds will grow and be ready to break through.

Chapter 11: Ready for a Breakthrough

All major breakthroughs begin with making a decision to change. But how do you change? What do you decide to change? What is the goal? How do you get there? Change must start with figuring out where you want to go. If you are familiar with *Alice in Wonderland*, there is a great scene where Alice asks directions from the Cheshire Cat. The Cat says, "That depends a great deal on where you want to get to." Alice replies, "I don't much care where." And the Cat responds, "Then it doesn't matter which way you go." You cannot be an aimless Alice, and expect to have a breakthrough.

Many of you have been seeking change for some time now, but don't know where to turn or which direction to go. You've been reading all the right books about success and happiness, but somehow the more you read, the more perplexing it gets. Don't you find it confusing that all the business and success books contradict many of the self-help inner-peace books? The business books say, "Business is business" and "There's no crying in baseball," whereas the self-help books say, "Follow how you feel," "Get in touch with your emotions." I don't know about you, but I cannot keep up with that. If I try to put it all into practice in a daily existence, I would need an on/off switch for my heart. Turning your emotions off to function at work, and turning them back on for a personal life is a disaster. What happens when you get a personal call in the middle of the day? It could soften you up and throw off your meetings for the rest of the afternoon.

The point is, having no aim will get you nowhere. Repeating the same thing and expecting different results will get you nowhere.

Adding confusion to the mix will only encourage you to stick to what is safe, which is what you know, which is your habits, which will not produce different results; so again, you are getting nowhere. For us Type A's, that means that instead of focusing on a destination of wealth, fame, power, and control, we need to change our destination to fulfillment, love, joy, peace and wisdom if we're ever going to get there.

Once you know your destination, the next step is figuring out how to get there. There is another movie scene in the *Wizard of Oz* where Dorothy wonders which way she should go when at a crossroads on the yellow brick road. "That way is a very nice way," says Scarecrow, pointing in one direction. "It's pleasant down that way, too," he remarks, as he points in the opposite direction. "Of course, people do go both ways," he says, his arms of straw crossing in front of him as he points in both directions simultaneously. Bewildered, Dorothy asks, "Are you doing that on purpose, or can't you make up your mind?" Isn't this exactly what the contradiction of business success and self-help books feels like? One of my favorite lines in the *Wizard of Oz* is later in that same scene. After explaining to Dorothy that he can't make up his mind because he doesn't have one, Scarecrow justifies his suggestions by noting that "there are some people without brains who do an awful lot of talking, don't they?" I'm not saying that people who write business books or self-help books don't have brains, but I am suggesting that neither category separately is capable of providing the fulfillment, love, joy, peace and wisdom you are seeking. It's got to be something else.

Most of us grasp at some level that our money, accomplishments, possessions, power, and fame will mean very little to us when we look back at the end our lives. And we somehow know that if we're looking back at a life of solitude and isolation, we'll feel even worse. Even if we subconsciously or consciously know we need to change, change is unfortunately easier said than done. It becomes something that we'll just have to deal with later, even if we don't know exactly when later is going to come.

It is so easy to convince ourselves that once we earn more money, have more status or power, or achieve a certain something, that it will be easier to change and go back to finding our true selves. But this is a never-ending treadmill, and later never comes. Even if we do achieve wealth, power and fame, we will not find satisfaction. As Lee Marvin said, "They put your name on a star on Hollywood Boulevard and you find a pile of dog manure on it. That's the whole story, baby." More wealth, power, and fame does not change who you are, and will not make you happy. Check out this quote from Cynthia Heimel, a New York City columnist who has known many celebrities since before they were "discovered," and followed them for many years through their careers:

> I pity celebrities. I really do. Sylvester Stallone, Bruce Willis and Barbra Streisand were once perfectly pleasant human beings. But now their wrath is awful. I think when God wants to play a really rotten practical joke on you, he grants you your deepest wish, and then giggles merrily when you realize you want to kill yourself. You see, Sly, Bruce and Barbra wanted fame. They worked, they pushed, and the morning after each of them became famous, they wanted to take an overdose. Because that giant thing they were striving for, that fame thing that was going to make everything ok, that was going to make their lives bearable, that was going to provide them with personal fulfillment and happiness, had happened, and they were still them. The disillusionment turned them howling and insufferable.

By contrast, did you watch the Ted Kennedy eulogies? Though I am from Massachusetts, I was never a big fan of his politics. However, the eulogies given at his funeral were an amazing tribute to his humanity. Not only did he accomplish a great deal professionally, but the stories told after his passing were all stories of a great friend. He was always the first one to pick up the phone when someone was in need. He was the one who spent countless hours by people's sides when they needed him most. He was not a man who said, "I'm doing something more important right now; how about we do lunch next month." After a couple hours of story after story, I began to wonder how he had time to accomplish everything he did. The only answer is that he placed high priority on humanity and friendship. He did not miss an opportunity to be a friend right here, right now.

I knew a guy who was on the fast track straight to the top, and everybody knew it. He didn't make time for people, but they still wanted to be around him to mooch off of his success by osmosis. He spent more of his time blowing people off than helping them. He strictly followed a personal policy not to talk to anyone below a certain level of production or status. As years passed by, and he received promotion after promotion, people tracked his career from a distance and through the rumor mill. More people are waiting for him to fail than cheering for him. Whether I ever said so or not, I always saw greatness in him as a person, and hope for the opportunity to tell him that someday, face-to-face. Hopefully he won't be too far gone by the time that happens.

Are you that guy? Are you sick of being that guy? Are you ready for change?

Self-help Won't Help Type A's

Are you sick and tired of business books that tell you to be heartless, and self-help books that tell you to follow how you feel? I find it confusing. Not only do they contradict each other, but neither one really has the answers for what I'm going through at any given point in time. These standardized self-help, self-empowerment, and self-discovery examinations dance around the core issue, without addressing the core itself. Even books about following your bliss or passion don't make sense. All they do is point out what you should be doing, but there is no roadmap how to get from where you are to where you want to be. What, am I supposed to just dive into the abyss and hope the universe takes over to make it happen? No wonder the upcoming generation is having quarter-life crises! None of these sources has the right answer!

If you are Type A like me, you have an automatic reflex response to most of these questions, which is another reason these outside-in approaches are totally hopeless. You are unconvinced of the process before you even start, so when the slightest thing does not go according to the book, it is easy to discredit it, blow it off, and keep living life the same way you have before. We are going to take a look at some of these questions. If you are Type A, you will completely understand where I'm coming from as I go through a few of them.

~A~

Self-help Question: Are you happy about where your life is right now? Why or why not?

Type A Responses: "Oh come on! Is anybody really happy about where their life is right now, aside from losers who settle for less?" *Or* "I will be in five years after I've accomplished all the things I am working so hard on right now." *Or* "I will be when I get that promotion, new car, new house, raise..." *Or* "I'm just not where I want to be in my career yet. Once I have more money and more power, things will be better."

Self-help Question: At what point (or phase) in life were you the most satisfied? Why? How did you get to this point in your life?

Type A Responses: "Oh come on! Satisfaction is for people who settle for less – didn't we already cover this in the last question?" *Or* "I believe it's a positive thing to never be satisfied. That way, you always keep striving for more, and you keep accomplishing more. Therefore, I don't ever want to be satisfied." *Or* "I'll be most satisfied in a few years when everything comes together." *Or* "My childhood, or college because I had no responsibility or stress."

Self-help Question: What do you think is the best thing about you? The worst?

Type A Responses: "My drive, determination, and my unending ambition are the most notable, respectable, and admirable things about me." *Or* "I'm the top producer (youngest one to make partner)." *Or* "I really like my car, and I know all the best places. A lot of people wish they were me." *Or* "The worst thing about me is, people say I'm too tough or competitive, but they are just wimps who don't get it." *Or* "The worst thing about me is, I just don't have a lot of time."

Self-help Question: Are you happy about where you are living? The community, culture, weather...?

Type A Responses: "Huh? As long as I'm climbing the ladder, I don't care where I am." *Or* "And yet another stupid question. Let me break it down for you. Outdoor activities include: going to the mailbox, walking from home to car, walking from car to office. Any questions?"

Self-help Question: Are you pleased with your romantic relationship? Your relationship with your spouse and children?

Type A Responses: "I don't have time for a relationship! What a stupid question! Ha! Yeah, I love my relationship with my desk, and my laptop! That's the romance in my life. Spouse and children – is this a joke?" *Or* "The relationship I'm in probably won't last because I work too much, so why would I even bother answering this question?" *Or* "Well, nobody's perfect, and he/she puts up with me, so..." *Or* "I don't get to spend as much time with them as I want to, but I provide a really good lifestyle and they will appreciate that someday!!" *Or* "I attend as many of my kids' games, recitals, plays, and school events as I can, and even though I'm on my BlackBerry the whole time, they know I'm there!"

Self-help Question: What are the recurring difficulties in your life?

Type A Responses: "Stupid people." *Or* "Things not happening fast enough, or according to my plan." *Or* "If only I had more money or more power, everything would be better." *Or* "People getting in my way and slowing me down."

Self-help Question: What have been the biggest disappointments in your life?

Type A Responses: "I'm always disappointed because I'm not where I want to be yet." *Or* "When so-and-so was chosen for the promotion over me, or out-performed me." *Or* "I'm usually disappointed by people. They are always letting me down. I can't count on anyone but myself."

Self-help Question: Do you consider your life to be balanced?

Type A Responses: "Are you serious? These questions are supposed to help me? Are you on crack? Don't waste my time. Of course, my life isn't balanced! I'm a workaholic and I know it, but there is nothing I can do about it right now!" *Or* "I'd like to be more balanced, but when I'm not working, I need to catch up on sleep!" *Or* "The imbalance I have in my life now will all be worth it when I get where I'm going."

Self-help Question: Are you fulfilled with your professional career? What would you do even if you didn't get paid to do it? What do you do in your free time? What is your vision of happiness?

Type A Responses: "Am I satisfied with my professional career? Not yet. However, I set goals, I achieve them. That is satisfying. I get recognized for my work. That is satisfying. So there!" *Or* "Work for free? Who would do such a thing? Where are these questions coming from, La La Land? Why does everyone ask that? That question is so cliché! And so stupid!" *Or* "I don't have any free time! If I have free time, I'm working!! If I'm not working in my free time, I'm sleeping!!!" *Or* "My vision of happiness can be found on my Dream

Board. Is that the last of these idiotic questions? I really don't have time for this. I have somewhere to be."

~A~

Aren't you sick of these questions, too? Aren't there times when you wish you could just start all over again? Do you ever wish you could go back to the beginning, rewind the clock, and just start over again? Do you think these questions are the beginning of major breakthrough and life-altering change? Diane Ackerman said, "I don't want to get to the end of my life and find that I have lived just the length of it. I want to have lived the width of it as well." I don't know about you, but I don't want to get to the end of my life and be a bitter old lady, or a cantankerous old man like the Economist from the Case Study in section one of this book. I don't want to be the guy in the movies who sacrifices it all for a mansion, yacht, and private jet. But even though I know I don't want to end up like that, I don't think that an outside-in approach to change is really going to change anything. Frankly, I am sick and tired of it.

Sick and Tired

Change is easier said than done and sometimes you have to hit rock bottom to initiate it. Since rock bottom isn't really a fun place to be, if you are lucky, perhaps just being sick and tired will be enough. Let's find out if you are really ready for change. Are you sure you are really ready for that? Have you had enough of where you are, who you've become, what you think you're supposed to be? Let's find out…

Are you sick and tired of

- ✓ Being afraid that you do not have enough?
- ✓ Always feeling strapped?
- ✓ Keeping up with the Joneses?
- ✓ Competing for everything and about everything?
- ✓ Never feeling good enough?
- ✓ Feeling worthless aside from your status at work and the

money you make?

- ✓ Being concerned about what others think as your security?
- ✓ Being bullied or being a bully?
- ✓ Not living up to your own expectations?
- ✓ Not living up to the expectations of others?
- ✓ Insecurity about your short-term plans?
- ✓ Insecurity about your long-term plans?
- ✓ Disappointment with your work?
- ✓ Being motivated by fear, insecurity, guilt, pride, or reputation building?
- ✓ Feeling held back, even if you can't put your finger on why?

Service to the Idols of Money, Accomplishment, and Self will continually drive you back into feeling this way. Type A priorities cannot make you happy. The only satisfaction you will ever get out of a Type A life includes a temporary sense of satisfaction or accomplishment, short-lived ego gratification, a fleeting and occasional sense of joy, brief illusions of control, interim justification for your behavior, momentary attention and approval from others, and impermanent freedom of choice. None of these is lasting, and most of them feed the addiction into needing more money, more accomplishment, and more self-gratification in order to maintain the buzz. The addiction becomes the center of your life above all other things until you are worn out and beat up from keeping up with yourself. When you place any of these idols as top priority in your life, you become victim to it until it destroys you.

Living up to expectations, whether your own or those of others, is a nasty and dangerous treadmill that never stops. The only option is to dismount. If you want change, you have to renounce these idols and free yourself from their priorities. We will talk about this more in section three.

Are you sick and tired of:

- ✓ Lousy friendships and relationships?
- ✓ Finding out that an old friend you just reconnected with on Facebook is married and you're not?
- ✓ Feeling like a failure in personal relationships?
- ✓ Choosing the wrong people to trust?
- ✓ Needing an on/off switch for your emotions, if you even have emotions left?
- ✓ Being bored by most of the people around you?
- ✓ Feeling like you are missing out on the good stuff in life?
- ✓ Knowing that you are that guy in the movies who will get to the end of his life and wonder where it all went wrong?

We all need to feel like we are better than other people for some reason or another. There are cliques that pride themselves on being more successful, and cliques that pride themselves on being more laid back. As Type A's, the people we have the most in common with are serving their own Idols of Money, Accomplishment, and Self, which puts them in direct competition with us 99% of the time. Competition, no matter how friendly we claim it to be, is not the basis for healthy relationships.

Have you ever noticed that in high school and college, people keep telling you that "these are the moments," but then once you get into adulthood, they stop saying that? Does that mean that these aren't the moments anymore? No. These are always the moments. Now is always the moment. The difference between people who have real, lasting, deep friendships and people who do not is one word: time. If you have no moments available, you will have no moments to remember. If you do not prioritize love, you will not have love. The Europeans are so much better at emotions than we Americans are. I noticed this particularly in Scandinavia, and especially in contrast to my puritanical New England heritage. They take time to celebrate today, this moment, right now. They take time to cherish each other, speak from the heart, show others how they feel. They know that love is more important than money and accomplishments.

If you want change, you have to free yourself from the entanglement of image-building and seek authenticity. Renouncing idols is one thing, but you also need to replace them with an alternative that will grow and develop from the inside-out and blossom in the form of new results. We will talk about this more in section three.

Are you sick and tired of

- ✓ Dissatisfaction?
- ✓ Loneliness?
- ✓ Disappointment?
- ✓ Anxiety?
- ✓ Feeling foolish?
- ✓ Acting out your public profile?
- ✓ Being Type A?

Have you ever had a time in your life when you knew you should be satisfied, but you weren't? Have you ever had a time in your life when everything seemed wrong, and yet you were satisfied? What was the difference? I'll bet the difference was that the time you were not satisfied but "should" have been, despite everything appearing great, you still had an inner hunger for fulfillment, love, joy, peace and wisdom. Even though everything seemed terrific on the outside, there was an emptiness and starvation for satisfaction on the inside. Like a stomach growling for food, your spirit growled to be nourished. To satiate yourself, you have to keep hunting for satisfaction.

What happens when you go to the grocery store when you are hungry? You wind up buying a lot of stuff you don't need and probably won't ever eat, or you wind up gorging on junk food. That's what we are doing in our lives as we try to feed our spirits. We are gorging on substitutes and temporary fixes, aka spiritual junk food. We all know you can live on junk food for a little while, but eventually the side effects are deadly. At the grand buffet of feeding your spirit, the only food that idols have to offer is junk. If you want change, you've got to start feeding your soul, and start a diet of spiritual nutrition. We will talk more about this in section three.

Are You Ready?

As if being sick and tired of all those things isn't reason enough to change, I'm going to give you more incentive. I am a positive person, and I bet you are, too, so I prefer to focus on possibility rather than negativity. Here's an examination to see if you are ready for change from a positive point of view...

Are you ready to

- ✓ Feel abundant?
- ✓ Have authentic relationships?
- ✓ Be surrounded by real friends? Be a better friend?
- ✓ Feel a sense of accomplishment, to the point that you can rest?
- ✓ Feel satisfied with where you are in life – right now?
- ✓ Not be trapped in your own image of what you've become?
- ✓ Get over the past?
- ✓ Be more generous? Be "a giver?" Be an encourager to others?
- ✓ Be more compassionate?
- ✓ Smile more?
- ✓ Feel more grounded?
- ✓ Be more in control of your thoughts and fears?
- ✓ Know your worth based on who you are, not what you've done?
- ✓ Know what you stand for?
- ✓ Feel acceptance for everything that happens?
- ✓ Feel that you are accepted? Accept yourself?
- ✓ Live in the moment?
- ✓ Know your purpose?
- ✓ Have a happy spirit, no matter what life throws at you?
- ✓ Be well with your soul?

✓ Be a kinder, gentler you?
✓ Be a new, improved you?
✓ Be a better you than ever before?
✓ Be fulfilled, loving, joyful, at peace and wise?
✓ Have a breakthrough?

Are you ready for change? Do you really want fulfillment, love, joy, peace and wisdom? Do you want to know how to get them? Then I think you are ready for section three.

Intermission: Time to Change

You say you are ready for change. Here are a couple of side stories to get you thinking.

~A~

There's a Hole in My Sidewalk

This is a paraphrase of Portia Nelson's autobiography in five short chapters:

Chapter One: I was walking down the street, walking down the sidewalk. There was a hole in the sidewalk. I didn't see it. I fell in. It's not my fault. Man, it's hard to get out of here.

Chapter Two: I was walking down the street, walking down the sidewalk. There was a hole in the sidewalk. I pretended not to see it. I fell in. It's not my fault. Man, it's hard to get out of here.

Chapter Three: I was walking down the street, walking down the sidewalk. There was a hole in the sidewalk. I saw it, but I fell in anyway. I've been here before and I hate it. It is my fault. Man, it takes a long time to get out of here.

Chapter Four: I was walking down the street, walking down the sidewalk. There was a hole in the sidewalk. I walked around it.

Chapter Five: I took a different street.

~A~

Lessons of the Motorcycle

Have you ever driven or ridden a motorcycle? Really, really fast? My friend Joe was preparing me for my first motorcycle ride. We were in the Hamptons in the off-season, so the roads were ours, and Joe planned on showing me what 120 miles per hour feels like. He was showing me hand signals to prepare me for the ride, and then said this, "If we skid out or get thrown off, Do Not Get Up. Even if you think you have stopped moving, even if you think you are ok. No excuses. No matter what, do not get up until someone is there to help you. Let me explain: We will be moving at such a rate of speed, that even if you think you have come to a complete stop, you may still have kinetic energy moving through your body. If you try to stand up with this momentum still in you, it will throw you off balance. You could stumble around into traffic or down a ditch, and even if you were fine before getting up, you could really hurt yourself by trying to get up too fast without assistance. If that happens, and you live to tell about it, you'll still say you got injured in a motorcycle accident to sound cool, but deep down you'll know it's really because you were just a stumbling idiot. The point is, don't get up too fast or without help."

~A~

Have you ever made a mistake in your life, or had a time when you realized you had messed up in a huge way? You recognize the mistake, you think you have come to a complete stop, and you think you are ok... So you pick yourself up, a survivor of that mistake, trying to make new choices to avoid making that mistake again... But somehow you're living in the same world with the same pressures and the same vulnerabilities... And somehow you make an even bigger mistake in the process of trying to avoid making the same mistake... And somehow you damage yourself more because you got up too soon or without help... And even though your intentions were good, deep down you feel like a stumbling idiot?

It's time to get up and not stumble. It's time to take a different street. It's time to change.

Section Three

A New Life

Chapter 12: Inside-Out with the Old

So, how do you go about getting fulfillment, love, joy, peace and wisdom? That's a great question. It's also a question that a lot of people have been trying to answer for you for a very long time. But they don't have the answer for you. Even I don't have the answer for you. Remember how I told you this wasn't going to be a self-help, or 12-step, or "ten things to do" kind of book? I'm standing firm in that. Reading more of those books is not going to help. It's not about a formula that you can plug into a computer and out pops a better life. It's not about a prescription that heals you and takes away your pain. It's not about secret knowledge that only special people have, and now for $14.99 you can have it, too. There is no outside-in method that could ever solve your life. There is no outside-in approach to creating fulfillment, love, joy, peace and wisdom. That's because fulfillment, love, joy, peace and wisdom are bi-products of something else, something more, something true, something greater than ourselves. As Beth Moore said, "In search of truth, we will be driven beyond ourselves until all we find is God." A heart-to-heart, one-on-one relationship with God is the only path to fulfillment, love, joy, peace and wisdom.

Now don't freak out, roll your eyes or be presumptuous that you know where I'm going with this. There are oftentimes major differences between the truth of *what is written* when compared to *what is practiced.* So before you start with pre-canned push-backs, please hear me out. It does not matter what religion you were brought up with or what religion you are now. Though I am going to cite Biblical scripture as a means of *checking the source,* we will not get bogged down in religious dogma or practices, and we're not even

147

going to try to "be religious." It has been said, and I believe, that R-R=R. That stands for Rules minus Relationship equals Rebellion, and this is what many of you have probably and unfortunately experienced. However, that is not what I am here to talk to you about.

What I am going to focus on with you is building a personal relationship with a highly personal and relational God. He is the only one that has the answer to your fulfillment, love, joy, peace and wisdom; the only One who can give it to you; and even better, He wants to give it to you. If there is only one message I want you to get out of this entire section, it is this: God loves you. God loves you, God loves you, God loves you. Mother Teresa said, "God has created us to love and be loved, and this is the beginning of prayer – to know that God loves me, that I have been created for greater things." That's what we're going to talk about. So please, keep an open mind and an open heart. You owe it to yourself to keep reading.

Experts agree that permanent paradigm transformation must start at the core. This is why the outside-in approach of self-help is completely ineffective. You can soak yourself in new practices, attempt to change your thoughts and "Fake it until you make it" all day long, but it still won't seep in or change your innermost self. No matter how long you marinate a piece of chicken in steak sauce, it still doesn't become a piece of steak. The only option is to begin the process of change at the nucleus, and let all other changes stem and flow from the new foundation. There are various illustrations for why inside-out is the only approach that works, so here are a few to get you thinking:

- ✓ Beliefs become thoughts. Thoughts become words. Words become actions. Actions become habits. Habits become character. Character becomes results.
- ✓ Motives shape choices. Choices shape habits. Habits shape character. Character guides decisions we make even when tempted or stressed.

✓ Roots become shoots become trees become forests.
✓ A tree is known by its fruit. (Matthew 12:33)

The self-help response has been an overwhelming concentration on self-empowerment, and there are hundreds of available titles about it. Frankly, self-help and self-empowerment is the industry of the Idol of Self. *"It's not what other people think of you, it's what you think of yourself,"* or *"Don't let anyone get in the way of your dreams,"* and *"You can do it,"* or *"Believe in yourself."* They ask you questions like the ones we've already discussed and rebuked with Type A retaliations, and then make suggestions for external changes including altering your work life, changing your thought patterns, journaling your feelings, breathing exercises to clear your mind, and even stress relievers like getting a dog and taking up gardening. This proposition inherently admits its own inadequacy. If it were capable of delivering satisfaction, additional stress relievers would not be required.

True self-discovery and actualization is not about the two extremes of either changing who you are or becoming a caricature of yourself. Purposeful self-awareness has to do with understanding yourself and your role in the big picture. Changing your work life from the outside-in without changing the idols you are worshipping *(such as the Idol of Money or the Idol of Accomplishment)* is likely to produce the same long-term results. Changing your thoughts from the outside-in is far too oversimplified and still doesn't get to the crux of the matter. For example, when people attempt new affirmations to change their thought patterns, they often hear that little voice popping up that doesn't actually believe the affirmation. Outside-in approaches neglect to address this little voice, or dismiss it with the flippant suggestions of ignoring it until it goes away, or telling it to shut up. With this approach, your innermost self is not convinced, the affirmation is infertile, and optimism is not enough.

Similarly, journaling your thoughts does not change them. You wind up journaling more of the affirmations you are trying to convince yourself of, or you journal from the negative side of your doubts. If you are journaling because you believe the answer is already deep inside of you, then you are wasting your time. That's like asking 20 people for their opinion about what they think you should do, and then doing what you want to do anyway. What's the point? The same goes for breathing exercises to clear your mind. Clearing your mind does not change your mind. If you are even capable of clearing your mind, all you've done is empty it out to be filled back up with your own thoughts. If you haven't replaced your thoughts with foundational truths of purpose-driven beliefs and motives, you are likely to continue circling around the same life patterns over and over again.

The only path to transformational change is to start with the fundamentals of what is driving your decisions. As a Type A, your decisions are mostly being directed by the Idols of Money, Accomplishment, and Self. If you continue in service to those idols, then no matter how many cosmetic improvements you make to your outlook or attitude, you are still going to produce the same results. The only option is to renounce these idols and place God as the most important decision-driver in your life. First, you have to admit you are serving the idols, then you have to walk away from them, and then you have to choose God instead. This is a lifetime process and a journey, and you have to be committed to doing whatever it takes to stay on track. As a Type A, you are used to taking a *whatever it takes* approach, so this is just a new application of the theory.

This means that instead of changing your work life, you must discover your God-given purpose. Instead of changing your thoughts, you must begin a dialogue with God and believe in His promises. Instead of affirming yourself, you must allow God's love to neutralize your hurt and pain. Instead of clearing your mind, you must fill it with the truth of God to fortify your faith, deepen your wisdom, enhance your vigilance, and strengthen your steps. Instead of helping yourself, you must ask God for His help, and allow Him to help you. God loves you. He wants what is best for you. He is your path to fulfillment, love, joy, peace and wisdom.

When I talk about God, people ask me if I am spiritual or religious. My response is, both and neither. Spiritual people have the essence of a divine relationship, but tend to lack accountability. Religious people are so dogmatic or legalistic, they tend to be overly judgmental and lack grace regarding anything out of the box of their beliefs. Neither one works as a stand-alone. It has to be a combination of relationship plus cooperation on our part to follow God's path for us. We have been given free will. If we acknowledge God in all our ways, He will make our paths straight. (Proverbs 3:6) Kind of like those investment company ads on television, where they lay out the path in front of you. You don't have to stay on the path, but if you stray, it's not your advisor's fault.

It is my belief that many of the negative religious experiences people have suffered are based on practitioners who either don't read or don't follow what the Bible actually says. God did not say, "*I want to add to your stress and anxiety, make you feel guilty, or increase your burdens,*" or "*I am here to subject you to the judgment of others who claim to follow Me.*" Though, unfortunately, that is what many people regard as religion. Legalistic, do-and-don't, judgmental Christians are a disservice to God and the spreading of His love for mankind. Moreover, emphasizing external obligations and rules is the opposite of Jesus' teachings. Scripture is clear that a relationship with God trumps any human effort to "follow the rules." (Galatians 2:2-3) That's not to say that there aren't boundaries, but the boundaries of love, truth, and justice are there to enhance our freedoms, not to squash us.

More unfortunate religious experiences include messages that are hard to digest and apply in everyday life. Some hymns, for example, can be an awful way to think about God! To generalize, here's a summary of some hymns. Sing along with me: "*Everything here is bad, but it will all be good in Heaven. I don't deserve anything here on earth, but I'll get it after I die. The more miserable my life is here, the happier I'll be in Heaven. Hopefully, I can suffer some more this week before I come back next Sunday. Guilt and shame, guilt and shame, guilt and shame. Please have mercy. Amen."* Sorry, but I have no interest in that religion. Further, this is not the message of Biblical teachings. In scripture, God makes over 100 promises to us, many of which pertain to benefits He wants to give us during our lifetime here on earth. "That we may have life and have it more abundantly." (John 10:10)

The cultural response to negative religious practices has been a buffet-style approach to picking and choosing from various religious teachings according to personal preference. Intellectuals especially like to do this and then pepper it with some scientific theory. Unfortunately, this is very confusing, and nearly impossible to practice. Who knows which religion to choose when? What happens when they contradict each other? Where is the accountability, and to whom?

Don't get me wrong, I am not against open-mindedness. I believe we must walk in love and compassion for one another and our differences, each of us as ambassadors of our faiths, explaining, discussing, and understanding our distinctions. However, I believe we can do that without weakening or blending who we are and what we believe. Further, unless you have done the homework on all of the religions and all of their practices, you cannot claim to be a follower, even in part. Moreover, if you are buffet-style blending your religion, the result is that you are no better than the ancient Greeks and Romans. They had a god for every occasion and their primary pursuit was to enjoy the good life while they were here. Basically, that means if we are following them, then our society has reverted to paganism. Or, eating what I call Religion Soup. Here's the recipe:

Recipe for Religion Soup

✓ Religion Soup Broth: Everybody is saved unless they screw it up. Good people go to Heaven, and instead of calling it God, call it the Universe or a Higher Power.

✓ Add a little bit of Jesus (because he seems like a nice guy, and I want to keep my Christmas tree).

✓ Add the five pillars of Islam, (except I'm not sure about that Mohammed guy because of those whacko extremist followers, plus I don't like the outfits or the fasting or all that praying all the time, and minus the pilgrimage trip to Mecca because that's expensive, and I'd rather go to the Caymans).

✓ Add a Jewish rabbi (or substitute with a few Barbra Streisand CD's).

✓ Add a handful of reincarnation (because that's just super-cool).

✓ Incorporate some yoga (even though it's not a religion, it's Buddha-like).

✓ Add a teaspoon of quantum physics and metaphysical stuff (because it's trendy nowadays).

✓ Add a dab of Khlyst and Kama Sutra (so I can be sexually promiscuous – and good at it).

✓ Top it off with the Tao of Pooh.

✓ Season to taste.

If you actually tried to follow this recipe and put it into practice, you would be weary and bewildered. Do you know the rules of each one? If you don't know the rules, how do you know where you stand? Are you in the habit of playing a game without knowing the rules first? You would never run a business this way, would you? And aren't you the same people that are whining about your kids celebrating all the holidays in school?

Now, before you start thinking that I'm some Pollyanna religious girl, which by the way, if you've been reading the first two sections of this book, you know I'm not, please know that I have done my homework on this topic. I am not a religious scholar by any means, and I was not even raised in a religious household, but I have been seeking answers over the course of many years, applying full Type A *need-to-know* to my layman's approach. I have read the entire Tao Te Ching several times, I have studied Jewish beliefs and traditions, I have familiarized myself with the pillars and beliefs of Islam, I have read Chopra and Tolle, watched *The Secret,* and done yoga. I even read a book where the author set out to prove why coincidences happen, and his conclusion was that there are no coincidences. In studying these various messages, there are similarities, particularly about what is right and wrong. Beyond the surface level, however, they are hugely different, and quite contradictory to each other. Experts agree, they can't all be right.

So we have choices. The first option is to try to keep up with Religion Soup, meaning start adhering to all the combined required practices or continue to be blurred-out of solid beliefs. The second option is to choose to serve idols, which Type A's have most likely already been doing. The third to let everyone else make your decisions for you and your soul. And the last is to serve God. If you choose, like I have, to serve God, then we must get rid of a lot of the "religious" impressions that have clouded the truth and turned a lot of people away from faith, and replace that stuff with new perspective. Marcel Proust said, "The act of real discovery is not in finding new lands, but in seeing with new eyes."

I must be clear that I am not here to judge you, and this is not my attempt to force conversion on anyone. That being said, I am a Christian and therefore base my faith on Biblical truths. There are negative connotations with the title "Christian," mostly based on extreme examples that do, indeed, exist. Bear in mind that this is the same as judging Islam, a very peaceable religion, based on their extremists. Neither is a fair assessment. I believe that if you want to know the true and pure message of a faith, you must *check the source* for yourself. For a Christian, that means studying the Bible and what it says about everything. I'm not certain what you have come to know of the Bible, or how much you have studied it, but it is amazing. Even if you are not Christian, will never be Christian and do not believe that the Bible is the Word of God, you've got to admit, there's some pretty good stuff in the Book. In our journey together through this last section, I will cite several references directly from the Bible. I encourage you to look them up for yourself and begin your own adventure with this phenomenal treasure.

You may be wondering with all the research I have done, why the Bible rose to the top of the pile and gained authority in my life. The answer is, it pursued me. I didn't even own one until it beckoned me... literally. About six months prior to my conversional experience with God, I was sitting at home, and this strong craving came over me. Except this craving wasn't for chocolate, it was for the Bible. The little voice in my head was telling me, "Go get a Bible," and it kept repeating itself like a broken record. Though this did seem strange to me at the time, I usually follow my cravings (especially for chocolate), so I went to Barnes & Noble, chose a Bible and bought it. I had no idea where to start, so I just allowed "the Universe" to show me, and I opened to the first page of the Book of Proverbs. I've been hooked ever since. Furthermore, through the course of my study, I have also come to the conclusion that any "Christian" practice that does not resonate with Biblical truth should be eliminated. Jesus himself did not come here to start a religion or a religious system. He came as the Prince of Peace and a Messenger of God's love for you. (Isaiah 9:6)

As I delved into the Bible, still as a non-believer, it resonated with me. It makes sense and it covers everything you are going through right now that you think they couldn't possibly have known about thousands of years ago. I see in hindsight that God was using this study to prepare me for the inception of my faith. On that note, the details of my conversion experience will have to wait for another book; however, the basic outline is as follows: I was in a situation that didn't seem right, and I needed to know how to get out of it. I prayed to God with a proposition, making a deal with Him that if He showed me the right way out, I would believe in Him, accept Jesus as my savior, get baptized, and follow after Him. Within 24 hours of that prayer, God completely rocked my world, hence my need for a whole other book to tell the tale. My life was literally turned upside down, but I was grateful that God had suddenly made things so obvious. "I was blind and now I see" had a whole new meaning to me. Blindness wasn't just for weak idiots that couldn't keep up with me. I, myself, had been blind.

It's important to note that when you make a deal with God, and He does His part, it's imperative that you follow through with your end of the bargain. Let's just say, I am not naturally a submissive person. I'm almost laughing out loud just writing that, and Beth Moore said it better when she said, "Submission and subservience come about as naturally to me as cuddling baby porcupines." However, God had delivered on His part of the deal, so it was my turn to step up and follow through. Therefore, no matter how blind I felt at times, I cooperated with Him, continued to study His word, and I was baptized in the Gulf of Mexico the following summer on August 21, 2005.

After becoming a believer, and during the process of building my relationship with God, I heard people talking about the "change of heart" that happened to them. I never really understood what they were talking about and was sometimes cynical if this was just *Christian-speak*, or authentic. I was a skeptical believer, not a faithful servant. Good thing is, God was working on me, had a plan and a hope for me, and never gave up on me, no matter how stubborn

I was with my Type A ways and my worship of the Idols of Money, Accomplishment, and Self. I've made many mistakes along the way, but He was persistently and finally able to get through to me.

My metamorphosis began not just with belief, but with placing God first in my life. This book, particularly this section, serves as only a fraction of my testimony. It has been written out of dutiful service to Him, and is my attempt to help you experience the same transformation. We'll talk more about some of my personal change throughout this section, but as I said before, the purpose of this book is not autobiographical. I use vignettes from my experience of making God the center of my life to help you on your journey to the fulfillment, love, joy, peace and wisdom that God wants to give you.

I've asked you for an open mind and an open heart. If you really want fulfillment, love, joy, peace and wisdom for yourself, then I need to make another request of you. For at least the remainder of this book, I ask that you forget what you know of self-empowerment and self-help and stop weakening your faith with a diet of Religion Soup. If you are really serious about getting fulfillment, love, joy, peace and wisdom, then at some point you will need to make a full commitment to this path and invite God into your life. We'll talk more about that later, but let's not get ahead of ourselves. Before you can bring something new into your life, you have to make room...

Out with the Idols

"You shall have no other Gods before me." (Exodus 20:3) St. Augustine said that one of the biggest problems or habits of mankind is loving good things too much, and loving them more than God. When we love things, even good things, more than we love God, it distorts our emotions and logic. And since actions flow from thoughts, if our logic is distorted, the consequences of those actions are bound to be unfortunate. Dr. Timothy Keller referred to it as "turning good things into ultimate things." If anything but God is an ultimate thing in your life, there is no room for God to be the only ultimate thing in your life. It's like trying to be a little bit pregnant. All other idols have to go. "Throw away the foreign gods that are among you and yield your hearts to the Lord." (Joshua 24:23)

Idols can be anything we put in the place of God. We previously discussed the wide gamut of idols that people are worshipping nowadays, and more importantly, we discussed the most common idols for Type A's: The Idol of Money, the Idol of Accomplishment, and the Idol of Self. Money, accomplishment and self are all good things, but when you turn to them for your identity, worth, and value, or use them to bind your wounds and cope when things do not go your way, then you have turned a good thing into an ultimate thing.

The problem with loving or idolizing anything in the place of God is that you become captive to it. It will force you into service by controlling you and consuming you, until it destroys you. Any idol taking the place of God in your heart is deceiving you. It is incapable of doing what God can do for you. Remember how the Idol of Money puts you constantly in fear of never having enough? Remember how the Idol of Accomplishment puts you constantly in fear of keeping up? Remember how the Idol of Self puts you constantly in fear of not being good enough? No matter how much you make, how high you climb, or how much you reinforce your ego, these idols take delight in savoring your fears. They delude you with promises of grandeur and then misguide you to your ultimate defeat. Scripture warns that following these idols puts us on the same path as past generations who "consecrated themselves to that shameful idol, and became as detestable and loathsome like that which they loved." (Hosea 9:10) If you don't change now, no matter how much you resist, you will lose yourself and be destroyed by what you are idolizing.

The first step in walking away from these idols is to recognize that you are, indeed, worshipping them, and admit to yourself the truth that they are incapable of keeping you satisfied. If you go back to chapter 9 of this book, the descriptions will shed light on your own servitude and enslavement. Conceding to the truth will help you disallow their power over you. "You will know the truth and the truth will set you free." (John 8:32) Be honest with yourself, and know that you are not alone. Don't feel bad; if I hadn't been serving them myself, I wouldn't be writing this book right now.

As you go through this process, always remember that the Idols of Money, Accomplishment, and Self do not love you. You are just a number to them, a tool they use for their own devices. Remember the Dr. Keller quote, "If you are struggling for your own glory, power, or fame, you are on a collision course with God"? If you are in servitude to the Idol of Money, the Idol of Accomplishment, or the Idol of Self, they are using you and sending you into battle to die for them as they seek to glorify themselves. More importantly, God does love you. God especially loves it when people leave their idols in the dust, and run to Him.

Once you come to grips with this important first step, there is only one more thing to do to regain your freedom. All major breakthroughs begin with making a decision to change. Leaving these idols is a once-and-for-all decision to wholly and permanently renounce them and reject their influence on your life and decisions. Stop placing them first in your life. Stop striving after them as your top priority. End your enslavement to them immediately. As Romans 12:2 says, "Do not conform any longer to the pattern of this world, but be transformed by the renewing of your mind." This may seem strange, confusing and completely the opposite of everything else you've heard from Religion Soup and self-help approaches, but it is the only path to fulfillment, love, joy, peace and wisdom.

I don't want to make it sound over-simplified because it is actually quite difficult and very counter-cultural. Abandoning something you have depended on for self-worth is not easy. Not worshipping Money, Accomplishment, or Self is the opposite of everything our society encourages. And believe me, the Idols of Money, Accomplishment, and Self will rear their ugly heads as often as they can to try to recapture you. We'll talk about that more in a bit.

Unless you replace these idols with something else, you may feel hopeless, alone, and drifting for a while. But again, I warn you: Shifting to another idol of empty promises will be useless, inadequate, and incapable of providing fulfillment, love, joy, peace and wisdom. Therefore, the idols must be replaced with a relationship with God. You have to love God more than Money, Accomplishment, and Self. He has to be first in your life above all other things. Our culture endorses the goal of complete and total independence, self-sufficiency and autonomy. By turning our lives over to God, our goal becomes growing into complete and total dependence on Him. "By myself, I can do nothing." (John 5:30) "I can do everything through Him who gives me strength." (Philippians 4:13)

Renounce your idols and make room for God to come into your life. If you do your part, God will do His.

Transformation, Inside-Out

It's very trendy nowadays to be living your purpose or finding your purpose. People are struggling every day to know what their calling is and find a deeper meaning for their life. The only One with the answers is God. Outside-in, Religion Soup and self-help approaches have been going on for centuries. Thousands of years ago, Jeremiah was exasperated by people trying to worship idols just like we are today. He exclaims, "These people, who refuse to listen to my words, who follow the stubbornness of their hearts and go after other gods to serve and worship them, will be... completely useless!" (Jeremiah 13:10) Centuries later, when John realized that many people were attempting outside-in approaches to change, he exclaims, "Brood of snakes! What do you think you're doing? Do you think a little water

160

on your snakeskin is going to make any difference? It's your life that must change, not your skin!" (Matthew 3:7-10, The Message)

Making fulfillment, love, joy, peace and wisdom an outside-in goal is inappropriate and self-serving. By contrast, accepting God's gift of fulfillment, love, joy, peace and wisdom by allowing Him to transform you from the inside-out, and keeping Him first is purposeful and lasting. C.S. Lewis said it best when he said, "Your new self will not come as long as you are looking for it. It will come when you are looking for Him... Give up yourself, and you will find your real self... The more we let God take over, the more truly ourselves we become." Letting God take over will not come naturally at first. Believe me, cherishing the invisible over the visible is not an easy thing. And yet, scripture teaches that we must completely abandon our illusions of control, give up our worldly desires, and desert our man-made plans by surrendering it all over to God. Most of you Type A's are probably sarcastically smirking, "Yeah, right."

Yeah! Right!

I'm not telling you to go off and be a monk. I'm encouraging you to embark on a journey to finding the best you, and being the most you you've ever been. I strongly believe that what society is saying can't get you there. The biggest frustration I hear from people all the time is, "I did everything right, but yet I still feel totally empty." Are you wondering, like in the Pet Shop Boys' song, "What have I, what have I, what have I done to deserve this?" You didn't do anything but follow the messages of the world. The messages of our culture and the idols we are worshipping are wrong. This is why I asked you to forget what you know of Religion Soup and self-help, and this is why you have to renounce the idols that our society wants you to worship. You've tried everything else; isn't it worth a shot to try the truth of God instead?

For example, our society and the Idol of Self say it's not what other people think of you, it's what you think of yourself. Scripture says, "Are you trying to win the approval of men or the approval of God?" (Galatians 1:10) Our culture and the Idol of Accomplishment say God helps those who help themselves. Scripture says, "Trust God from the bottom of your heart; don't try to figure out everything on your own. Listen for God's voice in everything you do, everywhere you go; He's the one who will keep you on track. Don't assume you know it all. Run to God!" (Proverbs 3:5-7, The Message) Our society and the Idol of Money say money makes the world go 'round. Scripture says, "God will supply all your needs according to His glorious riches." (Philippians 4:19)

In the next few chapters, we will be emphasizing a paradigm shift – at the core – replacing the worship of idols with the love of God, and how God wants to transform you from the inside out. I said it before, but I'll say it again: It does not matter what religion you were brought up with or what religion you are now. If you have had unfortunate religious experiences, like messages of fear, or hell and damnation, or anything other than the love of God, I am truly and deeply sorry. I also understand that I cannot ask you to turn yourself over to a God you do not know. You may have a lot of preconceived notions about who God is, but I encourage you to start talking to Him and getting to know Him yourself. Think of it this way: Has anyone ever judged you without getting to know you first? Has someone believed a rumor about you, or just decided they didn't like you based on a brief encounter? Wouldn't you say this is really unfair? But all you can do is continue to be yourself regardless of what they've heard, and hope for the opportunity to demonstrate your character to them at some point in time. God is no different in wanting and waiting to demonstrate Himself to you. God loves you, and He's waiting for the opportunity to show you that.

Which leads me to another question: Can you imagine if we treated our relationships with people the same way many people treat their relationship with God? He calls out to you, you don't call Him back.

He reaches out again, you ignore Him. You believe what other people tell you about Him without getting to know Him yourself. You don't believe His promises and always expect the worst from Him. All He wants to do is be your friend and give you great things, but you can't be bothered, and you don't have the time. Many people are the kind of "kid" to God who calls only when they need something. I have to wonder if perhaps the hesitation many people feel about beginning a dialogue with God is not because of His behavior, but because of their own towards Him. Why would anyone give you the chance after you'd treated them that way? But God is waiting patiently for you, ready with overflowing love and acceptance. Give Him the chance to show you what He wants to do for you.

Allowing God to transform your life includes multiple components of having a relationship with Him, studying His truths and promises, and following His instruction in your life. Without all of these, you will inevitably become discouraged when God's perfect timing takes longer than you would like it to. Without a multifaceted approach, you are likely to become frustrated and doubtful and may come to the conclusion that God does not love you. But this is not true and will never be true. It is the times when you are feeling discouraged, frustrated, and doubtful that placing God first in your life requires a little extra effort on your part. Just because you put God in charge, doesn't mean you don't have work to do, and it is the extra work that most people neglect. F.F. Bosworth noted, "People wonder why they don't have stronger faith, but they feed their body three hot meals a day, and their spirit one cold snack a week."

Everybody wants to know their purpose, but few people are willing to do the work. You can't expect God to take over and do everything for you. That's not how it works. David says to his son Solomon in 1 Chronicles 28:20, "Be strong and courageous and do the work." If you want to grow in faith, so that God can transform you from the inside-out, then you have to do the work. Doing the work means

163

talking to Him all the time about everything. "Do not be anxious about anything, but in everything, by prayer and petition... present your requests to God." (Philippians 4:6) Doing the work means researching, studying, and reminding ourselves of the Biblical truths, for "faith comes by hearing, and hearing by the Word of God." (Romans 10:17) Doing the work means allowing God to show you His purpose for your life, following His path for you and overflowing with His fulfillment, love, joy, peace and wisdom for the benefit of others. God says to us, "I know the plans I have for you, plans to prosper you and not to harm you, plans to give you hope and a future." (Jeremiah 29:11) In this section, we will talk more about all of this.

When God instructed me to write this book, I wondered, "What on earth am I going to write about?" and "What am I an expert at?" In examining my past, I discovered I'm an expert at screwing things up by being a Type A instead of following His plan for me. In examining my present and looking toward my future, I discovered a sense of wholeness that I had never experienced in my entire Type A life. I cannot take credit for that wholeness, because I know it is a gift from God. It is that wholeness, and the fulfillment, love, joy, peace and wisdom He has given me on my journey with Him that I want to share with you. I write as a servant to Him, not as an expert. I again ask for you to keep an open mind and an open heart, and hear me out. I pray from Psalm 19, "Let the words of my mouth and the meditations of my heart be pleasing in your sight, O Lord, my Rock and my Redeemer."

I will do my best to ever-so-briefly outline observations from my journey to get you started on yours, but please know that I have an overwhelming sense of insufficiency as a stand-alone guide. This is my humble attempt at a brief introduction and invitation to your own relationship with God. To clarify what I mean by *introduction*, imagine you and God and I were all attending the same networking event. I would walk over to you, guide you over to God and say,

"God, here is someone who would like to meet You." After conversation began, I would walk away and let you continue from there. Now the ball is in your court. If you prefer *invitation*, please remember that an invitation gives an outline of the details of an event or happening. An invitation is not the event or the happening itself. No RSVP required, but the onus is on you to attend.

Being a Type A, you are used to being on the fast track. Unfortunately, there is no fast track with God. God is not a formula. He loves you, and all He wants to do is love you. Therefore, the only way to over-achieve in the eyes of God is to love Him, and place Him first in your life above all other things. It's just that simple. And it's just that challenging. This inside-out journey to fulfillment, love, joy, peace and wisdom is a process of discovering God's love for you and, overflowing from that love, to becoming the best you possible. God wants to give you purpose and meaning, wisdom and fulfillment and, most importantly, love. Every other change you will experience in your life is a reflection and overflow of that new relationship with Him. There will be challenges along the way, but God will be with you.

Catherine Marshall asks, "Are you serious about wanting God's guidance to become the person He wants you to be? The first step is to tell God that you know you can't manage your own life; that you need His help." This is just the beginning of your journey. I could not possibly address all of God's grandeur, nor am I qualified to guide you on your personal expedition. Remember, this is an introduction and invitation, not a roadmap. I encourage you to go get a Bible of your own if you don't have one, or if the one you have doesn't make sense to you, get an easy-to-read translation, like New International Version; or check out BibleGateway.com to look at all sorts of versions translated in various languages. Look up the passages given in this book and explore from there to find the ones that speak to you. As Charles Swindoll said, "It's right there, ink on paper. Count on it – that book will never lead you astray." I have also included a list of recommended reading at the back of this book and I encourage you to use it on your journey.

If you do your part, God will do His.

Chapter 13: Building on the Rock

First things first: God loves you. God loves you. God loves you. "God is love." (1 John 4:8) God loves you. You may be wondering how much God loves you. Take the deepest love you have ever felt for someone and the deepest love anyone has ever felt for you (that may not be the same person, by the way), add them together and then multiply them by infinity. That is how much God loves you.

In addition, God's love for you is not just any kind of love. The word *love* is often overused and has been distorted in our language. "I love pizza" does not equal "God loves me." The Greeks have four different words in their language for love. One for natural affection, one for sexual attraction, another for friendship, and the last is *agape*, which is unconditional, unwarranted, sacrificial love. Agape is the only kind of love God knows how to give. It has been observed that without God, there is no love, for it is God's love that loves through us. It is constant, unwavering, and overflowing.

John Hagee described that even if we don't have separate words for different kinds of love, we still have distinctions. He identifies three kinds. The first is *if* love: the kind of love that says, "I love you *if* you succeed, *if* you meet my expectations, *if* you do this or that for me." The second is *because* love: the kind of love that says, "I love you *because* you are good to me, *because* you are beautiful, *because* you are rich." The last is *in spite of* love: the kind of love that says, "I love you *in spite of* your faults, *in spite of* your failures, *in spite of* your weaknesses, *in spite of* everything that's happened, because I see your potential." *In spite of* love is the only kind of love God knows how to give, because He sees your potential and He wants you to fulfill it, regardless of your past and anything you may have done.

Realizing for the first time how much God loves you is an overwhelming, emotional, and life-changing experience. Get your tissues out, you're going to cry. Yes, you. If you don't cry the first time you fully grasp how much God loves you, then you don't really get it yet. Even a hardened, cynical, and emotionless Type A can be disarmed by the love of God. For me, the realization that I am God's child, and that no matter how much I screw up, He is there to hold me and comfort me; no matter what wonderful thing I accomplish, His smile is 1,000 times bigger than mine; and no matter what I face in life, He is right there by my side encouraging me, strengthening me, and cheering me on, was one of the most powerful experiences of my life. God's love is bigger than all my problems, past, present and future, and He is bigger than yours, too. God is love and God loves you.

There is a familiar passage that is often read at weddings, that describes God's love for you. From The Message translation: "Love never gives up, love cares more for others than for self, love doesn't want what it doesn't have, love doesn't strut, doesn't have a swelled head, doesn't force itself on others, isn't always 'me first,' doesn't fly off the handle, doesn't keep score of the sins of others, doesn't revel when others grovel, takes pleasure in the flowering of truth, puts up with anything, always looks for the best, never looks back, but keeps going to the end. (1 Corinthians 13:7-9)

So if God is love, then why do people fear Him so much? What's with all the hell and damnation stuff? It's a good question. In my opinion, the whole *fear of God* thing has been exaggerated and overdone by many. In the Old Testament, fearing the Lord was an expression of a man's sense of morality, as evidenced by his behavior, self-control, and hatred of evil. When you see, "He does not fear the Lord," it's the same as if it said, "He has no morals or self-control." By contrast, the New Testament tells us, "For you did not receive a spirit that makes you a slave to fear." (Romans 8:15) Just because the Idols of Money, Accomplishment, and Self had you in fear of never having enough or not being good enough, does not mean that God operates in the same way. The idols do not love you. God does love you.

Appropriately fearing the Lord is the same as respecting His authority over our lives. It could be paralleled to the way you fear your boss in the corporate world. Your boss has some level of control over your professional future, so you want to keep your boss happy. I remember attending a conference on a Saturday once where I had been told the dress was casual, but everyone (except me) showed up in a suit. When I re-inquired about the dress code and asked why so many people wore suits, the response I got was, "Everyone's boss is here." Fearing the Lord is the same as wanting to impress your boss, show Him your best, and leave a good impression. Show Him some respect.

I would encourage you to replace fearing God with this type of healthy respect for who God is. Appreciate His preeminence based on the many titles He holds. Here is a brief assortment: God, Lord, Abba, Heavenly Father, Alpha and Omega, Creator, Sovereign... and the list goes on. In addition, some of His traits include: All-Knowing, All-Powerful, All-Present, Wonderful, Marvelous, Glorious... and the list goes on. Geez! Can you imagine meeting someone with these credentials and qualities? I think you'd be a little nervous, aka fearful, out of deference, reverence, and regard for their supremacy and authority. It's good to respect God, but not to the extent that you are too afraid to talk to Him. Heavenly Father and Abba also mean He's your Papa or Daddy, and He loves you as such, so you can talk to Him familiarly. We'll talk more about communication with God in a bit.

We are also reminded that "there is no fear in love... perfect love drives all fear out." (1 John 4:18) Hannah Whitall Smith remarks, "When once we are assured that God is good, then there can be nothing left to fear." God's love drives out all fear, anxiety, hurt, pain, and offenses.

Think of it this way. Imagine a glass full of dirty water. Your objective is to fill the glass with clean water, but you are not allowed to tip the glass or dump the dirty water out. Instead, you must replace the tainted liquid with unpolluted water, until all the water in the glass is clean. You have an unending supply of clean water for this process. As you imagine pouring this fresh water into the glass, the dirtiness flows out and over the top until the water in the glass is fully pure. This is the feeling in your heart as God's love drives out fear, anxiety, hurt, pain, and offenses. There are times when you can literally, physically, feel this process happening in your heart. Each pulse of your heart is flooded with a tsunami of love, followed by a recess of unworthiness; only to be inundated again with grace and forgiveness, followed by an undercurrent of humility and gratitude; until the steady constant stream of each heartbeat is a simple and effortless mutual adoration and wonder, and all you can say is *thank You*.

We are all broken and bruised from the process of being human. There is no such thing as a perfect life. We have all been damaged somewhere along the way. All the king's horses and all the king's men (i.e., Religion Soup and self-help) cannot put you back together again, but the love of God can. Only the love of God can heal you, make you whole, and give you the overflow of fulfillment, love, joy, peace and wisdom that it takes to be the best you possible. There are times that your tears are the pouring out of that dirty water of pain, but once the tears are gone, what is left inside of you is purity and renewed chastity.

God loves you. God loves you. God loves you.

The more you realize just how much God loves you, the easier it is to allow Him to take over in your life. Surrendering to Him is the foundation of faith, no matter how unnatural it feels at first. The only reason it feels foreign is that our culture has no way of relating to unconditional, undeserved, and un-ending love. As Ken Boa noted, "For people who have experienced the pain and rejection caused by performance-based acceptance and conditional love, unconditional love seems too good to be true." We are cautious, insecure, and afraid that if we reveal who we really are inside, we will suffer rejection from God as we would from other people. But God doesn't work that way. He already knows who you are and what you've done. He still loves you. When you start allowing Him to take over in your life, you'll find that as you relinquish things you once thought defined you, in actuality, by giving them up you are able to become more truly yourself. That's because God wants what is best for you. God loves you.

Intellectuals want to dismiss the unexplainable by looking down their noses and questioning how anyone could be stupid enough to believe in God. The problem with their proposition is that knowing God and spiritual truths will escape you if you try to limit the divine quest to an intellectual or academic pursuit. Just because you can't figure something out, doesn't mean it doesn't exist. Furthermore, it is fitting that these intellectuals would pooh pooh belief in God for a number of reasons. Number one, God *doesn't* help those who help themselves. If you think you can do it without Him, He will certainly let you have it your way. That's what free will is all about. Good luck with that. Number two, I imagine these intellectuals are way out of their comfort zone when they exit the academic arena and enter into the supernatural realm. Once they can't explain something with logic, they have to run away from it, or all those degrees on their wall might be worthless and their pride and reputation would be damaged. The best way to maintain their image as the best brains in the world is to repudiate the existence of anything they can't explain. This is not only very self-serving, but utterly insufficient. Someone recently equated the likelihood of the universe and every living creature in it being the way we know it to be, as having the same scientific odds as a marksman accurately hitting a target the size of a dime from 20 billion light-years away. I could continue, but you get the point. A relationship with God is not an intellectual thing, and should not be reduced by theological, cultural, emotional, or mental filters.

God can do things that humans, no matter how smart they are, will never be able to figure out or explain. God the Creator can give rise to something that didn't exist before; He can invent, design, and construct the perfect solution to every problem you have, and He can produce it from a base of nothing. God the Almighty can change people's minds, alter every circumstance, and choreograph unfathomable events to favor you. God the Healer can breathe life back into people on their death-beds, perplexing the greatest medical minds, and deliver inexplicable miracles. But God doesn't want you to try to figure it out; He just wants to love you, and have you love Him in return. Jesus gave one commandment: "Love the Lord your God with all your heart and with all your soul and with all your mind." (Matthew 22:37) Have you ever had a problem that you thought you needed a shrink for because you think that analyzing your problems will make them go away? Sometimes figuring things out does help, but it is never the solution. Love is the solution. Sometimes you don't need therapy, you just need a hug. God wants to give you that hug. God loves you.

You may feel uncomfortable in your own wrestling with faith as you begin your relationship with God. That's a good thing. If you do not wrestle with believing in something you can never see, you are either extremely naïve, or your faith has never been put to the test. Walking the walk of faith is not easy. There will be many times when wandering away from faith will seem so much easier than sticking to it. Following God is warfare against our natural tendencies and inclinations, warfare against the idols we've been worshipping and warfare against our Type A desire to control everything. I guarantee you will stumble from time to time, especially in the beginning. Scripture even makes room for this by saying, "We all stumble in many ways." (James 3:2) But just because you stumble, slip into old patterns, or face new challenges doesn't mean God isn't working. The point is to recognize when you falter, get back up, turn around, and run back to abiding in the love of God.

God's love is unconditional and "He will not turn His face from you if you return to Him" (2 Chronicles 30:9), so you don't have to worry about Him taking you back or not. This is another very difficult thing for human beings to wrap their minds around. That's because many human beings profess unconditional love, but are unequipped to follow through. If more people understood unconditional love, we wouldn't have the divorce rate we have. Then there are those who profess unconditional love, but their love could be better classified as permanent, not unconditional. They have committed to loving you, but you can measure the ebb and flow of their love for you based on their actions towards you, which they are basing on your actions towards them. This is still performance-based, and therefore, by definition, conditional. With God's unconditional love, there is absolutely nothing you can do to make Him love you more than He already does. With God's unconditional love, there is absolutely nothing you can do to make Him love you less. His love is bigger than anything you could possibly do, or could have possibly done, and there is nothing you can do to separate yourself from His love. As a matter of fact, the only sin unequal to all others is hardening your heart to God, and even then, though I'm sure He's a little disappointed, He still loves you. The point is, there is no method of earning God's love. It is there. Unending, undeserved, unconditional, and overflowing.

This is why throwing away your pre-conceived notions about God is an imperative part of getting to know who He really is. Religions and zealots tend to manipulate scriptural truths to support their own agenda of trying to measure up to deserving God's love and grace. The truth is, you could never possibly measure up by anything you did, and He still gives you *agape* love and loves you *in spite of* your shortcomings. Experiencing the true love of God means that we don't have to be anything to anyone, and our only job is to love Him wholeheartedly. In His eyes, no amount of acting "religious" could ever compare to that.

Additionally, while the self-help world says, "It matters only what you think of yourself," thereby encouraging self-love and ego-inflation, instead, we are better suited to make an attempt to understand and accept the way that God loves us, reminding ourselves again that performance is not relevant.

To gain a glimpse of understanding this, try to put yourself in God's shoes, *only for a second*, and only for the purpose of looking at yourself the way that God looks at you, and loving yourself the way that God loves you. Here's what I came up with when I did this. If I were God, looking down on Wendy, I'd be thinking, "There's My child Wendy. She can be so stubborn, but she is strong. She has a big heart, but she hasn't protected it as well as I would want her to at times. She has a sharp mind, and sometimes a sharp tongue, but she is growing in wisdom with My guidance. She is a courageous adventurer, and sometimes I have to reel her back in, but she always comes back. If she sticks close to Me, I can do great things with her strength, heart, mind and courage."

What would God say about His love for you? Instead of constructing the answer to that question yourself, I recommend asking God what His answer is. You may be surprised, but He will answer you back. God always answers when you call. Scripture tells us, "But if you seek the Lord your God, you will find Him if you look for Him with all your heart and your soul." (Deuteronomy 4:29)

What God Wants to Do For You

Once you know how much God loves you, the next step is gaining understanding of what God wants to do for you. Here are a few things God says to those who know and follow Him: "I will bless you and I will make your name great, and you will be a blessing. I will bless those who bless you, and I will curse those who curse you," "I will throw open the floodgates of heaven and pour out so much blessing that you will not have room enough to receive it," "I will also supply and increase your store of seed and enlarge your harvest... you will be made rich in every way." (Genesis 12:2-3, Malachi 3:10, 2 Corinthians 9:10-11)

Blessed or *blessing* is another word that is used too casually with various meanings in our culture, lessening and distorting its value. If someone says, "I'm blessed" in a certain way, it can be taken as pride that they have a blessing that you do not. On the other hand, if someone is saying, "It's a blessing" in another way, it can be taken as false humility. People "say the blessing" before they eat, so does that mean if they want to bless you, they want to eat you? Then there is the saying of "Bless you" after you sneeze, which comes from a legend that your soul can be thrown from your body when you sneeze, and blessing you is your only protection against attack by the devil. And of course, let's not forget our good southern friends who love to say "Bless your heart," an expression with an inverse meaning. If you offend a southerner, instead of saying, "Go play in traffic" as a northerner would, they say, "Bless your heart." Or, it is commonly used when talking about someone who is not present, such as "She's the stupidest fool I've ever met... bless her heart."

None of these expressions quantify the type of blessing or the way that God wants to bless you. Godly blessing is all-inclusive and overflowing in every category. Good health, harmonious relationships, abundance, courage, protection, victory, and favor. Oh yeah, and I forgot to mention, fulfillment, love, joy, peace and wisdom. But not just a little bit... A LOT.

Think of it this way. Go fill a pitcher of water to the top. Then, go find an empty shot glass. God is the pitcher, the water is the blessing and your life is the shot glass. Pour the entire pitcher into the shot glass. As the water quickly fills and flows over the brim of the shot glass in a long and steady avalanche of blessing, know that this is the kind of blessing overflow God wants to provide in your life. God loves you and He wants to bless you. "Put your hope in God who richly provides you with everything for your enjoyment." (1 Timothy 6:17) You have to learn to trust Him, trust in His ability to fill you up, and trust in His ability to supply overflow. "Good measure, pressed down, shaken together and running over, will be poured into your lap." (Luke 6:38)

Everything you have is a tribute to God's grace and generosity. God gave you the ability (Romans 12:6), the intelligence (Daniel 2:21), the means (Deuteronomy 8:18), and the advancement (Psalm 75:6-7) that you have experienced since birth. I know average middle-class Americans really don't like to think of it this way, but it is true, nonetheless. For Type A's, that can be very difficult to wrap your mind around, but it is true whether you understand it or not. Even if you think He didn't give you that new car, He gave you the talent and smarts in order to make the money, in order to afford the new car. You may not be wealthy, but you are probably not poor. You want to take credit for what you have and where you are in life because you work hard; but there is so much more involved in how you got to where you are than hard work could possibly explain. Every moment, opportunity and happening in your life is a choreographed coordination of so many factors, most of which are completely out of your control, and all occurring in such a sequence that you couldn't re-create it if you tried. Let me approach this from various perspectives to articulate more clearly.

The wealthy, to generalize, have a better sense of the poverty in the world than the middle class do. Why? Because once you achieve a certain level of wealth (true wealth, not just the guy with the biggest house in your neighborhood), philanthropy becomes a part of your social agenda. That's not to say that those skinny, Botox-filled desperate housewives are down in the trenches serving supper to the destitute. However, they are solicited on a regular basis to give. Give to this, give to that, come to this luncheon, attend this black tie for $500 per person, and so forth. No matter how fancy these events, luncheons and black tie affairs may appear, the speeches made at them are a call to action to support the cause and give to those less fortunate. The events are glamorous, don't get me wrong, and that is why, at a certain level of wealth, it is an essential part of your social program. Seeing and being seen are of utmost importance, and being known as a philanthropist adds to your prestige. That's not to say that reputation-building is the right motive for giving, because it is not. However, you'd have to be deaf, blind, and heartless to attend these events and not become aware of how much more you have than the down-trodden. Furthermore, if the non-profit organization is doing its job correctly, it is at the precise moment during the course of the event that you become overwhelmed with this realization that they ask you to get your checkbook out.

The poor, to generalize, have a better sense of poverty in the world than the average American because they are living it. Not necessarily to the level of Africa-poor, but their lives are hard and an unceasing struggle. Their children are more likely to go to prison than they are to go to college. They are always the underdogs and they suffer constant shame and embarrassment. Yes, shame and embarrassment. Wait, you didn't actually think they want to be impoverished, did you? Living in Scandinavia was very interesting because there is practically no homelessness there. You can be homeless if you want to be, but the moment you decide you are finished being homeless, you go to the government and they provide you with housing, plus perhaps a job. I don't want to turn this into a political statement, but I am far from liberal in my fiscal opinions. However, the point I'm making here is that when given the choice, nobody *chooses* to be homeless. You might be thinking, "duh," followed by whatever rationalizations are popping into your head. But trying to explain and justify to yourself why they are poor, homeless, and suffering and why you are not is really just an exercise of frigidity.

The only reason you are not where they are is because, by the grace of God, you were born with different circumstances. If you weren't born in the ghetto, then you started life with more advantages than they had right from the get-go. Looking at impoverished children, why poverty exists and who is to blame, Dr. Timothy Keller has a great sketch about how the liberals blame it on social injustices and the conservatives blame it on the breakdown of family structures, but nobody says it's the kid's fault. If it's not the kid's fault that he was born in the ghetto, then can you really take credit for the circumstances given to you at birth? I said it before, but I'll say it again: God gives us the ability, the intelligence, the means, and the advancement (Romans 12:6, Daniel 2:21, Deuteronomy 8:18, Psalm 75:6-7) through His grace. It would be nice of you to start giving Him some credit and possibly even saying thank You to Him.

Grace, by definition, is getting better than you deserve. As you grow in your relationship with God, He wants to show you more grace, give you more than you deserve, and provide more for you than you can even imagine. (See Isaiah 64:4) In fact, walking in the grace and favor of God is like having the Red Sea part before you every day. Things come naturally, people want to help you, and "coincidences" start happening with mind-boggling frequency. "If you have faith as small as a mustard seed, you can say to this mountain, 'Move from here to there' and it will move. Nothing will be impossible for you." "Everything is possible for him who believes." "God is able to do immeasurably more than all we ask or imagine, according to His power that is at work within us." (Matthew 17:20, Mark 9:23, Ephesians 3:20) This is not to say that God gives you super powers to part the sea or move the mountain, but when you walk in faith and love for Him, He will part the sea and move the mountain for you, and bless your path beyond imagination. If you want examples, go check out the Book of Hebrews, chapter 11, for a long list of those who were all delivered, preserved, anointed, or empowered through their faith and by God's grace.

Hopefully, as you gain in understanding of how much God loves you and how much God wants to do for you, you will be encouraged to start talking to Him. God wants to bless you. God wants to show you His grace. God wants to give you overflow. What would you do if you had bought a really great present for someone, but they never made time to come and visit, stopped communicating with you, and generally wanted nothing to do with you anymore? Would you send it to them anyway, or would you give it to someone else? Are you giving God the opportunity to bless you, or are you acting in a way that He may be inclined to give it to someone else? Going back to the analogy, what do you think would happen if the shot glass tried to hold all the water from the pitcher? It would either burst, or the pitcher would have to stop pouring once the shot glass was full. Essentially, 95% of the blessing would still be in the pitcher because it had nowhere to go. God wants to bless you. He is waiting for your call. "He longs to be gracious to you." (Isaiah 30:18)

I must give you a word of caution on this. In gaining understanding of God's gifts and promises, we must be careful in wanting or expecting more than is proper. Just because God has limitless resources to supply your every need, want and desire, does not mean you should mistake God for a wish-granting machine or magic genie. Our desire for God must be stronger than our desire for any gifts He can give us. Otherwise, we are approaching God with the same line of attack we utilized in worshipping our idols, which is misguided. Service to idols is not rooted in grace and love, whereas worshipping God and receiving God's gifts and delivery on His promises is. The more you understand this, the more you will want to place Him above all other things in your life.

How God Communicates

God will answer your call. "Call to me and I will answer you and tell you great and unsearchable things you do not know." (Jeremiah 33:3) Pray about everything. D.L. Moody suggests, "Some people think that God does not like to be troubled with our constant asking.

But, the way to trouble God is not to ask at all." Scripture says, "Ask and it will be given to you; seek and you will find; knock and the door will be opened to you. For everyone who asks receives; he who seeks finds; and to him who knocks, the door will be opened." (Matthew 7:7-8) It didn't say "only special people" get to talk to God; it said "everyone." So go ahead. Ask, seek and knock. Then wait for the answer. God has a couple of ways to respond to any question you may ask Him, so be on high alert for His answer. The first is internal through His Spirit, and the second is external through His management of everything happening around you.

The Spirit of God is with you already. God reveals Himself to us "by His Spirit. The Spirit searches all things, even the deep things of God. For who among men knows the thoughts of a man except the man's spirit within him? In the same way no one knows the thoughts of God except the Spirit of God." (1 Corinthians 2:10-12) Because God loves you, His Spirit is the voice in your head that always knows what is best for you in every circumstance. The Spirit always wants you to do what is right, to do what is good.

The Spirit is your own personal messenger from God to guide your path as clearly as a GPS navigational system in the car that tells you "right turn ahead" or "turn around as soon as possible." Scripture says, "Your ears will hear a word behind you saying, 'This is the way, walk in it' whenever you turn to the right or whenever you turn to the left." (Isaiah 30:21) However, similar to a GPS in the car, you don't have to listen if you think you know a better way... running the risk of winding up very, very lost.

Again, the self-help community has come up with many alternative names for the Spirit, such as your inner voice, intuition, gut feeling, or conscience. These are self-aggrandizing and rest on the assumption that you know all the answers to all your questions already. Do you really feel like you know all the answers? God is God, you are not, neither am I. C.S. Lewis notices, "Almost our whole education has been directed to silencing this shy, persistent, inner voice; almost all our modern philosophies have been devised to convince us that the good of man is to be found on earth."

I used to think of the Spirit as the Chairman of my own personal Board of Directors. The Board would assemble in my brain, debate the issue and take a vote. But this was entirely unnecessary and led to some disastrous decisions. The Spirit always knew what was right, whether or not the Board of Directors agreed. If one of the other Directors is louder, more convincing, or has a quick-fix solution to the problem at hand, the other Directors may pass a vote to follow that path, even if it is wrong. And who's to say that all of the Directors really have your best interest at heart when they are influencing the Chairman? Listening to the Spirit can be difficult because of these types of battles that go on in our brains. It takes practice to understand that the other voices in your head are probably connected to other people's opinions, agendas, experiences (good or bad), or their own neediness or desired outcomes. It's easy to let yourself off the hook when all these other voices are conspiring against what the Spirit knows is right.

Other people have the image of the angel on one shoulder and the devil on the other. That's fine, as long as you understand that one of the most prevalent devils the Spirit is arguing with is you. It's named will, free will. Maybe you've heard of it. Isaiah 30:15 tells us, "You will receive the strength and calm you need when you stay calm and trust in Me. But you do not want to do what I tell you to do." There are times when you, yourself, do not want to do what the Spirit tells you to do. There are times when what the Spirit is telling you to do sounds absolutely crazy, but it is still always right. Your free will and the Spirit duke it out in your mind, and eventually you must take action one way or the other. Can you think of a time when you followed your gut, aka the Spirit, and everything went smoothly? Can you think of a time when you didn't follow it? In my experience, not following the Spirit creates a mess. Either a short-term mess that needs to be cleaned up right away or a larger, long-term mess that we'll be cleaning up later in life.

The only way to get in touch with the truth is to develop spiritual maturity where you are able to decipher the instruction of God through the Spirit, as opposed to your thoughts and feelings, and be willing to follow what the Spirit tells you. People often wonder how to tell the difference between the Spirit and your own thoughts. Charles Swindoll tells us, "God's voice isn't all that difficult to hear. He sometimes shouts through our pain, whispers to us while we're relaxing on vacation; occasionally, He sings to us in a song." The more time you spend with God, the easier it will be to hear what He is trying to tell you, and know that it came from Him.

This is another reason I am against the New Age counsel of "doing what feels good" or "Don't do it if you are not getting peace about it." Some of the greatest accomplishments of all time were done by very nervous people who didn't have peace about it, but did it anyway. Society has become so focused on feeling good that the moment we face a trial or don't feel good anymore, we change plans or abandon ship. The world is telling us to maximize our pleasure and minimize our pain, but sometimes God the Father tells us it's time to put our toys away. If our response is to throw a temper tantrum, say "I don't want to put my toys away," or just plain ignore Him, no one in our society will ever accomplish anything. Feelings lie, and most of you have suffered that truth already in some way or another. Feelings will lead you astray, and most of you can think of an example of this from your lives. But if feelings lie and lead you astray, then getting in touch with your feelings cannot be nearly as important as getting in touch with the truth, which never lies and sets you straight.

Keep in mind that even though God is capable of shouting, sometimes He chooses to whisper instead. If you want to hear Him more clearly, you have to get quiet and still enough to hear His voice. I also think of it this way. When I go to the gym, they always have music playing in the background. However, I put my iPod on so loud that I can hear only my music and not the music the gym is playing. Not that I have anything against their music, but I want to listen to *my* tunes. Occasionally, an earpiece will fall out of my ear, or there is a pause between my songs, and I can hear the gym music. Hearing the whisper of God is like that. No matter how much noise you put in your life to avoid hearing Him, He will be waiting for you to turn to Him and listen up. In actuality, the gym music is not that quiet, and neither is the whisper of God. But to hear from Him means that you've got to slow down, and sometimes completely stop what you are doing, in order to decipher the Spirit of God over the noise of your own thoughts. Again, the more time you spend with Him, the easier it will be to hear Him, and know the difference between the Spirit and your own thoughts.

Once you know you've heard from the Spirit, learning to trust and follow It is the next critical step. As a foundation, you must remember that God loves you, the Spirit is the voice of truth, completely incapable of lying, and always in pursuit of attaining and protecting your highest good. That does not mean, however, that you are guaranteed an easy ride, or that it will always *feel good*. Surrendering yourself to the will of God by taking the instruction of the Spirit will lead you on a long journey through changes, challenges and victories. In Isaiah 43:2, God promises, "When you pass through the waters, I will be with you; and when you pass through the rivers, they will not sweep over you. When you walk through the fire, you will not be burned; the flames will not set you ablaze." It does not say, *if* challenges come, but *when* they come, God is with you.

Since we know that trials will come, it is best to strengthen your trust in the Spirit through practice. Test It out on something simple to build your confidence, and then when you face a challenge, you will be ready and strong. It is what Dallas Willard calls the law of indirect preparedness. The things we practice in the background of our daily lives will prepare us for the unexpected times when willpower might not be enough. When things happen unexpectedly or when you are worn down or just plain tired, the Spirit does not automatically take over; your habits take over. Responding in the best possible way is a result of ongoing practice of listening to and following what leads us to our highest good, which is the Spirit.

Changing your habits, or in other words, getting your mind/actions and the Spirit on the same team, is a process of conscious trust-building over time and through commitment. Start doing two-second flash prayers at various points in your day. You don't have to close your eyes or drop to your knees. You can be at a conference room table, and just ask in your mind or whisper softly to yourself, "God, show me the truth." You can be driving your car (please don't close your eyes) and whisper softly, "Spirit, show me the way." You can meet a new person and ask, "God, show me who they are." You can be stuck on an idea or problem and request, "Spirit, be with me, help me." When you hear your answer, remember to say *thank You.* When you follow the answer, remember to say *thank You*, no matter what the result.

The more you learn to trust and follow the Spirit, the closer you are to following the path God has laid out for you. The more you realize that when the Spirit says, "No" or "Don't do it," you are probably dodging a bullet somewhere. And the more you realize that when the Spirit says "Yes," you must immediately and faithfully start running in that direction, you are on your way to abiding in God's love for you, understanding your significance, and pursuing your purpose.

The second way God communicates is through His sovereign control over everything happening around us. Lucky for us, as Ellen Debenport said, "Here is the good news: God is a nag. If we are destined to carry out some divine idea, we won't be able to shrug it off. For me, God doesn't just whisper within. If I'm supposed to get a message, I start to see it and hear it everywhere – books, sermons, television shows, conversations with friends." It has also been said that coincidences are God's way of remaining anonymous. God is signaling to you every minute of every day. You just don't see it, or you don't want to see it.

Whether we want to admit it or not, we all know that we have very little control over all circumstances leading up to and following each moment of our every day. Even if you are the greatest salesperson in the world, you cannot take credit for the decision being made by the client, or the fact that they were ready to change at the exact time that you knocked on their door. You don't take credit for the weather, you don't take credit when your computer crashes, and you don't take credit when you are stuck in traffic. What's the difference? I have been a big believer in the expression, "Everything happens for a reason" for a very long time. However, the closer I have gotten to God, the more that saying seems to lack gratitude for the source of everything that's happening. Now I say, "God is good," or "God has a plan," or "I don't know what that was all about, but God does, so let's go with it." There are no accidents, there is no such thing as coincidence. There isn't even irony, chance, or happenstance. Even a coin toss is decided by God. God is God, you are not, neither am I.

People wonder why there aren't burning bushes like there used to be. I say, there are burning bushes every day! People don't take notice of them, don't see them for what they are, or are just too busy to see them in the first place. When you are moving too fast, you do not notice the same things in the same way. Think of the difference in what you see walking vs. highway driving. It is impossible to pick up the same level of detail. So while you are buzzing through life, and right past that burning bush, you simply cannot properly internalize what it is or what it means. Another reason people don't see burning bushes is because they don't want to. Acknowledging a burning bush from God doesn't allow them to take credit for something themselves. Scripture encourages us to "Ask whatever you wish, and it will be given to you." (John 15:7) So, in following that, people ask, receive, and then take credit for making it happen themselves. What could have been a building block of faith and praise for God, somehow instead gets distorted into ego-masturbation and self-aggrandizement. This is just the Idol of Self trying to rear its ugly head again.

Another extreme of looking for God to produce results is the whole "God's got until Saturday" approach. What nonsense! Do you really think that God reports to you? Besides, if you are testing something from that standpoint, you have either already decided what results you want or you want to distance yourself from the results as much as possible, so you're trying to bring God in to make Him take responsibility for whatever happens. So, to summarize, you don't even talk to God that often and now you are asking Him to perform-on-command or be your fall-guy. That is just the Idol of Accomplishment trying to tell you that you won't get anything done if you really wait for God. We are told to "Delight yourself in the Lord and He will give you the desires of your heart." (Psalm 37:4) Scripture does not say, "Use the Lord for your purposes, and call on Him only when you need help."

Hearing from God through the Spirit and His signals involves giving Him credit for what He is saying and doing. The more you listen to Him, the more He'll have to say to you. The more you say, "Thank You, God; I know that was You and not me," the more clear everything will become. "I was blind and now I see." God is not a formula, and God cannot be rushed. We humans want a prescription, so we don't have to think; but wisdom comes when you admit that your thoughts are useless when they are not guided by God. Vance Havner said, "Nothing is more disastrous that to study faith, analyze faith, make noble resolves of faith, but never actually to make the leap of faith." God gives wisdom to people who have a history of asking for it, receiving it, and applying it. If you want to hear from God, you have to listen and look for it. I assure you, He's been trying to get through to you for some time now.

How to Talk to Him (aka Prayer)

Are you there God? It's me... Not only a familiar title, but also something many of us have wondered from time to time. You may be hesitant about how to talk to God. You can call it prayer, but I recommend starting by talking to God like He is your best friend. He is. It may feel awkward at first, but the more you do it, the more you realize that even though God has the wisdom of the ages and deserves your respect, He is also very contemporary. He knows what's going on in the world, He has seen it all before, and nothing surprises Him. So, just be yourself. Be authentic with Him. You don't have to speak the King's English. Instead of saying, "God, it is I, wherefore art thou; why hast thou forsaken me?" you can say, "Dude! What's up? What's the deal?" Some people might think that is disrespectful, but I contend that it is more respectful to talk to Him than it is to ignore Him. So, go for it. Talk to Him about everything. He understands. He loves you. He's happy to hear from you. He's glad you called. "I sought the Lord and He answered me, He delivered me from my fears... The eyes of the Lord are on the righteous, and His ears are attentive to their cry." (Psalm 34:4, 15)

When something goes your way, thank Him. This is hard for Type A's, and believe me, I've failed at this in the past. Sometimes when we feel like we've got everything under control and we're fat and happy, we completely forget that it's God who gave us everything in the first place. No matter what, everything you have now, have ever had, and will ever have is a gift from God. God gives us the ability, the intelligence, the means, and the advancement. (Romans 12:6, Daniel 2:21, Deuteronomy 8:18, Psalm 75:6-7) Since you can't send Him a thank-you card, make sure you express your gratitude and praise. To God be the glory! Thank You, God! Amen!!

When things don't go your way, tell Him how you feel. Ask Him why it happened and what He is trying to teach you. The whole, "There are starving people in the world, so finish your dinner" thing has a tendency to make us think that we are not allowed to complain or be disappointed from time to time. Scripture does tell us to "give thanks in all circumstances" (1 Thessalonians 5:18), but that doesn't mean that we aren't entitled to each and every one of our human feelings, including dissatisfaction and frustration.

If you don't believe me, look at the Psalms. Every kind of emotion any of us has ever felt is poured out on the page. David wrote most of the Psalms, and reading them you can hear him in today's language saying, "God, don't leave me all alone out here!" or "Protect me, God, I'm freaking out!" or "Wow! Thanks God, that was a close one!" or "I am so sorry, God, I really screwed up! You have no reason to forgive me, but I beg that you do!" or "God, I don't understand You. What am I supposed to do now?" or "Thank You!! Thank You!! Thank You!! You are so awesome!!" If you feel weird talking to God out loud, I encourage you to write you own modern-day psalm to Him, just like David did. Here is a psalm I wrote during a major turning point in my life.

Heavenly, Father: Why have You given me this life of torment? Why do I feel I am starting all over again, and behind the 8-ball all the time? I will resist the temptations I have fallen for in the past, Father, and I have tried to demonstrate my resolve to You through the new decisions I have been making. God, I want to follow the path You have for me, but I can't do it without You. I feel so drained right now by every circumstance around me. I don't know what to do, and sometimes I wonder if I'm being too passive waiting to hear from You. What do You want me to do, Father? I have been stepping out on faith, but I need You to come through for me now. I am lost without You. Please show me, God. Please guide me. Please help me. I cry out to You as I have been crying. Do not forsake me now.

Write your own psalm about whatever you are feeling. Be in touch with God in any way you know how, just keep on communicating with Him. Talking to God is one of the best ways to figure out how you really feel, and give all your worries and struggles to Him in the process. You can tell Him anything, and you can ask Him anything. Remember that He loves you and there is nothing He hasn't heard before.

On a side note, two days following my writing of that psalm, I had asked God for something, and He gave me ten times more than I had asked for. God is good! Looking back now, I can also see that the delivery of ten times more was not just a blessing in the moment. In hindsight, I see that if God had not delivered that much at that point in time, then other aspects of my life and service to His commands would have been greatly thrown off schedule in the months to follow. Our sight is so limited. Our scope is so narrow. That's why Elisabeth Elliot said, "Today is mine. Tomorrow is none of my business. If I peer anxiously into the fog of the future, I will strain my spiritual eyes so that I will not see clearly what is required of me now." God is God, you are not, neither am I.

Talking to God is not a duty, but an opportunity. Prayer should be ongoing, even continuous, and done freely, not structured, sequestered or forced. Colossians 4:2 says, "Devote yourselves to prayer, being watchful and thankful." Prayer is a dialogue and conversation with God, unencumbered from the rituals or practices that come to mind for most. Ken Boa defines prayer from a Biblical perspective: "It is the meeting place where we draw near to God to receive His grace, to release our burdens and fears, and to be honest with the Lord." It is a chance to be yourself before God, take instruction and guidance from Him, and be restored and re-energized for facing the world.

Talking to God takes many different forms, and we will all gravitate to different methods. Sometimes along your journey, it is helpful to try various approaches to prevent your exchanges with God from getting stale, repetitious, or overly methodical. Some of these practices include solitude, silence, study, meditation, and journaling, or writing a psalm like I mentioned. All of these are forms of prayer when they are focused on enhancing your relationship and communication with God. It has been said that God is a gentleman and will never force Himself on you. Similarly, the Spirit is not pushy, so you have to invite It in. Prayer is how you do that.

I've mentioned a few quick flash prayers already, and I encourage you to use flash prayers all the time for everything. The more aware you become of your dependence on God on a minute-by-minute basis throughout the course of your day, the more prayer becomes your first response instead of your last resort. You develop your new relationship with God until listening to and following the nudging of the Spirit becomes like second nature. I'm convinced God sent me a Spirit that is Type A, because sometimes It answers me so quickly, I hardly have time to catch up! As you grow in your faith, you will also gain in knowing that the Spirit will never tell you to do something without also giving you the power to do it. It has been said that "the Will of God will never take you where the Grace of God will not protect you." And the more you follow the Spirit, the more you will become who you always wanted to be. Remember to say *thank You*.

For more formal and extended prayer time, make an appointment with God as if He were your best client. Then hold to that way of thinking throughout your time with Him. If you had a 15-minute appointment with your best client, would you be looking at the clock every two minutes? Would you say you had somewhere more important to be after only ten minutes? Would you seek to hit your main points and then close your notebook and leave as quickly as possible?

When you set aside these times with God, try to pray in silence. No external distractions. Find a quiet and comfortable place that you can consistently use as your silent spot. Start with 15 minutes once a week, and then advance from there to higher frequency or added time. Come ready with your issues, including anything you need God to take over or take away from you, or anything else you need. Invite God and the Spirit to join you and guide you. Then close your mouth, shut down your brain, and listen for what God wants to reveal to you. I'm not trying to oversimplify it, and I'm sure there are a few things in here that will be very awkward for a Type A at first. Being in the moment is a foreign, even alien experience for most Type A's. But in the stillness, the Spirit can reveal the solutions. Remember to say *thank You.*

For most of us, it is difficult, if not seemingly impossible, to be silent and still, especially for Type A's. The Idol of Accomplishment will be reprimanding you and lying to you that you are wasting your time and could be getting so much more done. Yet, scripture tells us, "Be still, and know that I am God." (Psalm 46:10) Father Thomas Keating said, "Silence is the language God speaks and everything else is a bad translation." Stillness and quiet time with God will profoundly change you.

If absolute stillness and silence is too much, try study or Biblical meditation. Study the Bible, familiarize yourself with it. "All Scripture is God-breathed and is useful for teaching, rebuking, correcting, and training in righteousness, so that the man of God may be thoroughly equipped." (2 Timothy 3:16-17) Flip through its pages until it starts to fit together like pieces of a puzzle. When you first start, you will get overwhelmed with the major points and the minutiae because they are sometimes hard to tell apart. As you grow, you'll be able to cross-reference from book to book, Old Testament to New Testament, story to story, lesson to lesson and promise to promise. Further along, when someone says something that causes you to doubt, turn back to scripture to find the answer.

Similarly, Biblical meditation is not an act of clearing your mind, but filling your mind with the truth of the Word of God. To meditate on the Word is to pick a passage and let it sit in stillness on your brain until its nuances and synchronicities are revealed to you. A scripture that you have meditated on will be at the tip of your tongue when a trial arises. Therefore, you will find steadiness, comfort, and wisdom because you are deeply rooted in the truth, and it is written on your heart. Meditation is a great defense against our own preference for pleasant illusions over truth. It has been said, "None are so blind as those who do not wish to see." However, being armed with the truth, it is more difficult to be blinded.

Prayerful journaling can also be an effective form of prayer. Write a psalm, as I mentioned earlier. Or make a list of how you are feeling and replace it with scriptural truths. For example, if you think you are ugly, write "I am ugly," cross it out and next to it write, "I am beautiful in the eyes of God." Journal your testimony as a collection or list of ways or times when your faith in God or following the Spirit has pulled you through to victory or spared you some unfortunate situation. Praise God for what He has done for you. When you are feeling weak in faith, return to this list, read it, add to it, and remember that God is God, you are not, neither am I. Remember to say *thank You.*

There are times when a prayer list is a good idea to keep you focused on specific items in your life or in the lives of others you may be praying for. However, there are other times when simple silence is best. Martin Luther said, "The fewer the words, the better the prayer." God already knows what you need and what you want. Saying it a different way doesn't change what He already knows. Besides, if you are talking throughout the prayer, you haven't given Him the time to give you any answers. A friend of mine also referred to her time with God as an opportunity to spend 15 minutes with the most intelligent person in the entire universe. If you had that chance, who would you want to be doing most of the talking? Remember to say *thank You.*

We all know that giving it to God is easier said than done. However, true faith includes giving and surrendering ALL of it to Him. Once you give something to God, scripture says to rest, "Be still and know that I am God." (Psalm 46:10) Relax, God's got it all under control. If you can't rest or relax, you didn't give it all to Him. Go back and try again. Some people believe that you should pray for something only once, and then follow it with praise for God's decided best possible outcome for you regarding that issue. They contend that if you pray for the same thing six more times, you pray six times not believing that God answered you the first time. I can understand where they are coming from, but I also believe that persistent prayer helps God to see our obedience and helps us to remember Who is in charge. God keeps His promises. Persist in prayer, and when the timing is right, everything will happen instantly. Remember to say *thank You.*

I have personally tried all of these prayer methods for communicating with God. I vary them, so I don't feel like it is a duty or a routine, and also so I can hear God more clearly. Just so you know, God is a Man of few words. When He talks to me, it is usually very brief sentences. For example, one time during five minutes of meditation, all He said was, "Trust Me." On another occasion, the longest phrase I heard from Him was, "What are you waiting for?" and that's only five words. Keep that in mind if you are expecting something else.

Also, I've found that the self-help or business-empowerment questions are harder to get out of your head than you think. Therefore, I've had to convert the self-help questions we are all so tired of hearing into purposeful prayers that will have meaningful answers. Here are some suggestions for you:

Instead of: *Are you happy about where you are in your life right now?* ***Pray:*** God, show me the path you want me to follow. Protect me; give me strength and courage to submit myself to Your will. "You can make many plans, but the Lord's purpose will prevail." "The Lord directs the steps of the godly. He delights in every detail of their lives." (Proverbs 19:21, Psalm 37:23, both New Living Translation [NLT])

Instead of: At what point were you the most satisfied with your life and why? Or, How did you get to this point in your life? **Pray**: God, show me how I can use my unique history/experiences for Your purpose in my life. "A man's steps are directed by the Lord. How then can anyone understand his own way?" "Misfortune follows the sinner, but prosperity is the reward of the righteous." "And we know that in all things God works for the good of those who love Him, who have been called according to His purpose." (Proverbs 20:24 and 13:21, Romans 8:28, all NLT)

Instead of: What do you think is the best thing about you? The worst? **Pray**: God, show me how my unique character traits, personality, and experience can serve Your purpose for my life. "But I have raised you up for this very purpose." "I cry out to God Most High, who fulfills His purpose for me." (Exodus 9:16, Psalm 57:2)

Instead of: Are you happy about where you are living? The community, culture, weather... **Pray**: God, where do you want me to be right now? "I am with you and will watch over you wherever you go... I will not leave you until I have done what I have promised you." (Genesis 28:15)

Instead of: Are you pleased with your romantic relationship? Your relationship with your spouse and children? **Pray**: God, show me how to be a better partner and parent. "A wife of noble character is her husband's crown." "Train a child in the way he should go, and when he is old, he will not turn from it." "Husbands, love your wives and do not be harsh with them. Children, obey your parents in everything, for this pleases the Lord. Fathers, do not embitter your children, or they will become discouraged." (Proverbs 12:4 and 22:6, Colossians 3:19-21)

Instead of: What are the recurring difficulties in your life? What is your part in those difficulties? **Pray**: God, forgive me for my transgressions. Please show me my pattern of temptation and strengthen me to make new decisions. "No temptation has overtaken you except such as is common to man; but God is faithful, and will not allow you to be tempted beyond what you can bear. But when you are tempted, He will also make the way of escape, that you may be able to bear it." (1 Corinthians 10:13)

Instead of: *What have been your life's biggest disappointments?* ***Pray***: God, take these burdens from me and heal my wounds. "The Lord is close to the brokenhearted and saves those who are crushed in spirit." "I have promised to bring you up out of your misery, and into the land flowing with milk and honey." (Psalm 34:18, Exodus 3:17)

Instead of: *Do you consider your life to be balanced?* ***Pray:*** God, please fill me with enough inspiration to joyfully carry out Your unique purpose for my life, and thank You for allowing me to rest on Your promises, which You always keep. "For anyone who enters God's rest also rests from his own work, just as God did from His." "Their days of labor are filled with pain and grief; even at night their minds cannot rest. It is all meaningless. So I decided there is nothing better than to enjoy food and drink and to find satisfaction in work. Then I realized that these pleasures are from the hand of God. For who can eat or enjoy anything apart from Him?" (Hebrews 4:10, Ecclesiastes 3:23-25)

Instead of: *Are you fulfilled with your professional career?* Or, *What would you do even if you didn't get paid to do it?* Or, *What is your vision of happiness?* ***Pray***: God, what is Your unique purpose for my life? How do I go about making that happen? "You will show me the path of life" so that "Your will be done on earth as it is in Heaven." (Psalm 16:11, Matthew 6:10)

Hopefully, that is enough to get you started or rejuvenated into prayer and conversation with God. Pray about everything. Pray about decisions, pray about your friends, pray about your needs, pray about your problems, pray about people you meet, pray about your schedule and life balance, pray about everything. Mark 1:35 tells us that Jesus prayed "very early in the morning, while it was still dark… in a solitary place." My friend Michelle follows that example, and the results are flabbergasting. She is so grounded in the Word and with the Spirit, she can spot a lie a mile away. She sees things, or rather sees through things, to the extent that you think she has special powers. Wouldn't you like to have that type of clairvoyance? You can. Give it to God, and start talking to Him. "But when you pray, go into your room, close the door and pray to God who is unseen. Then God, who sees what is done in secret, will reward you." "According to your faith, it will be done to you." (Matthew 6:6 and 9:29)

"Everyone who hears these words of mine and puts them into practice is like a wise man who has built his house on the rock." (Matthew 7:24)

Chapter 14: Fight the Good Fight

Some people think that following God and allowing God to take first place in your life is a passive approach to life, but this couldn't be further from the truth. There are plenty of other people and things that want to be the top priority in your life, including the Idols of Money, Accomplishment, and Self who are yearning to have you back under their captivity, longing to be your main concern.

I've already assured you that there will be challenges, and we need to be strong enough in our faith to overcome these hurdles. Scripture relates us to athletes and tells us to "fight the good fight of faith." At the end of his life, Paul writes, "I have fought the good fight of faith, I have finished the race, I have kept the faith." (2 Timothy 2:5, 1 Timothy 6:12, 2 Timothy 4:7) And we are told "We are more than conquerors through Him who loves us." (Romans 8:37) If life with God were so passive, why would we need to train or conquer anything?

Let me paint the picture for you. In the beginning, God will likely give you some very clear indicators to let you know He is there. There may seem to be more coincidences, modern-day burning bushes, a series of unexplainable events that come together in your favor, or you may even have some wishes granted. In the beginning, you will likely have a fire in your belly for God and want to get your hands on anything and everything you can in order to reaffirm your faith. You'll be oozing God to everyone around you, and life may seem trouble free.

Then it will happen. Something you set your heart on will not come to pass, you will not hear from God as readily as you had before, or you will not receive an obvious sign or signal that you requested. This is where the rubber meets the road. Your faith cannot be based on expectation of sudden experiences or a series of experiences directed by God on your command or request. Though these experiences will happen, they are all on God's timing. In order to remind you of that, God will pull back from you from time to time, testing your faith and commitment. That's when it's time for your faith to grow, through "doing the work" and "fighting the good fight." We can never assume that we can figure God out, or know His plans. We must also never think that God is not working, even if we feel blind at times. We must always remember, as Thomas Carlisle reminds us, "God is always working on us and walking with us."

C.S. Lewis in the *Problem of Pain,* makes a wonderful observation that as God's creations, each of us is a work of art in His eyes. It is because He loves us so much that He treats us like masterpieces that need work, care and correction. He says,

> Over a sketch made idly to amuse a child, an artist may not take much trouble: he may be content to let it go even though it is not exactly as he meant it to be. But over the great picture of his life – the work which he loves, though in a different fashion, as intensely as a man loves a woman or a mother a child – he will take endless trouble – and would, doubtless, thereby give endless trouble to the picture if it were sentient. One can imagine a sentient picture, after bring rubbed and scraped and re-commenced for the tenth time, wishing that it were only a thumb-nail sketch whose making was over in a minute.

God is perfecting us through trials and challenges, erasing parts He doesn't like, layering on new attributes and faculties, constantly working on us. We must have faith that He loves us and trust His motives for us. Scripture is clear He has a plan to prosper us, not to harm us. (Jeremiah 29:11) Max Lucado said, "God is God. He knows what He is doing. When you can't trust His hand, you can trust His heart." The *Parable of the Sower* (Mark 4:1-8) makes it plain that seeds deeply rooted in faith will grow to be the tallest trees, as opposed to seeds planted shallowly that will serve as food for the birds. It's normal to feel blind. Walking by faith is quite ambiguous at times. Even Moses begged God in Exodus 33 to let him in on the plan, but God only reassured Moses that He would be there through to the end. Romans 8:28 reminds us to "know that in all things God works for the good of those who love Him." God is God, you are not, neither am I.

If you need an example of a man who had to work hard to keep the faith when God was distant, read the Book of Job in the Bible. I was particularly inspired by Job because he was a wealthy man who, in a test between God and the devil, had everything taken away from him, but never lost faith. I could relate to Job while he tries to figure out why and how all of this had happened to him. I could especially relate since I was a believer, just as he was a devoted man of God, so how could this have happened? It's a great story, and you should read it and know that in the end, as a reward for his faithfulness, Job is blessed with double of everything he had ever had before. God loves you and God has a plan for you. God's plan for you is the path to fulfillment, love, joy, peace and wisdom.

Still, keeping the faith is easier said than done. Following God is warfare against our own tendencies, temptations, and habits, and particularly for Type A's, it is warfare against the Idols of Money, Accomplishment, and Self. There is nothing the idols want more than to recapture you and bring you backwards until you are fully enslaved to them again. I don't want to freak you out, but in my view, the Idol of Money, the Idol of Accomplishment, and the Idol of Self are all foot soldiers of the devil himself. There is nothing the devil likes more than to see you dissatisfied, lonely, disappointed, anxious and feeling foolish, and his soldiers will use fear, temptation, and lies to lure you back to captivity.

For example, the Idol of Money will try to tempt you away from your faith in God by telling you that following God will make you poor and pitiable, instead of prosperous, or that with enough money you don't really need God anyway. The Idol of Accomplishment will try to tempt you away from your faith in God by telling you that waiting for God is way too passive, and you'll never accomplish anything that way. The Idol of Self will try to tempt you away from your faith in God by telling you that you should do it your way and that you'll never amount to anything by being faithful to God.

These idols will even team up on you when they have to, and society will chime in to help them. Following God is counter-cultural, and there is nothing society wants more than to convince you that you are an idiot for believing God and reading the Bible. It is easy to be pulled back into the "You are in control," "Greed is good" and "God helps those who help themselves" mantras of the world, but this is why we pray, "Lead us not into temptation." (Matthew 6:13)

Steadfastness and commitment to fighting the good fight is difficult, but scripture reassures us that "if we give our entire lives to the pursuit of God, everything else of value will find us." (Matthew 6:33) Further, God does not leave us defenseless or unprotected. Ephesians 6:10-20 gives us the Armor of God, which I recommend putting on daily. I used to call my power suits my armor because when getting dressed in the morning, I consciously felt empowered and prepared to face the harsh brutality of the corporate world. Now, I put on the Armor of God daily and feel empowered and prepared against any plot to pull me away from God and His purpose for me. We are told to "be strong in the Lord and in His mighty power. Put on the full armor of God that you can take your stand against the devil's schemes. For our struggle is not against flesh and blood, but against the rulers, against the authorities, against the powers of this dark world." (Ephesians 6:10-12) Paraphrasing the remainder of the passage, this is how you put on the Armor of God:

I put on the full Armor of God with the undergarment of love;
God's love for me, my love for Him, and His love through me
for others. I put on the belt of truth around my waist, the
breastplate of righteousness, and the footgear of the gospel of
peace. I take up the shield of faith, which extinguishes the
flaming arrows of the evil one. I put on the helmet of
salvation, and take up the sword of the Spirit, which is the
Word of God. I stand firm and protected in the full Armor of
God, with God's glory as my rear guard. I refuse to pay for
the same ground twice, and only goodness will follow me all
the days of my life.

Now that you have your armor on and are prepared for battle, let's
look at some of the obstacles in more detail. The initial and ongoing
obstacle for any believer is unbelief and doubt, and Type A's are no
different. The temptations faced more specifically by Type A's will
be the tactics and tools used by the Idols of Money,
Accomplishment, and Self because that's where Type A's are most
vulnerable. The Idol of Money uses the tools of prosperity and
hardship, the Idol of Accomplishment uses the tools of legalism,
accusation, and restlessness, and the Idol of Self uses the tools of
pride and personal history, all of which are used against you to try to
bring you down.

These are only a few of their tactics, but there are many more. I will
give you a brief outline to give you a taste of what I'm talking about,
but please don't stop here. Do the work for yourself, know your own
patterns of temptation, reinforce yourself with scripture, and check
out the books on the recommended reading list at the back of this
book.

In the beginning, and even at certain points of your journey with
God, unbelief and doubt are normal and natural. I've already
mentioned that loving an invisible God takes some effort on your
part, and wrestling with your faith is to be expected. Believing in
God is entirely different from believing God. Trusting that He is

there is different than trusting what He promises. Unbelief and doubt surface as these questions in your mind: "Does God really exist?" or "Does God love me?" or "Can God take care of me?" or "Will God take care of me?" or "How is God going to make this happen?" These questions are the surfacing of worry and fear, which is the opposite of faith. As George Mueller said, "The beginning of anxiety is the end of faith, and the beginning of true faith is the end of anxiety."

Especially for a Type A, with your do-it-yourself attitude, your well-educated mind and intellect and your control-freak tendencies, this is going to be a challenge. You will have to go through this for yourself, but I can tell you from my experience that when my faith is strongest, my decisions are based in love and wisdom, and I have a calm peace in all situations. When my faith has been weakened by doubt, I become vulnerable to predators and weak to temptation. You've already heard some of the results of those decisions.

Unfortunately, all it takes to make you vulnerable is just the slightest glimmer of apprehension. When you don't feel faith overflowing your heart, then faith has to be a decision in your mind. The inception of my faith was a deal with God that I would believe, whether I wanted to or not, and my whole life changed. Believe it or not, even Billy Graham had a momentous experience of doubting God's Word. He broke through his skepticism and hesitation by making a conscious decision to believe the Word of God in full force and rely on it totally as his source of truth. This was the major turning point that launched his career.

Decide to believe. Choose faith. Believe God. Accept the Bible's authority. To wrestle unbelief to the ground, keep scriptures of God's promises everywhere around you. On a slip of paper in your wallet, on the mirror while you get ready in the morning, by your bedside, in your office, anywhere you feel that doubt could creep in, solidify and strengthen your faith with the Word of God. Matthew 6:30-35 says, "O you of little faith... do not worry, saying, 'What will we eat?' or

'What will we drink?' or 'What will we wear?' For the pagans run after these things, and your Heavenly Father knows that you need them. Seek first His kingdom... and do not worry about tomorrow, for tomorrow will worry about itself. Each day has enough trouble of its own." Warren Wiersbe puts it this way, "One day at a time. No person, no matter how wealthy or gifted, can live two days at a time. God provides for us day by day." Even the most widely known Christian prayer requests, "Give us this day our daily bread" (Matthew 6:11), not tomorrow's bread or next week's, and not the Type A five-years-from-now bread. God knows what you need. Trust Him. Eventually, you will be able to trust any outcome as God's design. You will be able to say something like this paraphrase of 2 Timothy 1:12: "I really don't understand what I'm going through right now, but I know God, and therefore, I am not ashamed. I don't turn my back because I know He is able to guard me and guide me."

The Idol of Money uses the primary tools of prosperity and hardship to lure you away from your faith in God. Prosperity gives you the inclination to believe that you don't need God. The more you succeed, the less dependent you think you are on God, and the more you want to take credit yourself. C.S. Lewis noted, "Prosperity knits a man to the World. He feels that he is 'finding his place in it,' while really it is finding its place in him. His increasing reputation, his widening circle of acquaintances, his sense of importance, the growing pressure of absorbing and agreeable work, build up in him a sense of being really at home on earth." Prosperity can be a trap of the Idol of Money to lure you away from your faith.

Hardship, on the other hand, makes you blame God because He didn't create prosperity. You wonder why God is doing this to you, why He is angry with you, and you even get angry at Him. The truth is, sometimes God allows your plans to fails in order to show you the correct path. Sometimes God allows hardship to teach you a valuable lesson you need to learn in order to create prosperity in the future.

Sometimes we are like cell phone batteries that need to be completely drained to zero before we can be recharged to our fullest capacity again. But since you get frustrated not knowing God's plan, it's a great tool for the Idol of Money to separate you from your faith.

You see, the Idol of Money tricks you into this backwards equation of thinking that when you face hardship, it's God's fault, and when you're prosperous, it's your fault. Hmm... sounds fishy to me. Thomas Merton reminds us that "we must be ready to cooperate not only with graces that console, but with graces that humiliate us; not only with lights that exalt us, but with lights that blast our self-complacency."

Personally, I have experienced times of prosperity and hardship over the course of my life. For me, it is easier to connect with God when things are tough, because I have a tendency to feel independent and self-sufficient when things are going well. I have found that for a Type A who is driven, recognized, and prosperous, scripture guides us to "remember the Lord your God, for it is He who is giving you power to make wealth." (Deuteronomy 8:18) I have this scripture in big bold letters on my excel spreadsheets where I organize my bills and accounts. Other people turn from God in times of hardship, and return to Him when things are going well.

Your only defense against allowing prosperity or hardship to dismantle your faith is scripture and the truth of God. Scripture is the most amazing tool because it is the only text that can humble you when you are overconfident and fortify you when you are fragile. I am a broken record repeating these passages, but if you need to be humbled, remember that God gave you the ability, the intelligence, the means, and the advancement (Romans 12:6, Daniel 2:21, Deuteronomy 8:18, Psalm 75:6-7); and if you need to be reinforced, have faith that God will give you the ability, the intelligence, the means, and the advancement.

The Idol of Accomplishment uses the primary tools of legalism, accusation, and restlessness to lure you away from your relationship with God. Legalism is anything that comes close to any of those preconceived notions you had about what you had *to do* to be "religious" or pleasing to God. It is also the origin of hypocrisy and exploitation. Being the victim of legalism makes you feel accused that you are not doing enough for God. However, if obedience comes from anything except reciprocating love to God, performance quickly replaces passion and purpose. You start looking at things with a microscope instead of a mirror; and doing "religious" things or acting "religious" replaces prayer and relationship. You convince yourself that doing something more tangible for God is better than the simplicity of just talking to Him. But we have all seen examples of victims to the Idol of Accomplishment through legalism because we all know people who are so "religious," you can't see the love of God in them anymore.

Accusation is when you use legalism against others. Just because you are establishing your relationship with God doesn't mean you get to be the judge of everyone else around you. To paraphrase Romans 2:1-4, "Who are you to pass judgment on anyone else? When you point your finger at someone else, you are condemning yourself. Do you really think that passing judgment on someone else is a substitute for what you do?" Accusation is an obstacle to faith because it makes you quite unpleasant to be around with your obnoxious and condemning criticism, until you are ultimately alienated. But since you made these accusations in the name of God, you'll blame your loneliness on Him.

Personally, I have met plenty of believers who think that if you aren't a Christian, you are not "in the club;" and there are times when I have felt judged, condemned, or looked down upon by people who are supposed to be full of grace and love. As a Type A, it is also tempting to want to be the best at whatever you do, but trying to be perfect for God is an exercise of futility. Scripture teaches that we all have value and we all have unique gifts, and not one of us is any better or worse than any other. "Each one of us should use whatever gift he has received to serve others, faithfully administering God's grace in its various forms." (1 Peter 4:10)

The problem with legalism and accusation is that you are basing your worth and value on what you and others are ***doing*** for God, instead of finding your significance through God's love for you, and your love for Him. As I said earlier, legalism, and accusation are a disservice to God, and against Jesus' teachings entirely. Jesus taught that we have only one commandment with two parts: "Love the Lord your God with all your heart and with all your soul and with all your mind and with all your strength. The second is this: Love your neighbor as yourself. There is no commandment greater than these." (Mark 12:30-31) In other words, combat legalism by reminding yourself that God loves you, God loves you, God loves you; and combat accusation of others by reminding yourself that God loves them, too.

Restlessness is also a tool of the Idol of Accomplishment, and this is a slippery slope for Type A's. Since you are used to working at lightning speed, waiting for God's timing seems to take forever. Then you start turning to devices like, "God's got until Saturday" or "God helps those who help themselves" or "I can't wait for God right now" or "God's not working fast enough." You feel overly passive, like you are not doing enough, but this is exactly what the Idol of Accomplishment wants you to think. Sometimes God is giving you a time of rest to prepare you for what's ahead, but the Idol of Accomplishment would rather have you stressed out and weary.

You know what you want, but God knows what you need. Waiting for God's timing is not passive. Trust in the process is not *que sera, sera*. Sometimes it takes more courage to wait for God than it does to get up and do it yourself. Restlessness was particularly difficult for me when my life came to a screeching halt. I thought the more I did for myself, the faster I would achieve results. This, of course, is nonsense. My activity has no bearing on God's perfect timing, and moreover, God was giving me a gift of time that I had never had before. The best way to combat restlessness is to fill your time with study and keep on walking in faith. Trust Him. Trust His timing. "Those who wait for the Lord will gain new strength; they will mount up with wings like eagles, they will run and not get tired, they will walk and not become weary." (Isaiah 40:31)

The Idol of Self uses the tools of pride and personal history to lure you away from believing God, and is used with affirming and negating techniques. In the affirmative, pride creeps in when things are going well in your life. You want to treat God like a doctor that you visit only when you are sick. You want to send God a thank-you card for helping you through life's transitions, but at the end of your note you say, "I'll take it from here, I've got it under control." In the negative, pride holds you back from making strides of faith and fulfilling your purpose. Those negative voices in your head saying things like, "What will people think?" or "I can't," or "I don't have the experience or education," or "I've got to be crazy to be doing this," or "I'm not good enough," or Type A's, "It's not perfect."

Personal history amplifies these two ends of the spectrum with our past experiences. Success/failure or joy/pain, or fulfillment/emptiness serve only to magnify our belief in what we can or cannot do. Personal history also includes family history. Sometimes "generational curses" dictate the voices we hear in our head, either positive or negative. Family patterns have been known to repeat themselves until someone is strong enough to stand up against them. Though we are commanded to honor our mother and father, we must also stand firm that their issues are theirs, not ours.

Personally, my biggest struggle has been with pride and personal history. Oftentimes the tough Type A exterior makes arrogance an easy trap to fall into. On the other end of the spectrum, in quiet time alone, that arrogance is hollow, and thoughts are riddled with negativity and doubt. This is a delicate balancing act of replacing arrogance for yourself with confidence in God. Change "I can do anything" to "With God's help, I can do anything" and "By myself, I can do nothing." (John 5:30) Replace the self-help answer of "Get over it" with "Give it to God." Lastly, stop a generational curse with faith that "fathers will not be put to death for their children, nor children put to death for their fathers; each is to die for his own sin." (Deuteronomy 24:16)

I have also found prayerful journaling to be an effective tool for reinforcing the truth according to God. One very tearful night, I wrote out two columns, which was a clear demonstration of the battle being fought. In one column, I wrote everything I thought was bad about myself. Then in the other, I wrote out the scriptural truths according to God. I gave you the example previously about replacing "I am ugly" with "I am beautiful in the eyes of God." On other occasions, when I feel my ego taking hold, I remind myself that God can always use someone else for His purposes if I'm going to get in His way. I ask Him to help me get out of His way, and He does.

The problem with pride and personal history is that you are not allowing God to be God by centering your viewpoint on what you can or cannot do, instead of what God can do. Therefore, pride and personal history must be replaced with God's love for us and what scripture tells us we are. Again, it is time to turn to scripture to reinforce the truth, bring you down when you are arrogant and build you up when you need a boost. Pray for humility and praise God for what He's done, or reinforce with God's promises of victory and triumph. Here is a small list about who you are with God on your side. You are a child of God (Romans 8:16), justified (Romans 5:1), sanctified (1 Corinthians 6:11), led by the Spirit of God (Romans 8:14), strong in the Lord (Ephesians 6:10), blessed coming in and going out (Deuteronomy 28:6), above only and not beneath (Deuteronomy 28:13), more than a conqueror (Romans 8:37), walking by faith and not by sight (2 Corinthians 5:7), casting down vain imaginations (2 Corinthians 10:4-5), a laborer together with God (1 Corinthians 3:9), the light of the world (Matthew 5:14), kept in safety wherever you go (Psalm 91:11), getting all your needs met (Philippians 4:19), casting all your cares on Him (1 Peter 5:7).

As I mentioned, maintaining humility will be the biggest challenge for Type A perfectionist, control-freak overachievers. Especially in high-ranking, power-based positions, it is very difficult to stay grounded. Since you don't get paid for things you didn't do, you've got to put your stamp on everything you touch. Since you won't get promoted unless you're promoting yourself, you peacock around so everyone notices. And since nobody else is going to make you important, you become self-empowered and self-important. It is ingrained in us to leave our mark and be noticed for what we do. But "How can you believe if you accept praise from one another, yet make no effort to obtain the praise that comes only from God?" (John 5:44)

Society will only make this more challenging. Even if you are not trying to leave your mark, people around you will want to give you credit, and will want you to take credit for the wonderful things you do. For example, the movie *Gifted Hands* is a true story about Dr. Ben Carson, a gifted surgeon with a very strong faith. In the "Making of the Film" part of the DVD, the real Dr. Carson is interviewed. He is a humble, gentle, mild-mannered man who acknowledges his gift is from God and does the best he can with the gift he has been given. Most of the other people interviewed, including producers, directors, actors, and contributors talk about the story as one of "human determination" or "perseverance," and "You can do anything you set your mind to." Do you see the incongruence between the two? No doubt, Dr. Carson is gifted, but if he exalted himself based on his accomplishments, I'm sure he'd be an insufferable, narcissistic egomaniac. My belief is that perhaps God has given Dr. Carson more exceptional gifts than most because Dr. Carson knows how to handle them and use them for the good of others.

Now, keep in mind that humility is not a contest. You can't fake humility, but you can stop taking credit for things, and start giving the credit to God. "Fake it until you make it" will not make you humble. If you are a Type A, I strongly recommend praying for humility... a lot. Here's a prayer for humility you can use if it suits you:

Father God, I ask of you, out of Your great goodness and compassion, to search my mind and heart for any and every kind of pride. Lord, take away from me any illusions of becoming great and famous, for You alone are those things. God, help me to get out of Your way. When my pride wants to stand up for itself, help me knock it down. Awaken me to the truth in all things, and let this truth give me natural humility. From this humility, I give myself to You, Lord, and ask that You use me for Your purposes, and give me the strength to see it through for You.

Still, humility will not come easy for a Type A. The best method I have found is to keep a ticker tape running at the bottom of my mind's eye that says "To God be the glory." Every time I am habitually inclined to take credit or gratification for something, that ticker tape is running, reminding me that I couldn't have done any of it without God. It makes it easier to say, "To God be the glory" instead of taking credit myself, which is dismissive and exclusionary of God altogether. It should also be noted that when someone gives you credit or acknowledgement, you should still politely say *thank you*. I have found that since giving the credit to God is so counter-cultural, if you say, "To God be the glory," all the really self-empowered people will think you are being too humble and persist in acknowledging you until you break down and take the credit. So, until people get used to, "To God be the glory" from you as a stand-alone, the combination of "Thank you... to God be the glory" is your best bet. The point is, God is the only one who deserves the credit. Always.

Hopefully, this has given you an idea of what you are up against on your path to finding fulfillment, love, joy, peace and wisdom through a relationship with God and keeping God first place in your life. You will be faced with obstacles and temptations, so be alert and prepared. The devil's appeal to many people through the ages has been, "Why worship God when you can be one yourself?" But scripture is clear that "you shall have no other Gods before me." (Exodus 20:3) "No one can serve two masters," and more specifically, "You cannot serve both God and money." (Matthew 6:24) Type A's will be most vulnerable to the Idols of Money, Accomplishment, and Self, but there will be other temptations along the way.

For most of you, following the path God wants you to follow is going to require some major short-term and long-term changes in your life. None of these is to be taken without full appreciation, understanding or consent. Do not rush. Allow these changes to become clear to you in a gradual way, in order to build your confidence before each leap of faith, and build your certainty that you are really following God's directive and not being wooed into old patterns of behavior. Take your time. Don't limit your hopes or expectations to any singular outcome. Don't try to manipulate anything for God; He is highly capable of moving things around for Himself. Don't try to control things. Remind yourself that God is in charge. Don't compare yourself and your faith to anyone. Mature faith is impossible to measure externally because it is completely unrelated to life experience, age, or appearances.

Do the work. Fight the good fight. Talk to God about everything. Research, study, and reinforce Biblical truths. Allow God to be first in your life and trust in His plan for you. God builds your faith by guiding you through obstacles that sometimes seem insurmountable. Without Him, they are. The overriding and ongoing challenge is to constantly remember that the goal is not independence and self-sufficiency, but complete *dependence on God.* This is why we need scripture, the only resource that can humble us when we are proud, and reaffirm us when we fail. When you succeed, remember that everything you have is a gift from God; when you fail, remember that God promises victory. We all want to know what the next step is before we take it. But the next step with God is always the next leap of faith. Leaps of faith are the only way to grow in faith, and God wants you to grow. Don't settle for being a spiritual child. 1 Corinthians 13:11 tells us, "When I was a child, I talked like a child, I thought like a child, I reasoned like a child. When I became a man, I put childish ways behind me."

Growing in faith and following God's path and plan for you is the only way to overflowing fulfillment, love, joy, peace and wisdom. God knows the plans He has for you, plans "to prosper you and not to harm you, plans to give you hope and a future." (Jeremiah 29:11) "We walk by faith, not by sight." (2 Corinthians 5:7) Trust God to transform you and lead you to your overflow.

If you do your part, God will do His.

Chapter 15: Transformation, Purpose, Overflow

Depending on where you are right now, God either has a little or a lot of work to do on you. If He has a little work to do, you will notice changes here and there; or there may be one big change that swells into changing everything else. If God has a lot of work to do, fasten your seatbelt and get ready for the ride of your life. Everything is subject to change without further notice, including, but not limited to: your job, your location, your lifestyle, your friends, your thoughts, your perceptions, and even your image of yourself. You said you were ready for change, right? Don't wimp out now!

Everybody wants to know their purpose, but there are processes of change that need to occur before you are ready to be called. The process of getting onto God's path will include growth, pruning, victory, purposeful defeat, and lessons to be learned on the path to ultimate triumph. Knowing you want to get on God's path is one thing, but cooperating throughout the journey is entirely different.

This is why building your relationship with God is the critical precursor to transformation. You have to know beyond a shadow of a doubt that God loves you. You must dare to believe that if everything else in your life changes or goes away, that God is enough. He is. You must continually do the work of building that relationship through conversation with Him, study of His Word, fighting the good fight and taking leaps of faith in order to grow. Mary Manin Morrissey said, "Parachutes weren't proven trustworthy by having people carry them around on their backs. The device showed its reliability once someone jumped. God, too, can be trusted with our lives, which we discover once we take a leap of faith." As you develop and grow in your relationship with God, He will require you to take this leap of faith over and over again. It starts with believing that God can do the impossible. It starts with admitting the futility of doing it yourself. It starts with believing in God's love for you, and believing that blessings follow obedience.

I was fortunate. Returning from Europe with no job, no man, and no home of my own, I didn't have certain entanglements that can be so complicated. I'm not certain if I would have been able to grow in faith as precipitously as I have without this level of autonomy. Even though it looked like my life was a disaster from the outside, it is the disintegration of my Type A life that lead to my breakthrough and transformation. Besides, I had plenty of other challenges to conquer. Even though it seems unusual, I praise God for the hardship. If you do not have the same level of freedom, you are going to have to trust God to walk you through your obstacles step by step. He will.

God's approach to transforming each of us is custom-tailored like an expensive suit. There is no reason to think that you will be transformed the same way that I was because what fulfillment, love, joy, peace and wisdom mean in my life will be different than what they mean in your life. Our transformations may be similar because of our Type A relation, but truth be told, there are parallels and resemblances in God's transformation of all of us. He is following a prototype. We will talk more about the prototype in the next chapter, but for now I'm going to articulate to the best of my ability the flowchart of Godly transformation.

First, God removes the blindfold you've been wearing so you can see where you've been going wrong. Then, God provides new opportunity for you to make different choices. God continually forgives you for your mistakes, past, present and future, enough so that you can also forgive others. God continues His process by supplying you wisdom and changing your motives. Once you are prepared and equipped, God calls you to a purpose, your purpose in life. He continues to transform you into a messenger of His love and blessings, calling you to give to and serve others. As your transformation becomes apparent in all aspects of your life, God will authenticate and exfoliate your relationships. Finally, once God's transformational process is complete, your fulfillment, love, joy, peace and wisdom are overflowing.

This process never ends. God is never finished with you. You are never finished with God. He will do His part, and you have to do your part. You and God are partners on this. He knows what you need. He may not transform you in this exact order, but these are the general components of allowing God to change your life.

He is constantly perfecting you, His masterpiece, just like the artist with the painting from the C.S. Lewis quote in the previous chapter. Each time we achieve fulfillment, love, joy, peace and wisdom, God will remove another blindfold you didn't realize you were wearing, to reveal to you a new level of understanding, and the process starts again. You will stumble, you will make mistakes, but that is how you learn. God never says, "You should know this by now." He only says, "I'm here, try again." Obedience to God is not just about appetite or enthusiasm, but also willingness to follow through. God wants us trained and ready in these practices to strengthen us in the execution of His greater purpose for us.

There are plenty of books written on each of these stages of growth and the overall process itself, which will support the abbreviated version I'm about to give you. I'm trying to communicate to Type A's the best I can, based on what I have gone through, based on my research and study, and based on observing and listening to others who have been transformed. Remember to look into the books on the recommended reading list at the back of this book. I encourage you to do the work on your own path of discovery.

A Quick Note on Attitude

There are parts of this section that may appear to be in opposition to the inside-out approach I am so passionately supporting. But I assure you, it is not a contrast. God will do His part of transforming you, but you have to do your part, too. This is your journey to fulfillment, love, joy, peace and wisdom, so I assure you, it is worth the work. Before we get into the stages of transformation, we must discuss appropriate attitude to ensure that this is, indeed, an inside-out transformation. Without the right approach to attitude, your journey will be lackluster, monotonous and shallow at best.

My pastor, Dr. David Chadwick, has a system of "G's" to help us remember what following God is all about. I'm going to use his G's as signposts, but explain them in my own words. The first set of three G's pertains to how you approach doing your part for God's transformation process. Since I've already made it clear that this is not outside-in, executing your obedience to God with the right mindset and intentions is critical to your success. If you cannot do your part with the right attitude, your quest will be ineffective.

At any stage in the process, DO NOT PROCEED IF:

1.   you are doing so out of Guilt
2.   you are Grumpy about it
3.   you are doing it in order to Get something.

Guilt: It has been said that guilt puts pressure on you from the outside without changing you on the inside. Believe me, Italian and Jewish mothers specialize in guilt, and I know because I have one. My Sicilian grandmother not only specialized in guilt, but she always had the wooden paddle labeled "Grandma's helper" hanging on the wall to remind us who was in charge. Excuse my digression, but the point is, when you are forced into doing something because you feel guilty, it doesn't really change your mind, or more importantly, your heart.

It is also important not to mistake guilt with a proper level of humility. For example, I don't talk to you about the needy children in order to *guilt* you into doing something or make you *feel guilty* that you have more than they do. Rather, I inform you about the realities in this world in order to assist your *gratitude* for what you have and hence your *humility,* so you can consider doing your part for positive change.

The point is, do what you do for God with pure intentions, modesty, and graciousness.

Grumpy: If you are feeling down or negative about moving forward with your transformation, don't do it. That means thoughts along the lines of *"It's not going to make a difference anyway,"* or *"What a pain,"* or *"I have to do what?"* When you have these thoughts, it is best to wait to move forward until you are thinking thoughts such as, *"It's the least I can do,"* or *"I wish I could do more,"* or *"I cannot wait to do this!"*

When God instructs you to do something, He will make Himself clear with His instructions, and He is persistent. When God gives instruction, He also gives power and capacity in order for you to walk with assurance while carrying out His purposes. That doesn't mean that it will always "feel good," and you may be nervous at times, but hopefully you can tell the difference between nervousness and grumpiness. Sometimes doing the right thing isn't the most fun, but it is still the right thing.

The point is, do what you do for God boldly and willingly.

To Get: If you are doing anything for God in order to get something back from Him, don't do it. Karma has become the culturally accepted reason for doing anything good, but following God and being obedient to His transformational process should be done with praise and appreciation. You don't get to negotiate with God or build up an account.

Getting something back includes bragging to other people about what you are doing for God to get recognition for it. To paraphrase

Matthew 6:1-4, "Be careful not to do your acts of righteousness to be seen by other people. If you announce your good deeds to be recognized by men, you have already been paid in full. If you do your good deeds in secret, where only God is your witness, then God will reward you in the way that only He can." For you karma-loving people out there, that means that if *what goes around comes around*, then when you do a good thing to get recognized for doing it, what *came around* was the recognition. Karma circle closed. Essentially, you snubbed yourself out of a much greater reward.

The point is, do what you do for God for no other reason than to worship Him, place Him first in your life and submit to His divine authority. As Rick Warren points out, "Worship is not for your benefit, it's for His benefit."

Now, we are ready to begin by taking a deeper look at each stage of God's transformational process for your life.

God Removes the Blindfold (aka Confession)

It's amazing how people justify their actions nowadays for even the simplest things. *"It's not my fault,"* or *"I had no other choice,"* or *"I had a rough childhood,"* or *"It's because of my boss,"* or *"The devil made me do it,"* or any other form of blame and pointing the finger, just to avoid saying, *"Uh-oh, I messed up."*

As you grow in your relationship with God, He will gradually and gently reveal the truth to you. He has to do it gradually or you would most likely be crushed under the burden. If God revealed everything at once, it would be like a Looney Tunes character having a ten-ton weight dropped on them, and we'd all be flattened like pancakes. When God knows you are ready, He will show you more. As you grow closer to God, and you look back over your life, small things will be uncovered and exposed, and even though you were not sorry for them at the time, you realize now that they were amiss or at the very least, misguided. Patterns of temptation become easily identified, and knowledge of the pattern is the first step to abolishing it.

"We all stumble in many ways," (James 3:2) and there are times when we make mistakes, slip up, or even sin. It's hard enough admitting it to yourself, much less to someone else, or even God. As the blindfold is removed, a sense of "What have I done?" washes over you, and your instinct is to hide it and keep it a secret, but that will only make it fester and come back stronger at some point in the future. The only way to be freed from your mistakes is to admit to them. Fess up. In the beginning, this will not come naturally, especially for a perfectionist Type A. Similar to the foreignness of giving credit to God for everything you already have, nobody likes to admit when they are wrong or have made an error, and most people don't like to think of themselves as sinners.

As a matter of fact, in the beginning, it is very common for people to say, "I'm not a sinner." I know that's where I started. It's not ingrained in us to be sorry for what we've done or think we've done something bad. On the contrary, with all the sex and violence constantly playing out before us, our society has distorted our concept of what sin is. In our culture, especially as driven Type A's in the corporate world, where the ends justify the means, rogue-ness is commended. A rogue maverick doesn't apologize! If he does, it's only part of his plot to be more rogue and more maverick-y! The point is, we all sin sometimes whether we mean to or not. Not admitting your mistakes or even worse, ignoring or covering up your faults, is really not the path to positive change.

The closer I got to God, the more He revealed to me about the incompatibility between "I am not a sinner" and the truth. Even scripture says that "if we claim that we're free of sin, we're only fooling ourselves. A claim like that is errant nonsense. On the other hand, if we admit our sins – make a clean breast of them – He won't let us down; He'll be true to Himself. He'll forgive our sins and purge us of all wrongdoing. If we claim that we've never sinned, we out-

and-out contradict God – make a liar out of Him. A claim like that only shows off our ignorance of God." (1 John 1:8-10, The Message) Believe me, I am not a bad seed, and was always trying to do the best I could, just like you are. However, good intentions do not neutralize mistakes. Resting on good intentions is the same as not allowing God to remove the blindfold. Only confession can move you forward.

I'm sure some of you Catholics out there are rolling your eyes and really don't want to think about confession. I'm not saying you need to go to a priest to confess, but I'm afraid I cannot let you off the hook of talking to God and acknowledging things you've done that might not be fully kosher. That's why I'm calling it *God Removes the Blindfold*, because before you can change, you need to see and acknowledge where you are and what you are doing now that is blocking you from pursuing your purpose and having your best possible life. Transformation starts with looking at what you are doing wrong and trying to do it differently and better.

I know that this is really not a fun thing to think about, but we are all sinners who fall short of God's glory and perfection. Nobody wants to feel naughty or dirty, but instead of feeling bad about it, please know that there is a certain exquisiteness in realizing that you are broken, imperfect, cracked, screwed up, and just as whacky as the next person. There is a certain effortlessness to just surrendering to the idea that you are not perfect, never can be, never will be, and shouldn't really bother trying to be. For so many years, I expended all my energy into being as perfect as I possibly could. Everything had to be in its place: every hair on my head, every decoration in my home, every item on my computer, and every piece of information on my desk. Now, I can see how thoroughly irrelevant and unproductive all of that effort was. I am much more comfortable in my own skin, and I have become my own version of imperfectly perfect.

If you don't know what to confess, ask God. God's truth will penetrate the innermost places of your heart. Things you thought you had moved beyond already, hurts you didn't realize were still in your heart... God's truth hones in on all of it in order to purify you and prepare you to move on with your life. One awe-inspiring experience of mine was during a time of asking God to reveal truth to me in confession. He showed me how my life had been a trail of dominos. In my mind, I watched one domino, a misguided blooper many years ago, topple onto the next domino, and the next after that, until an entire trail had fallen down, bringing me to the recent past. Let's just say, it brought new meaning to, "I was blind and now I see." The beauty of confession lies in that ability to see. Use this prayer as a guide, based on Psalm 139:23-24 from The Message:

Heavenly Father, Investigate my life and find out everything about me. Cross-examine me and test me to get a clear picture of what I am about. See me for who I am, and show me if I have done anything wrong. Let me know where I have gone astray and what I have done right. Reveal to me the truth of my actions, past and present. After You reveal the truth to me, God, please forgive me for my offenses, and lead me to a better path for my life.

God knows what you've done, and it's no surprise to Him. He has seen it all before. He even understands, and more importantly, He wants to forgive you. You have to be honest with Him in order to move forward. If you are still having difficulty with the whole "I'm not a sinner" thing, go back to the Seven Deadly Sins chapter. Start with the Seven Deadly Sins as a guide, and take it from there, based on your own history. If you are really Type A, you can start by apologizing to God that you are always trying to do His job for Him. The hardest part is getting started, but once you break through your resistance, God will start a full and thorough housecleaning of your heart. The more you pray for exposure, and the closer you get to God, He will raise your standards and reveal to you more clearly the mistakes of the past in order to increase your wisdom for your new steps. Soon enough, instead of "I'm not a sinner" or "It's not my fault," you'll find yourself regularly saying, "Whoops! God, I messed up, sorry about that." It's ok to admit your mistakes.

It has been said there is no sin so great it cannot be forgiven, and no sin so small it does not need to be forgiven. James 4:8 reminds us to "Come near to God and He will come near to you. Wash your hands and purify your hearts." Confession is an act of obedience, but it does as much for you as you think it's doing for God. You do not need to go to a priest to have a private time of confession with God, though a more advanced form is confessing to other believers. This is more difficult because we often place more emphasis on what other people think of us instead of what God thinks of us. I recommend starting confession privately with God. If He wants you to fess up to anyone else, He will let you know.

Ask God to remove the blindfold for you, so you can begin your transformation. "When you cry out to the Lord for help, He will show you His favor, and He will answer you as soon as He hears you. At first, you may eat the bread of trouble and the water of suffering, but He will be your teacher, and will not hide Himself anymore." (Isaiah 30:19-20, Reader's Bible)

God Provides New Opportunity (aka Repenting)

Once God has removed the blindfold so you can see more clearly, He will also provide a new opportunity to make a new choice. "No temptation has overtaken you except such as is common to man; but God is faithful. He will not allow you to be tempted beyond what you are able, but with temptation will also make the way of escape, that you may be able to bear it." (1 Corinthians 10:13) If you have noticed any of those recurring themes in your life, be ready to not be victim to them anymore. Now that you can see what they are, you will intentionally endeavor not to continue repeating them.

The first time I heard "Hole in My Sidewalk," a light went off about so many things in my life. I was able to see holes I had fallen in professionally, holes I had fallen in with men, holes I had fallen in with friends... the list goes on. It took the writer three times of falling into the hole to figure out and admit (confess) that it was her fault. What happened once she did? She walked around the hole and finally took a different street (repented). Every day is a new chance to "take a different street." In my experience, however, being able to see what your temptations are does not make them go away. As a matter of fact, in the beginning, it may seem that they are everywhere. God is testing you. He has given you clarity, and now it is time for you to demonstrate your mastery over this challenge. God did His part, now it is time for you to do yours.

A simplified definition of repenting is "making a change for the better." Throw away any images in your mind of repenting as spiritual imprisonment for your crimes, or having to "do your time" with no foreseeable end date in order to repay or repair your good name and good standing. Discard any ideas that if you don't do your time in spiritual prison, God will not forgive you. That's not how it works. Repenting is taking the opportunity God gives you to make a new choice, a better choice. It's your job to take that opportunity and make new choices. Remember Albert Einstein said that doing the same thing over and over again and expecting different results is the definition of insanity. That sounds more like prison to me.

Scripture says, "Repent, turn from your idols and renounce your practices, and you will be restored." (Ezekiel 14:6, Jeremiah 15:19) That simply means, the best way to truly repent is to turn around. Stop what you are doing. Don't keep doing it. Make a positive change. Make new choices, and things will get better. You can start doing that today.

Luke 15:10 says, "There is rejoicing in the presence of the angels of God over one sinner who repents." That's the part where God and all the angels are on the sidelines or in the crowd cheering you on louder than anyone else, prouder of you at that moment than ever before. Get the image of God and the angels with their pom poms watching you from the stands as you make new choices. When you make a new positive choice, they are high-fiving each other, hollering and clapping to encourage you on. When you stumble into repeating old choices, they are still rooting for you, encouraging you with shouts of, "Come on! We know you can do it! Next time! You can do it! We believe in you!!"

It will not be easy. People and situations around you will be begging you to continue doing things the way you have in the past. Your closest friends and relatives will wonder why you are acting strange, and will continue to view you as the type of person that is still falling in the same holes. They are not maliciously trying to hold you back, but it will take time to prove to them that you are now approaching things differently. When you start to feel weak or tempted, the Spirit will be screaming in your head, "Don't do it!" Listen to the Spirit. With your blindfold off, declare your power and authority over that temptation. If you cannot declare your own power, declare God's power and authority over it. God says, "Call upon Me in the day of trouble and I will deliver you and you will honor Me." (Psalm 50:15)

Remember that God loves you and wants you to succeed. Even though this is your part of walking in obedience, He is there to help you. Give it to God. Give it ALL to Him. Have you ever heard people say, "I'm working on it" when it pertains to changing their patterns or behaviors? Working on it means you haven't given it to God. This is an ineffective outside-in approach to change because you're still walking around carrying your burden with you. Then, when you get tired or frustrated, it is all too easy to revert to old ways of doing things and succumb, woefully as it may be, to the same temptations all over again. When you fully give it to God in repentance, He will give you the strength you need to make positive new choices. Shirley Dobson explains, "God conquers only what we yield to Him. Yet, when He does, and when our surrender is complete, He fills us with a new strength that we could never have known by ourselves. His conquest is our victory!" God is the only one who can cancel the behaviors you need to eradicate and make them no longer relevant to your existence. For example, at a certain point in my friend Audrey's journey with God, her mother made a comment that pertained to Audrey's old way of doing things. Audrey turned to her mother and said, "No, mother. That girl died."

Be strong. Be courageous. God will never leave you. If you want new results, you have to make new choices first. Take the new opportunity God gives you. "You're done with that old life. It's like a filthy set of ill-fitting clothes you've stripped off and put in the fire. Now you're dressed in a new wardrobe. Every item of your new way of life is custom-made by the Creator Himself, with His label on it. All the old fashions are now obsolete." (Colossians 3:9-10, The Message)

God Forgives

Here's the good news. God has more forgiveness than you need. The Lord says, "My grace is sufficient for you." (2 Corinthians 12:9) No matter how much forgiveness you require, no matter what you've done, no matter how many times you've done it, God is bigger than that. Additionally, God's forgiveness is always forgive-and-forget. It has been said that "there is no use burying the hatchet if you are going to put a marker on the spot." When God forgives, your offense is cancelled, eliminated, neutralized, defused, removed, purged, as if it never happened; you have a clean slate. The Black Eyed Peas say in a song, "Let's catch amnesia, and forget about all that evil." God catches permanent amnesia once you confess and repent.

As a matter of fact, if you try asking for forgiveness for the same exact incident more than once, God's response will be, "What are you talking about? I already forgave you for that. You are wasting my time. Go, get on with your life; I have bigger plans for you." And that is exactly what you can and should do: Move on. God's forgiveness does you no good if you can't let it go yourself. Accepting God's forgiveness is a major part of this process, and highly crucial to being able to move forward with carrying out God's purpose for you. Scripture says, "But because of your stubbornness and your unrepentant heart, you are storing up wrath against yourself." (Romans 2:5) Wrath against yourself does you no good, and only keeps you stuck. God's got bigger plans for you than that. Remember what I said about God being able to use someone else if you are getting in His way? This is one way of blocking Him. Get out of His way and accept His forgiveness.

The Greeks believe that rain is very cleansing. There was a time that I was praying while driving, confessing and asking for guidance. The skies opened up with what seemed like a monsoon, so much so that I had to pull over to the side of the road. It wasn't a burning bush, but through this storm, I heard God speaking to me that my sins and troubles were all being washed away, right in that moment with that rain. The tears streamed down my face while the storm raged on for a while. The Spirit reinforced me with scripture: "Those who sow in tears shall reap in joy." (Psalm 126:5) When I finally pulled back onto the road, I knew I had a fresh start.

Just because being forgiven is so easy, doesn't mean you can manipulate that to endorse continuing bad behavior. It's easy to let yourself off the hook if you think God's going to forgive you anyway, but that is an abuse of God's love for you. Don't be careless or cocky. However, if you do slip up and falter, which we all do, the point is to continually return to Him. Tell Him you know the blindfold is off, tell Him you know you screwed up, and tell Him you know that with His help, you will be able to discontinue these outmoded ways of doing things.

This is why there is a difference in forgiveness based on repentance, and why forgiveness is step three and not step two. Luke 17:3 states, "If he repents, forgive him." Forgiveness with repentance is when scripture says the angels are celebrating. (See Luke 15:10 above.) Your trust and status is fully restored if not enhanced. Scripture says, "God will repay you for the years the locusts have eaten." (Joel 2:25)

Forgiveness without repentance does not include that kind of restoration. There is a difference between forgiveness of the past and trust for the future. The demonstration of repentance is the key separator that dictates new steps moving forward.

For example, I shared with you about the time I was fired. Now, first of all, let me say that in the weeks leading up to this series of events, I had been praying to God for a breakthrough. Talk about not getting something in the way you expect. When all was said and done, as you read about in chapter 7, I was fired on a Wednesday morning. I spent most of the rest of the day on my knees in prayer. I confessed, I repented and I prayed for deliverance. This continued through Sunday when I went to church, bawled my eyes out, and made a biggie-size tithe with money I hardly had, purely as an act of obedience and demonstration of faith that God is my provider and will see me through this. On Monday, God told me to relax and He would take care of the rest. "Be still and know that I am God." (Psalm 46:10) I made one phone call and went to the beach. Within two weeks, I had a new job that paid me more than double in base salary, plus a generous bonus structure for performance. This is Godly forgiveness and restoration when repentance is involved.

Going through step one and two of God's transformation process, you've asked for God's forgiveness and you've asked for God to give you strength to make new choices. God loves you. Consider yourself forgiven. Starting immediately, you are no longer captive to your past.

The second part of the forgiveness process is forgiving others the way God has forgiven us. Yes, that includes the amnesia part. "If you hold anything against anyone, forgive him, so that your Father in heaven may forgive you your sins." (Mark 11:25) One of the most commonly used examples of forgiveness in the Bible is Joseph, in the Book of Genesis, chapters 37-50. Joseph was sold into slavery and left for dead by his brothers, yet *later* in life, when he had amassed great power, he forgave them completely. The Reader's version tells us that Joseph says, "Do you think I'm God? You planned to harm me. But God planned it for good." (Genesis 50:20) Joseph understood that God can use every circumstance to our advantage if we let him. Joseph also understood that God is God, you are not, neither am I, and neither was he. Scripture also teaches us that for every time someone comes to us apologetically in repentance, we are to forgive them. "Not up to seven times, but up to seventy times seven." (Matthew 18:22) For you mathematicians, that's 490 times. But seriously, once you get to 490, is 491 going to be too much to ask?

Remember that the demonstration of repentance is key to restoration. Forgiveness is always required, but restoration is not. For example, my constant prayer when I start dating someone is, "God, show me who he is." Since dating can be awkward at times and communication can get skewed, the point is to understand who the person is behind what they are saying and doing while trying to make their best dating impression. If they "mess up" once, I have the desire, ability and duty to forgive them. If they do it again, my desire may be fading, but I still have the ability and duty to forgive them. If they continue doing the same thing, I still have the duty to forgive them. However, repentance has clearly not been demonstrated, and they are not in the running to be my husband anymore. When there is no repentance, actions have consequences. In other words, we are called to be forgivers, not idiots.

If you are like me, as you go through this journey with God, you will realize that since you have turned your emotions off for the past decade or so, there's a lot of stuff stuck in your heart that really needs to get out of there. There are people who have hurt you along the way that you brushed off at the time, convincing yourself that you were tougher than that, or that you'd show them, or that success is the best revenge. If you are like me, you'll discover that those people hurt you more than you thought they did, and you have a lot more wrath built up against them than you thought. This is really unhealthy. Barbara Johnson says, "Grudges are like hand grenades; it is wise to release them before they destroy you."

To get these grudges and offenses out of your system, I suggest writing down the names of the people who have hurt you over the years through disloyalty, betrayal, lies, aggression, hidden agendas, exclusion, insults, or any other form of abuse. Then, systematically go through the list one by one. Say their name out loud, followed by "I forgive you for _____." Then crumple up the piece of paper and throw it away or burn it. If you feel strongly enough about it, write the person a letter. You can send it, or choose not to send it, but get it out of your system. If God instructs you to forgive them in person, set up a meeting. I put myself through this exercise and found it very cleansing. It inspired me to do the same thing with people I had wronged along the way. Following the same concept and steps, I made a second list of those I may have hurt, to ask for their forgiveness.

Accept God's forgiveness. Don't block Him by getting stuck in your past. Use His overflowing forgiveness to forgive others. Create a clean slate in every aspect of your life. "Do not judge, and you will not be judged. Do not condemn, and you will not be condemned. Forgive, and you will be forgiven." (Luke 6:37)

God Supplies Wisdom

One of God's greatest gifts in your transformational process is His wisdom. It's also good for your image: "Wisdom brightens a man's face and changes its hard appearance." (Ecclesiastes 8:1) Solomon had the opportunity to ask God for anything in the entire world, and he asked God for wisdom and discernment. The result is that under Solomon's reign, Israel reached its greatest geographical boundaries and enjoyed unprecedented peace and prosperity. Solomon authored the Book of Proverbs, encouraging us to seek after wisdom, knowing that the proceeds of wisdom are incomparably better than the profits of silver, fine gold, rubies or anything else you may desire. (Proverbs

3:13-15) Solomon submitted himself to the wisdom of God, telling us, "I hear counsel, I receive instruction, and accept correction," and "I lean on, trust in and am confident in the Lord with all my heart and mind and do not rely on my own insight or understanding. In all my ways I know, recognize, and acknowledge Him, and He directs and makes straight and plain my paths. I am not wise in my own eyes, but I reverently fear and worship the Lord." (Proverbs 19:20, 3:5-7)

Have you ever seen someone with tremendous disadvantages, no credentials, or no experience rise to the top through a series of supernatural circumstances? Have you ever seen someone with all the advantages, all the credentials, and all the experience get shot down? The singular difference is wisdom, Godly wisdom. You can have all the knowledge in the world, but if you lack wisdom, it is useless. Wisdom fills in the gaps where knowledge does you no good. The decisions you make in life rely more on wisdom than knowledge or skills or credentials. Who to marry, where to live, which profession and job to choose, who to hire or fire, who to trust; none of these answers are available on Google.

I have admitted to you that I have mistaken other things for wisdom, including my "old-soul/ahead-of-my-years" maturity, my intellect/ knowledge and my common sense. I now understand that they are no substitute for true wisdom, and sometimes serve as its enemy. When looking at the battle in your mind between your free will and the Spirit, there are times when your maturity, knowledge, and common sense gang up on the Spirit to try to have their way. The more mature, more intelligent, and more practical they are, the harder it is to allow the Spirit to have Its way. Wisdom steps in as the referee who sides with the Spirit and follows up with peace and confidence in the results to be revealed. Marie T. Freeman said, "Knowledge can be found in books or in school. Wisdom, on the other hand, starts with God... and ends there." Wisdom is not about denying the realities of life, or putting down your maturity, knowledge, or common sense. Frankly, the ultimate denying of reality is thinking that you are in control or know better than God. Instead, wisdom is an inherent understanding that God has purpose for everything, including a purpose for you, and acting on that purpose will not lead you astray.

Here are some additional truths consistently delivered in the Book of Proverbs: Wisdom is the ability to judge and act according to God's directives. Wisdom is the most valuable of all assets. Wisdom is available to anyone, but the price is high. Wisdom originates in God, not self. Wisdom and righteousness go hand in hand. In other words, God is God, you are not, neither am I.

Growing in wisdom is a process, and sometimes requires long stretches of faith before you see the outcome. Especially in our fast-paced world, making a wise choice instead of an urgent choice may temporarily make you look foolish to others. Your self-protecting ego will not enjoy that part, and the Idol of Self will be there coaxing you and trying to persuade you away from wisdom. However, with patience, the results are well worth being a temporary laughing stock, and over time, your wisdom-based decisions will be executed with unwavering serenity and poise. Cynthia Heimel said, "When in doubt, make a fool of yourself. There is a microscopically thin line between being brilliantly creative and acting like the most gigantic idiot on earth. So what the hell, leap." Scripture says, "Wisdom is proved right by her actions." (Matthew 11:10)

Take the leap of faith and put your trust in God's wisdom. Read the Book of Proverbs and apply it to your life. Ask God for wisdom every day, in every situation and about every person in your life. He will give it to you. "If any of you lacks wisdom, he should ask God, who gives it generously to all without finding fault, and it will be given to him." (James 1:5) We talked about how God removes the blindfold for you about your own life, but wisdom and discernment are the part where He removes the blindfold for you about everything else. "Wisdom is the principal thing. Therefore get wisdom." (Proverbs 4:7)

God Changes Your Motives

Wisdom and motives go together like peas and carrots. The more you pray for and receive wisdom from God, your motives naturally and sincerely become more righteous. If your motives are directed by following after God, seeking Him, placing Him first in your life, then He will fill you with wisdom to guide your path. If you are wise in willingness to wait forever for God to deliver on His promises, then He will not keep you waiting very long. "If it seems slow, do not despair, for those things will surely come to pass. Just be patient, they will not be overdue a single day!" (Habakkuk 2:3) If you are focused and content in acknowledging that God's timing is always perfect, then He will have plenty of burning bushes to light the way for you.

On the other hand, if you think you are in control, or that you know better than God does, you are not taking God seriously, and He has no good reason to meet your demands or guide you. "All a man's ways seem innocent to him, but motives are weighed by the Lord." "You want something, but don't get it. You kill and covet, but you cannot have what you want. You quarrel and fight. You do not have because you do not ask God. When you ask, you do not receive because you ask with wrong motives, that you may spend what you get on your pleasures." (Proverbs 16:2, James 4:2-3)

I admitted to you earlier in section one that I tirelessly prayed the Prayer of Jabez. Looking back, I did so with entirely the wrong motives. The Prayer of Jabez is familiar to many, but for those of you who do not know it, here it is: "Jabez called on God saying, 'Oh that you would bless me indeed, and enlarge my territory, that your hand would be with me, and that you would keep me from evil, that I may not cause pain!' So God granted him what he requested." (1 Chronicles 4:10) Scripture also tells us Jabez was more honorable than his brothers, so he had the right motives in this prayer. Basically, Jabez is saying, "Bless me first, and then I promise to bless everyone else." Praying this prayer with the wrong motives includes praying it while still worshiping the Idols of Money, Accomplishment, and Self. God can discern your motives when He considers your request.

Motives dictate results. God has prepared for you what your eyes have never seen, your ears have never heard and your mind has not conceived (Isaiah 64:4), but He's not going to do it on your terms for your purposes. The relationship with God is not about Him producing results for you, but rather you committing to follow His path. God is not a formula, no matter how much scripture you can cite. Proverbs are not promises. Wisdom is like a chiropractor for motives, and sometimes you can hear your motives snap, crackle and pop as they get back into alignment.

Along those lines, as you grow in wisdom, you will experience a paradigm shift in your motives, toward following His purpose and path for you. I spent years asking God to bless my path, instead of trying to get on His path for me. I prayed for abundance and prosperity, knowing that God was the "lamp to my feet and a light for my path" (Psalm 119:105), but I didn't take responsibility for my part of cooperating with His plans. I neglected to take into consideration that God was lighting His path for me, not my path for me. No wonder it kept getting dark.

I can see it now, God and me in the dark woods and He's got the lantern. I keep walking on a different path than Him, saying, "Come over here, God" and then wondering why He's not blessing me, and it's getting so dim and shady. God's standing there with the lantern lighting His path for me saying, "Come over here," but I keep doing my own thing on my own path, getting frustrated that God is not cooperating with me. What a dope I was.

Just because your motives aren't wicked or hurtful, doesn't mean they are submitted to cooperating with God. Godly motives are those that utilize your unique gifts and capacities for the benefit of other people instead of singularly for your own personal advancement. It is the difference between becoming a doctor because of your higher desire to help those who are ailing, or becoming a lawyer based on an inborn passion for justice, as opposed to becoming a doctor or a lawyer because you worship the Idol of Money, Accomplishment, and Self, and want to earn more, do more, and be more than other people.

"Do your work for God, not to impress other people." (Colossians 3:23) It's the difference between asking yourself, "What do I want to do with my life?" or "What do I want to be when I grow up?" as opposed to asking God, "What do You want me to do with my life?"

Examine your motives. Hold yourself to a standard of knowing that God knows the real reason why you are doing what you are doing. Are you serving the Idols of Money, Accomplishment, and Self, or are you motivated by keeping God first and getting onto God's path for your life? Before you do something, ask God why you are really doing it. The Spirit will speak up and let you know very quickly. Everything in my life changed when I finally asked God to help me get on His path for me instead of asking Him to bless mine. "Trust in the Lord with all your heart and lean not on your own understanding; in all your ways acknowledge Him, and He will make your path straight." (Proverbs 3:5-6)

Allow God to change your motives. "My counsel is this: Live freely, animated and motivated by God's Spirit. Then you won't feed the compulsions of selfishness. For there is a root of sinful self-interest in us that is at odds with the Spirit; just as the Spirit is incompatible with selfishness. These two ways of life are antithetical, so that you cannot live at times one way and at times another way according to how you feel on any given day... Choose to be led by the Spirit." (Galatians 5:16-18, The Message)

God Calls You to a Purpose

C.G. Jung said, "I have a sense of destiny as though my life was assigned to me by fate and had to be fulfilled. This gave me an inner security... often I had the feeling that in all decisive matters, I was no longer among men, but was alone with God." Can you honestly say that you feel that same way about what you are doing with your life right now? Vaclav Havel: "The tragedy of modern man is not that he knows less and less about the meaning of his life, but that it bothers him less and less." Have you gotten so bogged down in your daily existence that you have forgotten to search for your higher purpose?

Did the process of making a perfect Type A five-year or ten-year plan blot out the truest meaning for your life? Did other people's opinions, agendas, or even beliefs about you get you to where you are now? For example, I remember being in the second grade and telling people I wanted to be a writer. You know what their response was? "You don't make a lot of money being a writer." I figured out very quickly that I should tell people I wanted to be a lawyer instead. Nobody ever disapproved of that. When you look back at your life, can you see how society starts chipping away at you so early on in the process of figuring yourself out? Talk about misguiding your motives from day one!

Have you ever really thought about what God's calling for your life is? Has there been a recurring theme in your consciousness that is magnetizing you to a path different from the one you are on? Are there images in your head of you doing or being something, but you're not certain how it could ever come to be, how you get from here to there? If you are wondering if you are too far gone or too deep into your current path to change now, you are not. Don't fool yourself. I will not allow you to lie to yourself like that. You may have some changes to make to get to God's path from where you are, but He promises to guide you every step of the way.

235

Your calling is your purpose, your mission, your life's work; what you alone were sent into the world to do during your time here. A true calling is an assignment from God. It's not something you are capable of creating by human design. If you logically concluded that this was the right path, or you sensibly arranged the pieces together to seize the opportunity, you are following a man-made mission, which is not necessarily God's path for you. God will make His calling clear to you through prayer, wisdom, reformation of motives, and your own natural gifts. "Faithful is He who calls you, and He will also bring it to pass." (1 Thessalonians 5:24)

To paraphrase something I heard recently, "The difference between what you are doing now, and what God wants you to be doing, is that really big decision you've been putting off." Emile Barnes said it this way, "God has put into each of our lives a void that cannot be filled by the world. We may leave God or put Him on hold, but He is always there, patiently waiting for us... to turn back to Him." For those of you who already know your purpose, or calling in life, but "can't do anything about it right now," those statements probably just hit you pretty hard. For those of you who don't know your calling yet, keep praying and asking God to show you. When you are ready, He will let you know.

Once God has called you to an assignment, you will know with certainty that it is completely, undeniably, uncontrollably and unquestionably the path you must follow. No matter how long it takes, no matter what obstacles come in your path, no matter who says you can't, no matter what your parents think, no matter what happens for you or against you or to you, your assignment is what you are on this earth to accomplish. Of course, as with other parts of God's process, this doesn't mean that it takes no effort on your part. You have to cooperate. God is God, you are not, neither am I. If you do your part, God will do His.

I knew my calling for over five years before I acknowledged it. Instead, I continued living my life, my way, on my time, according to my Type A excel spreadsheets and To-Do lists. Even though the vision and magnetic draw of my purpose was always there, I just ignored it while I went along my merry way, asking God to bless my steps. As I said earlier, it was me and God in the dark woods, and I was on my own path. Oddly enough, even when I was ignoring my purpose, somehow I still instinctively knew it wasn't going to go away, and would be there when I finally decided I was ready to act on it. It became that "thing" I was going to do in ten years. Which, of course, became a perpetual, running, ten years starting *now* every time I thought about it, no matter how long it had been since I'd heard the calling in the first place. What's ten years got to do with it? Not much really. The point is, it was my way of saying, "I'll do it after I live my life, my way, according to my plans; or after I get married and have kids and the kids are enrolled in a good school; or after I save up enough money that I can feel secure enough to be crazy enough to take such a giant leap of faith; or _____; you fill in your own blank. (Yes, you know exactly what I'm talking about.)

Even more odd was once my life came to a screeching halt from following my own path, pursuing my purpose was not something that came immediately to mind. Part of it was my own persistence in worshipping the Type A idols I've mentioned. Part of it was my own negligence in walking the walk and practicing the things we'll discuss in the next chapter or two. Either way, I continued to seek after my man-made creation of what seemed logical for me to be doing. I kept perfecting my resume over and over again, basing my identity on money, accomplishment, and ego. As I searched ceaselessly for a job, I continued to ignore my calling. Guess what. Despite my qualifications, no doors were opening. I guess God was tired of waiting for me to catch on.

At the same time, and quite fortunately, my craving for the Bible was also restored. I knew I had made mistakes, I knew I had wandered away from God's plan for me, and I knew I had to turn around immediately. I delved into scripture, completed numerous Bible studies by myself (even ones that are intended for groups), watched Christian television, found a church in my new city, and got plugged in. I was incessant in prayer and dialogue with God, until finally it happened.

God bonked me on the head.

One evening, I was all dressed up in my suit, heading to a networking event to further my man-made agenda. But I was burnt out from being rejected and the networking cycle of "We'd really like to hire you, but we can't right now," or "I'm sorry, you are too overqualified," or "We're restructuring, call back in six months;" or my personal favorite from many men, "Let's get together to discuss some opportunities" and then, somehow, "opportunities" becomes them trying to take me on a date. As I drove to the event, I cried out to God, "I am sick of this! What is it you want me to do? Give me a sign!!" I agreed to do anything God asked of me. And that night, my life changed.

Though it sounds dramatic, there was no spectacular, extraordinary, or life-changing event. It was simply God's perfect timing and unbroken delivery on His promises. One of Bono from U2's favorite passages tells us to "Call to me and I will answer you and tell you great and unsearchable things you do not know." (Jeremiah 33:3) I called out, and God answered. Following the networking event, I went to dinner with the event's coordinator, who was already a friend of mine. Our relationship is one of affectionately abject irreverence, so it was not strange for him to fire off a series of questions that made my plans look like mincemeat. But the disintegration of my plans was like the curtains parting on the *Price Is Right*, revealing very clearly my *brand... new...* **life!** Finally, it was so all so clear. God bonking me on the head was His way of saying, "See! This is what I've been trying to show you!"

The next morning, I dropped to my knees and prayed about this revelation. Though I felt inspired and mostly certain, everything seemed so unclear. I knew I'd been given an epiphany, but I had no way of knowing how the pieces would come together. I had so many doubts and felt so unqualified and unprepared. My first prayer, which is something I pray on a regular basis when I am feeling doubtful about deciphering God, was, "God, is that you?" It was. My next questions included, what, how, when, where, and why me? God's reply was very clear. He said, "Follow My instructions. The time is now. What are you waiting for?" I was relieved and elated, assured and inspired. I took a two-week nap to drain out the exhaustion from months of accumulated frustration, and to recharge for what was ahead of me. I haven't stopped since.

Do you know your calling? Would you like to know your purpose? Are you longing to do something of significance? A great source of inspiration is the *Purpose Driven Life* by Rick Warren. Here's the first line: "It's not about you." Bob Buford, in his book *Half Time,* talks about a Final Exam we will all face when our life here is over. He talks about two questions we will each be asked, whether at the pearly gates or face-to-face with God Himself. One of the questions is "What have you done with the resources you were given in life?" We tend to think of resources as only financial, but that is not the case. Resources include everything about you: your blessings, talents, and special gifts; your hurts, failures, and experiences; your location, timing, placement, and vocation; your physical, mental, geographical, temperamental, and other advantages or limitations; your personality, race, and everything else about you that has made you uniquely who you are, set apart from every other individual on earth. "Do nothing out of selfish ambition or vain conceit, but in humility consider others better than yourselves. Each of you should look not only to your own interests, but also to the interests of others." (Philippians 2:3-4) Purposeful living is about making a lasting impression on the lives of others.

God will call you to a purpose that you are uniquely perfect for in every way. Your only job is to submit willingly to His plan for you, but that is not as easy as it sounds. You will block yourself (and God) with questions and thoughts such as, "What will people think?" "Can I earn enough money at it?" "How could I possibly attain this goal?" "I'm not good enough." "I don't have the right education or enough money to attain my dream." But that is not allowing God to be God. As Catherine Marshall says, "When the dream of your heart is one that God has planted there, a strange happiness flows into us. At that moment, all of the spiritual resources of the universe are released to help us." Remember, God is God, you are not, neither am I. If you do your part, God will do His.

Heed caution in trying to equate "dream in your heart" with your passions, as an indicator of purpose. Contrary to popular belief, your passions are not necessarily the best place to start. Starting with your passions is a misguided, outside-in approach that can be disastrous. Case in point, have you ever started a romantic relationship based solely on passion? How long did it last before it fizzled out? By contrast, with your purpose, you may feel blind to what the future holds or how it's all going to come together. As God molds you and moves you, He will require you to do things that may feel unfamiliar or uncomfortable, more like an arranged marriage or duty than a bliss-filled reverie. It will not always "feel good," and you will be called to take numerous leaps of faith in the process. Even Paul, in carrying out his mission, said to the Corinthians, "I was unsure of how to go about this, and felt totally inadequate – I was scared to death, if you want the truth of it... But the Message came through anyway. God's Spirit and God's power did it, which made it clear that your life of faith is a response to God's power, not to some fancy mental or emotional footwork by me or anyone else." (1 Corinthians 2:3-5, The Message) As you take your leaps of faith, you must be grounded in God's love and hopeful in expectancy that God will fulfill His promises. "Hope that is seen is no hope at all. Who hopes for what he already has? But if we hope for what we do not have, we wait for it patiently." (Romans 8:24-25)

Your purpose is not about how you can serve yourself and your own desires. Remember, motives count. God will call you to a purpose which will entail the complete surrender of yourself and your self-serving motives, and which will require your total commitment to staying on God's path for you. There will be times when the Idols of Money, Accomplishment, and Self will come along with what may look like a better offer, but do not be fooled by their counterfeit of what God has in store for you. Following your calling and God's purpose for you is not about how much you can make, how much you can pull off, or what you want to be when you grow up. It's about what God wants you to do as a participant in and faithful servant to His master plan. Once you are on God's plan, you gain the most powerful, most intelligent, most resourceful business partner you could ever imagine. "Commit to the Lord whatever you do, and your plans will succeed." "With men this is impossible, but with God all things are possible." "No one whose hope is in God will ever be put to shame." "Be steadfast, immovable, always abounding in the work of the Lord, knowing that your toil will not be in vain." (Proverbs 16:3, Matthew 19:26, Psalm 25:3, 1 Corinthians 15:58)

I wish it were easier to tell you what your unique purpose is, but I don't have the answer for you. If the Spirit has been screaming at you about something while reading this section, there's a good possibility that you already know your calling. If you don't know it yet, don't fret. Discovering it is a process of asking God continually until He makes your path clear, and then trusting in that path with every ounce of your being. Beth Moore articulates things so well; she said, "Only God's chosen task for you will ultimately satisfy you. Do not wait until it is too late to realize the privilege of serving Him in His chosen position for you... If you will receive the fact that God is determined where you are concerned, and you will get determined where He is concerned, your life will be radically transformed. You will experience huge, miraculous, unexplainable things."

Talk to Him. Ask Him. Petition Him for your purpose until you are certain you know what He wants you to do. I guarantee, if you keep asking, God will let you know sooner rather than later. Accept the assignment. Commit to doing the work. Surrender yourself to God's path for you. God will smile upon you and say, "Well done, good and faithful servant." (Matthew 25:21)

You Become a Messenger

As God continues to transform you through His truth, love, and purpose in your life, you are also called to become a messenger of His love and blessings. As you grow in wisdom and understanding that God gave you the ability, the intelligence, the means, and the advancement (Romans 12:6, Daniel 2:21, Deuteronomy 8:18, Psalm 75:6-7), you will want to share what you have been given with others. "We have three things to do to lead us toward that consummation: Trust steadily in God, hope unswervingly, love extravagantly. And the best of the three is love." (1 Corinthians 13:13, The Message) Billy Graham said, "God has given us two hands, one to give with and the other to receive with." The more you understand and acknowledge how much God has blessed you, the more naturally humble you become, and the more your pride and self-centered ways become irrelevant to your daily mission, and moreover, they tend to get in the way.

How can you tell if something is a priority? Look at your calendar and your checkbook. As you become a messenger of God's love and blessings, you will notice your calendar and your checkbook morphing into a conduit of hope. Instead of rebalancing your calendar and your checkbook the way you rebalance your portfolio to constantly feed back into your own prosperity, you will turn the spigot to let the abundance and overflow of your life be a blessing to someone else. As you become a messenger of God's love and blessings, you will grow in desire to follow God's protocol for giving and serving others. Doing so, you are making room for God to

242

bless you more. And He will.

> Remember this: Whoever sows sparingly will also reap sparingly, and whoever sows generously will also reap generously. Each man should give what he has decided in his heart to give, not reluctantly or under compulsion, for God loves a cheerful giver. And God is able to make all grace abound to you, that you, so that in all things at all times, having all that you need, you will abound in every good work. (2 Corinthians 9:7-8)

Giving and serving is not the path to God, but the proof of God in your life. As we discuss giving and serving, it is critically important to remember the G's about attitude. Do not give and serve if you are doing so out of *guilt*, if you are *grumpy* or if you are doing so in order *to get*. Give and serve because you want to give and serve, and not for any other reason. Philanthropy has become a marketing ground for self-promotion, but that has *"to get"* written all over it. Therefore, I encourage you to give anonymously without expecting or accepting any praise, thanks, recognition, or remuneration for it (e.g., buying a ticket to a charity event doesn't count – you benefit by attending the event). Serve without boasting or bragging. The sign of maturity in giving and serving is when you are selflessly focused on the pleasure and advancement of the recipient, taking your joy only from their delight.

Ok, a little politics. I can't resist. We don't need to be *taxed* into providing for the disadvantaged. If we were all purposefully and generously *giving to and serving* those less fortunate, a lot of our worldly problems would be solved. Scripture says, "Command those who are rich in this present world not to be arrogant or put their hope in wealth, which is so uncertain, but to put their hope in God, who richly provides us with everything for our enjoyment. Command them to do good, to be rich in good deeds, and to be generous and willing to share." (1 Timothy 6:17-18) If we give not only our treasure, but also our time and talent as a "hand up," not a "hand out," the world would start changing in ways beyond the vision of even utopian philosophers. The answer to the question, "How do we get from here to there?" is simple: Be a messenger of God's love and blessings. Give to and serve others.

God's protocol for giving and serving includes the second set of three G's of Dr. David Chadwick's system. Again, I will use his G's as signposts, but explain them in my own words. All of these are done as an act of gratitude for the blessings God has bestowed upon you. The more God blesses you, the more you are expected to bless those less fortunate. God will provide more than you need. There have been times when, by the standards of logic, I could not afford to give, but kept giving anyway, and somehow, God supernaturally provided. On one such occasion, God did the Hanukkah story on my checkbook! What was supposed to last only a few months lasted a year!

First things first: You knew I was going here, and I am. I have to start with tithing because that is supposed to come off the top. Tithing is payment to God, the first G, acknowledging Him with our first fruits. In case you've forgotten, tithing is 10% of your gross income, before you even think about spending the remaining 90%. Since everything comes from God, it's really not too much to ask. But God knows you're skeptical, so He says, "Test me. Bring your tithe into the storehouse and see if I will not throw open the floodgates of heaven and pour out so much blessing that you will not have room enough to receive it." (Malachi 3:10)

Another thing to mention, just so we're clear: God doesn't need your money. If you have seen or heard any misguided prosperity message from an imprudent preacher, let me shed light on what tithing is about. God doesn't want your money, He wants your heart. "For where your treasure is, there your heart will be also." (Matthew 6:21) God knows how near and dear money is to all of us, but money should never be *more* near and dear to us than He is. Scripture states, "You cannot serve both God and money." (Luke 16:13) If you need a refresher on this subject, go back in this book and read about worshipping the Idol of Money. God deserves your respect and your appreciation for what He has done for you. Little things like giving you a job and a paycheck in the first place, and big things like creating the world. If that still doesn't get you there, think of it this way. You pay your electric bill to keep the lights on in your house, right? When was the last time you paid your sunlight bill?

Your tithe is to be paid to the place that gives you spiritual nourishment and feeds your soul. In most cases that is the local church; in other cases, that will be a radio station or television preacher. You are not paying for the message you are receiving, you are supporting the spreading of God's love and blessings so others can come to know God as well.

As for serving, what would happen if you tithed 10% of your time and talent to God? On the basis that we are useful 12 hours of the day, and we have six days of the week to work with, (because we are taking one to rest, of course), 10% is equal to 7.2 hours per week. That is a little over an hour a day. I guarantee if you take one hour per day and give it to God through prayer, worship, scripture study, service to your church, or even just watching the right television preachers, your life will radically change. If that seems like too much, or you are still skeptical about the God thing, take one hour per day and research God through reading and on the internet. He will show you the way.

The second G is a "grace gift" or free-will offering above and beyond tithe, which can also be known as personal philanthropy or just plain generosity. Find a worthy cause that you believe in and give them a portion of your paycheck. Adopt a family in need and buy them groceries for a month, help an underprivileged kid go to college, buy Christmas toys for needy children; support boys, girls, research to cure cancer... whatever touches your heart. It doesn't have to be one thing. Give an additional 10% of your income away or figure out a percentage on top of your tithe that you can give. Push yourself. Go wild! Mike Murdoch encourages us to give so much away that later in the week, we have a moment of shock and terror thinking, *What have I done?* (The Chadwick G for this is "gulp gift" because we're gulping in uneasiness.) Once you have humbled yourself to the level of sacrificial giving, the level where you have to give something up yourself in order to give to someone else, you have finally figured out how much God has given you. God will reward your obedience. "The Lord will repay you for what you have done. You will be richly rewarded by the Lord." (Ruth 2:12)

Again, the same applies to serving. What if you gave additional time to a worthy cause? What else could you be doing for the world in your spare time? Keep in mind that service comes in many forms. It doesn't have to be a soup kitchen if you are not comfortable with that, though I do highly recommend you try it at least once. You can get involved as a volunteer with so many great causes, and they would love to have you. It doesn't have to be complicated. Serve in the form of your talents and natural gifts. Use your God-given skills to help someone who doesn't have that skill.

For example (this is not to boast, but to demonstrate and encourage you), I have a aptitude for business strategy and fundraising, so I've served in leadership positions on Boards of Directors for non-profit organizations and Chaired major charity events to raise money for causes I am passionate about supporting. I love food and can't imagine being hungry for days at a time, so I've served at soup kitchens to fill the bellies of those in need. Whatever you excel at, whatever your gifts are, go do it, and do it for someone else. "Do not forget to do good and share with others, for with such sacrifices God is pleased." (Hebrews13:16)

The third G stands for gleanings, also known as chump change. One night at our church, we did a gleanings offering of the loose change in people's pockets. Chump change amounted to over $40,000. When you empty your pockets or purses, put the change in a jar reserved for a cause you believe in. Give your loose coins to that homeless person the next time you walk by them. It's chump change to you, but it's a big deal to them. "He who gives to the poor, lends to the Lord, and the Lord will pay back what has been given." (Proverbs 19:17)

For serving, this means performing as many acts of kindness in a day as you possibly can. It doesn't have to be complicated. Hold the door for someone, help the lady with the baby stroller, carry a bag for the old guy with the cane, give someone a meaningful compliment – and mean it. Write someone a letter expressing how they have touched your life. Make the letter about them, not about you. Mail it. Start with one act of kindness each day, and increase your goal until it becomes a part of who you are. Whenever you think you are doing enough or have done enough, do one more. Turn your Type A *make one more call* into *do one more kind thing*.

Giving and serving is an act of obedience and appreciation that all you have was given to you by God. I certainly do not want to encourage you to give and serve in order to get, but I can tell you that when it becomes a part of your life, it will change you. Words cannot express how God softens your heart through this part of the transformation process. If you've ever heard someone say, *"I'm getting so much more out of this than I'm putting in"* about giving and serving, and wondered what it feels like, stop wondering and go try it!

Be a messenger of God's love and blessings in your life. "He who gives to the poor will not lack, but he who hides his eyes will have many curses." "If anyone has material possessions and sees his brother in need, but has no pity on him, how can the love of God be in him?" (Proverbs 28:27, 1 John 3:17)

God Exfoliates Your Relationships

When you are serving idols who do not love you, it is easy to allow yourself to be surrounded by people who do not love you. But as you become grounded in God's truth, it is easier to authenticate the sincerity of people around you, and as you realize how much God loves you, your standards for relationships go way up. Part of God's transformational process is exfoliating your relationships through His truth and love.

Exfoliating is something you think of when it comes to your face. You want to scrub off all those dead skin cells, and bring out the vigor in the clean and fresh skin underneath. Walking around with dead skin on your face makes you look old and wrinkly, and yet if you over-exfoliate, your good skin gets dry and irritated. I contend the same theory applies to your relationships and friendships. The wrong people weigh you down and make you look bad, and yet, if you treat your real friends too coarsely, they get aggravated and annoyed. Needless to say, it's a fine balance.

We are all surrounded by people every day. There are people who bring you up, and people who bring you down. People who ignite your passion, people who rain on your parade. People you learn from, people you teach. We are far too careless in labeling people as our "friends." Perhaps this is because of the social networking revolution, or maybe we've just gotten lazy in our relationships. Cynthia Heimel says, "Never judge someone by who he's in love with; judge him by his friends. People fall in love with the most appalling people. Take a cool, appraising glance at his pals."

Since you are a Type A, most of the people you have in your life are probably there because they are useful to you for some reason. Similarly, and especially with your hot-shot status, most people are friends with you because you are useful to them for some reason. The higher you climb, the harder it is to tell who your real friends are. "The poor man is hated even by his own neighbor, but the rich man has many friends." (Proverbs 14:20) Oprah Winfrey said, "Lots of people want to ride in the limo, but what you want is someone who will take the bus with you when the limo breaks down." It has also been said that "a true friend is someone who will take you to lunch even when you are not tax deductible."

We Type A's have cut ourselves off from our emotions for so long, we have become cold and hard towards others, like human Tootsie Pops. There is still a soft center in there somewhere, but nobody knows how many licks it will take to get there. You may not know it, but there are people who look at the wrapper of your Tootsie Pop and walk away. They will probably label you something like "emotionally unavailable," also known as "jerk." Other people will be willing to break their teeth biting into the hard outer shell, but really that's just to prove to themselves that they could get to the center. Once they do, it's either mission accomplished and they are gone, or they use their access to the soft center to manipulate you to their agenda. Finally, there are your friends. Your friends are the people who know your soft center, forgive you for the hard outer shell and feel compassion for your dichotomous existence.

The balance in relationships is finding people who are between two extremes, those being naysayers and flatterers. Naysayers are those totally negative people who drain your energy or fizzle your fire with their worry and doubt. Flatterers, also known as "yes men," are so complimentary, that even though you want to believe what they say, their feedback lacks credibility because they never say no. Neither one will keep you grounded, humble and real. "Wounds from a friend can be trusted, but an enemy multiplies kisses." (Proverbs 27:6) You need friends who will wag their tail like a dog every time you see them, no matter what is going on in your life. You need friends who will tell you the truth, even when it's difficult to hear. You need friends who believe in what you are doing and are protective of your greatest good. You need friends who bring you closer to God and keep you on track with God's purposes for your life.

Remember how in chapter 13 I talked about how I used to have a Board of Directors in my head instead of listening to the Spirit alone? Choosing the right friends is similar to that, except live in action. "The righteous should choose his friends carefully, for the way of the wicked leads them astray." (Proverbs 12:26) You can always find people to endorse whatever bad thing you are doing, even if you know you shouldn't be doing it. There will always be someone who is doing it worse than you, whom you use as an example to justify it to yourself. In contrast, there are also people who encourage you to do the right thing or the noble thing, following the truth, even if it is more difficult. Also remember that following God is counter-cultural. Society's aim is to be independent, self-sufficient, and completely autonomous. God's path for us is highly relational, inter-dependent on one another, unselfish, and totally dependent on Him. Once you get the love of God rooted deep in your heart, you could never look down on anyone else, you don't have to try so hard to overachieve everyone, you take pleasure in sharing your gifts with others and serving them without seeking your own interests first, and there is no room for one-upmanship.

As you get closer to God, and become unwaveringly committed to His path in your life, you will want to share with others what God is doing in your life. You will "go home to your friends, and tell them what great things the Lord has done for you, and how He has had compassion for you." (Mark 5:19) The more you do that, the more you will begin to notice things about people in your life that you didn't see before. It can be strange, observing people you have known for a long time in a whole new way. It will be strange for them to watch you change as well. There is something different about you, but they can't quite place their finger on it. As your priorities change, there will be people who are no longer relevant to your life and your path. There are people we need to spend less time with, and then there are people we need to cut out altogether. My friend Jen did a friend-inventory at one point, and asked me, "Why do I keep discovering that so many of my friends are jerks?" Something like this is not uncommon. The issue of exfoliating your friends is finding the ones who bring you closer to God instead of pulling you away from Him.

As you grow closer to God, He will also bring new people into your life whom you may never have been friends with before. People you may have looked down upon or may not have been able to connect with, you now, somehow, look at with admiration and respect. For example, I lead a Life Group through my church. There are people in this group whom I would not have thought to be friends with had God not put us together. And yet, those are the ones who have added the most value and dynamic perspective to my life, giving me deeper understanding and a new lens to see. As God continues to transform you, it is important to allow Him to show you who in your life to keep, and who to part ways with. He will let you know if you ask Him. Spend more time with the ones who bring you up, and spend less time with the ones who bring you down. We are called to love one another as God has loved us, but we must be mindful to "above all else, guard your heart, for it is the wellspring of life." (Proverbs 4:23) Who do you have in your life that keeps you accountable? Who in your life would you consider a truth-teller? Is there anyone you have avoided or undervalued as a friend? Who in your life brings you closer to God? Who in your life could benefit from more time with you? Who could you help get closer to God?

Here is a friendship prayer asking God to guide you with your companions:

God, please show me who in my life is good for me and who is not. Show me the truth of people's hearts and who brings me closer to You. Show me who I need to remove from my life, or remove them for me in the ways that only You can (e.g., they move across the country or get too busy to spend time with me). Show me who in my life needs extra encouragement from me, and how to help them.

God, when I am with a friend, help me to put myself in their shoes before giving flippant or quick answers; strengthen me to tell the truth when they need to hear it; and help me to speak the truth in a way they can receive it. Surround me with friends who help me grow. Most importantly, Lord, thank You for the gift of friendship and fellowship, that we may love one another as You have loved us.

Allow God to exfoliate your friends. Surround yourself with people who help you grow. Be the kind of person that helps other people grow, and you will grow more. Allow people to be human. Allow yourself to be human. Once your Type A Tootsie Pop exterior starts cracking, you will start becoming more who you always wanted to be. "Greater love has no one than this, than to lay down one's life for his friends." (John 15:13)

The Result – Overflow

God wants to give you overflowing fulfillment, love, joy, peace and wisdom.

God's process is never complete because He is never finished with you. He knows what you need and when you need it, and He will renovate every aspect of your life. Through His unending love for you, through guidance from the Spirit, through the truth and wisdom of His Word, through His amnesia-like forgiveness, through His purpose for your life, through encircling you with the right people, and through providing the right opportunities, God will raise you up, give you life and give it to you more abundantly. (John 10:10) "The fruit of the Spirit is love, joy, peace, patience, kindness, goodness, faithfulness, gentleness, and self-control." (Galatians 5:22-23) The results of God's process are fulfillment, love, joy, peace and wisdom. In sections one and two of this book, I listed the compliments you may receive at different points of your journey. Each of those lists includes positive characteristics that can be used for the benefit of God's purpose in your life, but this last list includes the most humbling and glorifying compliments you could ever receive, and will receive as God transforms you. *(Remember, to God be the glory!)*

List 3: Compliments for God's Humble Servants

You brought me closer to God.
I see God in you.
You helped me believe in people again.
You restored my faith.
God is doing great things through you.

God wants to make Himself recognizable through us. If you do nothing else but start living your life with an aim of hearing these words spoken to you, your life will change in every imaginable way. God will be pleased and He will say to you, "Well done, good and faithful servant." (Matthew 25:21) You will find fulfillment, love, joy, peace and wisdom. He will meet your every need. It's a promise.

God's Process, Recap

Transformation: God Removes the Blindfold (aka Confession), God Provides New Opportunity (aka Repenting), God Forgives. **Results**: Clean slate; fresh start; renewed purity to try again.

Purpose: God Supplies Wisdom, God Changes Your Motives, God Calls You to a Purpose. **Results:** Not making the same mistakes; doing things for the right reason; knowing your worth and significance.

Overflow: You Become a Messenger, God Exfoliates Your Relationships. **Results:** Blessed to be a blessing to those around you; surrounded by the right people; fulfillment, love, joy, peace and wisdom.

"Take on an entirely new way of life – a God-fashioned life, a life renewed from the inside and working itself into your conduct as God accurately reproduces his character in you." (Ephesians 4:24, The Message)

If you do your part, God will do His. Let God change your life. Invite Him in.

Chapter 16: Invitation

If you want God to transform your life, you have to invite Him in. All you have to do is "Love the Lord your God with all your heart and with all your soul and with all your mind and with all your strength." (Mark 12:30) That's it.

You have to make the first move. The ball is in your court. Loving and following the Lord is not on a 30-day receivables schedule where He performs a miracle for you, and then you pay Him later. Your love and obedience to God is paid in advance. It is not a process of, *"If I trust You, God, then You will_____,"* but rather, *"I surrender myself to you, and promise to follow Your lead."* Belief is not a feeling, it's a choice. "Faith is the substance of things hoped for, the evidence of things not seen." "We walk by faith and not by sight." (Hebrews 11:1, 2 Corinthians 5:7) I don't know where you are right now in life. I don't know where you are in the world. I don't know if you are in a corner office, on an airplane, in a mansion, or in a crack house. It doesn't matter. God loves you no matter where you are or what you've done.

There are many reasons for desiring God in your life, including wanting Him to deliver on His promises, desiring His purpose for your life, needing His love and comfort, or maybe you just have no other options and nowhere else to turn. James McConkey observed that "faith is dependence on God. And this God-dependence begins only when self-dependence ends. And self-dependence comes to its end, with some of us, only when sorrow, suffering, affliction, broken plans, and hopes bring us to that place of self-helplessness and defeat." I find it sad that so many of us need to be brought to our knees instead of getting on our knees voluntarily to turn ourselves over to God. It doesn't have to be that way.

Western culture is focused entirely on rationalism and materialism, what can be intellectualized and observed. Unfortunately, this leaves no room for the spiritual or the demonic, which other cultures acknowledge freely. It's nice to think about God up on puffy white clouds in Heaven, and I've met some very intelligent people who have paid the devil no regard, except for maybe a few movies here and there. However, denying the devil's existence doesn't make him not exist. Moreover, denying God's existence doesn't make Him not exist, either.

Alexander Maclaren said that God is "the magnet that draws, the anchor that steadies, the fortress that defends, the light that illuminates, the treasure that enriches, the law that commands, and the power that enables." God promises that His followers will walk in victory and favor wherever they go. (See 2 Samuel 8:6, Psalm 30:7.) But it is important to clarify that although God's love is unconditional, many of His promises are not. Some of you, especially my Christian friends, are probably thinking I've forgotten to mention something, or rather, some One. Don't worry, I haven't forgotten Him.

We've already covered Religion Soup, but the truth is there are only two kinds of religion in the world: religions based on works and a religion based on God's grace. *Good people go to Heaven* and *Everybody is saved unless they screw it up* seems to be the overriding consensus of our modern-day society. This is a works-based philosophy. Your fate is determined by what you do. Society says, *"Behave yourself and don't worry about it. Meanwhile, do whatever feels good now. If you do well enough, you'll go to Heaven, and then in your next life, you'll come back even better off."*

What if we were measured not only by what we are *not* doing, but by what we *are* doing, instead? Just because you are not doing the wrong things, doesn't mean you are doing all of the right things. To qualify as being a "good person," are you following all the Ten Commandments every day in every way and, on top of that, are you following all of the Levitical laws? Do you even know all of the Levitical laws, or that there are over 700 of them? Here are a few to see how you are doing. Do you: Give everything you earn away to charity every three years? Cancel all debts owed to you every seven years? Abstain from eating lamb, venison, antelope, or pig? Abstain from eating all animal fat? Take an entire day of rest every seventh day? *(Type A, yeah right!)* Lastly, have you slaughtered an animal lately to atone for your sins?

The list of rules is endless. If you want a glimpse at a man who tried to follow these to the letter for an entire year, read A.J. Jacob's book *The Year of Living Biblically*. He had to buy a stool to sit in his own living room after his wife discovered the law stating that a man cannot sit in a chair in which a menstruating woman has sat, and therefore decided to sit in every chair in the house when the time came. He even stoned an adulterer in Central Park, just to be obedient. The book is hilarious, and though I do not agree with some of Jacob's conclusions from this experiment, it does give a vivid picture of what true obedience to the Old Testament requires.

If you are thinking that the New Testament is the place where good people go to Heaven, you are unfortunately mistaken. As a matter of fact, the rules only get harder! "If your right eye causes you to sin, gouge it out and throw it away." "If your hand causes you to sin, cut it off." "If you want to be perfect, sell your possessions and give to the poor." (Matthew 5:29, Mark 9:43, Matthew 19:21) Even worse, not knowing is no excuse. Stand before a police officer or a judge in court and say, "I didn't know;" see how that works out for you. Scripture covers this, too: "If anyone sins unintentionally... even though he does not know it, he is guilty and will be held responsible." And, "unless your righteousness surpasses that of the high priests and teachers of the law, you will certainly not enter the kingdom." (Leviticus 4:2, 5:17; Matthew 5:20)

I know I'm repeating myself, but I find this *Just-be-good* stuff highly confusing, and these laws are impossible to keep up with and apply. Where exactly is the line between good people and bad people? What is a passing grade, 51%? And where is God while I'm living my life? Doesn't He care?

What about you? Are you still as "good" as you thought you were? How did you do on the Seven Deadly Sins chapter? Are you still trying to convince yourself that you are not a sinner? Have you sacrificed an animal lately to atone for your sins?

The good news is there is one religion based on God's grace, where you do not have to *be good enough*, and you don't even have to know all the rules. As a matter of fact, there is nothing you can do for God to measure up to the love and grace He gives you unconditionally and freely. Spiritual life is not about trying to measure up. There is no connection between the Ten Commandments and the love of God or getting into Heaven. Scripture is clear that "we are not justified by observing the law." "We have been released from the law so that we serve in the new way of the Spirit, and not the old way of the written code." (Galatians 2:16, Romans 7:6) But if you are not justified by being good or observing the law, then what are you justified by? What does it take to make God's promises as unconditional as His love? The question is not what, but Who.

"Ask whatever you wish in my name and it will be given to you." "The Father will give you whatever you ask in My name." "I am the way, the truth, and the life. No one comes to the Father except through Me." (John 15:7, 16:23, 14:6)

Who said those things? Jesus Christ.

"So the law was put in charge to lead us to Christ that we might be justified by faith. Now that faith has come, we are no longer under

258

the supervision of the law." "So let us fix our eyes on Jesus, the author and perfecter of our faith." "For God so loved the world that He sent His only begotten Son, that whoever believes in Him will not perish, and will have eternal life." (Galatians 3:24-25, Hebrews 12:2, John 3:16)

Let's be clear. Jesus did not come here to start a religion. If He had, there is a very good chance His years on earth would have been much longer, and His teachings would probably have been recognized as the Jewish reformation. But that's not what happened. Jesus came here to throw the system out because nobody was measuring up, and nobody ever could.

He came to measure up for us. He came so that we may be forgiven, that we may have a clean slate with God, that we may follow God's purpose for our lives as God transforms us. Jesus is the prototype that God uses when He is transforming us into Messengers of His love and blessings. He came to die on the cross to be the sacrifice and atonement for our sins. He came to take the punishment that we deserve. He came to change the requirements for us. He came so we don't have to be perfect; we just have to be forgiven. "For it is by grace you have been saved, through faith – and this not from yourselves, it is the gift of God – not by works, so that no one can boast." (Ephesians 2:8-9)

Historically speaking, Jesus did not blend well with the other religions, but everybody has really nice things to say about Him. Jews regard Him as an excellent Rabbi. Islam gives Him credit as a great prophet. There are great historical figures who have come to faith in Jesus by studying Him and His life. Napoleon said he was astonished by Jesus' life and teachings. C.S. Lewis was converted from atheism, in addition to many other atheists who became believers after embarking on a mission to disprove Jesus' claims.

The bottom line is, He either was or He wasn't who He claimed to be. Don't take my word for it. Do the work for yourself. Check the source for yourself. If you are on a quest for the truth, God will guide your path.

I understand that a lot of people do not care for the *exclusivity* of Christ. However, true followers of Christ are the most *inclusive* of all. Everybody is welcome to God's abounding love. This is not about gifts or talent because then it would be for only Olympic athletes; it is not about productivity because then Type A's would have a free pass. It is not based on performance at all. It is based on the love in your heart for God, placing Him first in your life, and being faithful to the opportunities He provides you to contribute to the greater good.

The more you know Jesus and what He did for you, the more you will be radically transformed into the you that you've always wanted to be. The more you emulate the practices of Christ, the more God will speak to you, give you wisdom and change your way of thinking, doing, and being. The more you understand the cross and Jesus' gift of salvation, the more you will be humbled and enabled to carry out God's purpose for your life. The more you understand that Christ already paid the price, the more fully and thankfully you will be able to accept God's gifts. The more you accept Jesus and make Him your friend, the more you will accept yourself and be a friend to those around you. The harder you fight the good fight of faith for Christ, the more you will realize that nothing can ever take you away from the love of God. "For I am convinced that neither death nor life, neither angels nor demons, neither the present nor the future, nor any powers, neither height nor depth, nor anything else in all creation, will be able to separate us from the love of God that is in Christ Jesus our Lord." (Romans 8:38-39)

You were put here for a purpose: "And we know that in all things God works for the good of those who have been called according to His purpose." "This is to my Father's glory that you bear much fruit." (Romans 8:28, John 15:8)

God loves you: "The Lord your God loves you." And Jesus said, "God himself loves you because you have loved Me and have believed that I came from God." (Deuteronomy 23:5, John 16:27)

God has a plan for you: "For I know the plans I have for you, plans to prosper you, and not to harm you, plans to give you hope and a future." "In all these things we are more than conquerors and will gain surpassing victory through Him Who loved us." (Jeremiah 29:11, Romans 8:37)

You are forgiven: Jesus said, "Take heart, your sins are forgiven." "Everyone who believes in Him receives forgiveness of sins through His name." (Matthew 9:2, Acts 10:43)

You will ask and you will receive: "Ask and it will be given to you; seek and you will find; knock and the door will be opened to you." "If you remain in Me and My words remain in you, ask whatever you wish, and it will be given to you." (Matthew 7:7, John 15:7)

Everything is possible: "I can do all things through Christ who strengthens me." "Nothing is impossible with God." "Apart from Me you can do nothing." (Philippians 4:13, Luke 1:37, John 15:5)

Choose Him; He has already chosen you: "You did not choose me, but I chose you and appointed you to bear fruit – fruit that will last." (John 15:16)

Invite Him in. Christianity is not meant to be a religion, but a relationship with God, with Jesus and with the Holy Spirit. Saying a prayer doesn't make you a Christian; placing your trust in God, and believing Jesus makes you a Christian. Becoming a Christian doesn't mean you have to attend hokey fellowship dinners in church gymnasiums with potluck suppers and old people. Becoming a Christian means accepting God's love, by grace through faith, and keeping God first in your life, so that you may be "overcome with joy because of God's unfailing love." (Psalm 31:7)

If you are ready for change, and you want God to transform your life so that you, too, can experience huge, miraculous, and unexplainable things, would you pray this prayer with me? Say it out loud, but more importantly, say it in your heart:

Heavenly Father,
I want to know You.
I admit I am not perfect, and I have made mistakes.
I need Your help. I cannot do this by myself.
I commit myself to You with all my heart, with all my soul,
with all my mind, and with all my strength.
I want to know Jesus. I accept Him as my Savior.
I ask that You replace the pressures of my life with His peace.
Show me Your Way, and help me keep You first in my life.
Help me fight the good fight as I repent of my sins.
I invite You to come into my heart.
You are my Lord, my God, my Rock, my Redeemer, and my Hope.
In Jesus name, Amen

If you prayed that prayer, you are on your way to a radical life transformation. Do the work. Renounce and resist the Type A idols of money, accomplishment, and self. Find a good Bible-based church and start attending. Start reading your Bible daily. Get baptized when you are ready. Use your positive Type A gifts, talents, and drive to serve others and do good in the world.

Be the light of the world. (See John 9:5)

Be the love in the world. (See 2 John 1:6)

"Well done, good and faithful servant." (Matthew 25:21)

God bless you.

Afterword

Friends, I hope you have made the decision to begin or revitalize your journey with God. He will take you places and show you things that you never thought were possible for you. Do the work, do your part, talk to Him, find a good Bible-based church, and when you are ready, get baptized as a symbol of your commitment. Place God first in your life. Thank Him for what He's done for you, and thank Him for what He will do for you in the future.

Friends, I want to thank you for taking this journey with me. God bless you, and to God be the glory always.

Give thanks to the Lord for He is good;
His love endures forever.

Psalm 118:1

Recommended Reading

Here are just a few titles to assist you in continuing your journey. There are many more out there. Keep on reading.

The Purpose Driven Life, by Rick Warren

Your Best Life Now, by Joel Osteen

Boundaries: When to Say Yes, How to Say No to Take Control of Your Life, by Dr. Henry Cloud & Dr. John Townsend

How Good is Good Enough? by Andy Stanley

The Search for Significance by Robert S. McGee

Prayer, by Richard J. Foster

The Case for Christ by Lee Strobel

Life of the Beloved by Henri J.M. Nouwen

Sacred Romance, by Brent Curtis & John Eldridge

If You Want to Walk on Water, You've Got to Get Out of the Boat, by John Ortberg

About the Author

Who I am and how I got this way... I don't know when being a perfectionist, workaholic, control-freak, and over-achiever started for me... birth, probably. I've always been on the fast track headed straight to the top. I've read all the right books and applied all the right messages like, *"You can do anything you set your mind to," "Don't let anybody stop you,"* and *"Don't care what anybody else thinks about you."*

And yet, somewhere along the line, I found myself dissatisfied, lonely, anxious, disappointed and feeling foolish. No matter how great my life looked from the outside, I was sad, empty, and unfulfilled on the inside. While society looks at my fast-track life and says, *"Wow!"* I look back at my fast-track life and say, *"How?"* how did I get here? How did this happen? How have I missed years, even entire phases of life?

I decided to once and for all, *give it to God.* Though major soul searching, blunt dialogue with God, and the complete surrender of my Type A ways, my life has been transformed into a life of abundance and happiness. I now have a sense of purposeful satisfaction that I never had before. I have experienced a complete metamorphosis.

I wrote this book for the purpose of demonstrating how this kind of breakthrough transformation can happen for you. I founded New Street, a non-profit organization dedicated to inspiring positive change through spreading the good news and demonstrating the loving application of compassionate conservative values. I hope you will join me. In fact, I hope you will share your journey with me by writing to me at wendy@recoveringtypea.com, and see *Spread the Message* at the back of this book for ways you can help.

Spread the Message

Help New Street carry out our mission to inspire positive change through spreading the good news and through the loving application of compassionate conservative values! If you have been inspired by the Recovering Type A message and want to support our mission, here are some ways you can help:

✓ Make a tax-deductible contribution to New Street, Inc. All proceeds will be used to carry out our mission. Your contributions, big or small, are so very appreciated and helpful.

✓ Order books! They are available on Amazon.com on the RTA e-store at www.recoveringtypea.com. For bulk or special orders, contact: info@recoveringtypea.com or fill out and mail/email the order form at the end of this book. For additional Recovering Type A offerings, visit: www.recoveringtypea.com, and follow *Recovering Type A* on Facebook and LinkedIn.

✓ Attend a workshop! *Confessions of a Recovering Type A's* author, Wendy Bowen, is available to speak to groups, or conduct Recovering Type A workshops for a more comprehensive and personalized approach to your own transformation. She also offers retreats several times a year and helps you stay on track with the Recovering Type A e-newsletter and tips.

✓ Other needs… From time to time, New Street will need additional forms of support, including volunteers for mission-based projects, business-related assistance, and prayers partners, to name a few. For more information, or to offer your assistance, contact: info@recoveringtypea.com.

✓ Pray for us! We believe that God hears your prayers. Pray that God grants us the means and privilege of carrying out our mission for Him!

To God be the Glory!

Thank you!

267

To receive Recovering Type A e-tips, learn more about speaking and workshop schedules, or support the Recovering Type A mission, follow *Recovering Type A* on Facebook and LinkedIn, or write to info@recoveringtypea.

Contact information:

New Street, Inc.
Box 30
7633 Pineville-Matthews Road
Charlotte, NC 28226

704-999-4908

I would like to support New Street, Inc. in carrying out its mission by placing the following order:

___ Book: *Confessions of a Recovering Type A* – $19.95

___ Workbook: *Recovering Type A (Your Confessions)* – $24.95
    (Coming soon)

___ *RTA @ Work, a Work-Life Balance Workbook* – $24.95
    (Coming soon)

___ T-shirt: Recovering Type A long-sleeve (baseball) t-shirt – $19.95
    Circle: Women's Men's S M L XL

___ I would like to make a tax-deductible contribution in the amount of
    $_____ .

Name _____

Address _____

City_____ State_____ Zip_____

Tel._____

Email _____

Total Order $_____ (include $5.00 for shipping)

Payment Method (circle): Check (mail only) Credit Card (CC)

    Name on CC: _____

    Card Number: _____

       3-digit code: _____ Exp. _____

Please mail this form to New Street, Inc., Box 30, 7633
Pineville-Matthews Road, Charlotte, NC 28226

Or scan and email this form to
info@recoveringtypea.com

Or call 704-999-4908

Thank you for your support!

*Note: All proceeds/royalties go to benefit New Street, Inc., a
non-profit organization*